WINGWALKER

From Wisconsin to Norway
The Larson Brothers and Clyde Lee

To Mary Jane Schanke
Bernice Lee Krippene

Bernice Lee Krippene

WING WALKER

From Wisconsin to Norway
The Larson Brothers and Clyde Lee

Bernice Lee Krippene

ISBN 0-938627-29-5

Publishing Services

Pre-press production & design
provided by:
New Past Press, Inc., Friendship, Wisconsin
Erika Hall, Publishing Assistant

Library of Congress Cataloging in Publication Data

Manufactured in the United States of America

Clyde Allen Lee

Contents

Acknowledgements

The author wishes to acknowledge the contributions of Leonard Larson and Viola Larson, who contributed generously to the information used in writing this book. They also supplied nearly all of the Larson pictures.

Thanks also to others who had recollections of events shared with Clyde: Bob Morgan, a buddy of Clyde's; Earl Iverson; Elmer Clark; Don Agrell; Carrold Manse; Eva Hallock Haese Jacobson; Enid Miller; Jack Perrigo; Loyall Larson; and Evelyn Lee Baxandall. Also a great deal of appreciation goes to Arleen Krippene who assisted in editing some of the information.

Elwyn West, in his taped conversation with Leonard Larson, contributed importantinformation regarding the flying experiences of the Larsons and Clyde Lee. Many thanks to Lee Baxandall for contributing the computer used in writing the book. Also Penny Sinclair who corrected my geography of Miami in 1929 and gave other input. And to Brett Krippene for his persistent insistence that I write the book.

This is a true story. In the interest of personalizing the account, some of the dialogue has been invented, but everything spoken of really did take place as related.

Bernice Lee Krippene

Foreword

When Clyde Lee banked his plane into a cloudless eastern sky on an August morning in 1932, he flew into the pages of history and wrote the final, tragic chapter to one saga of Wisconsin aviation.

With him he carried the dreams of the four brothers with whom he took his first flying lessons, made his first flight and first dreamed of attempting a transoceanic flight to Norway.

The Larson boys–Roy, Leonard, Newell and Clarence–were an enigma for their time and community. Orphaned while Leonard and Newell were still in their teens, they were on their own in a strictly conformist farm community.

When the boys used their inheritance to finance the first permanent airport in Wisconsin, the neighbors were aghast. One went so far as to draft a petition asking a local judge to intervene and put their money in trust, hoping the Larsons would come to their senses and go back to farming full time.

But such tactics were to no avail, the boys continued to build and tinker with planes, to give flying lessons to would-be aviators, and to purchase more and better planes.

When Clyde Lee entered the scene in 1923, it was only natural that the Larsons' enthusiasm for flying would sweep him along. At fifteen, he was an impressionable teenager who had been excited by his father's tales of flying during World War I. Given the opportunity to fly–the Larson airport was just across the road–there was no keeping him away.

Two years before Charles Lindbergh made his famous flight to Paris, Roy Larson was planning a transatlantic flight to his fatherland, Norway.

Eighteen-year-old Clyde dreamed with Roy and hoped he could accompany him, but death in a plane crash ended Roy's dream. Clyde dreamed on.

In January 1932, the city of Oshkosh, Wisconsin began to read about Clyde's dream. The *Daily Northwestern* reported Clyde's plans to rebuild a five-passenger Stinson airplane and fly it to Oslo, Norway.

"It will take a few months to rebuild my plane," he said, "but I hope to leave in June or early July while the weather is warm over the ocean. Later, ice forming on the wings would be a great hazard."

In early July, an accident at Oshkosh airport damaged Clyde's plane and delayed his departure. Even after he named the plane "The Oshkosh B'Gosh", his attempts to raise money for the flight in Oshkosh were unsucessful and further delayed his takeoff.

Despairing of reaching his July deadline, but still undaunted, he immediately began repairs and continued to seek financial support. More precious days passed and the atmosphere over the ocean continued to cool.

When the necessary sponsorships could not be found in Oshkosh, Clyde flew to Barre/Montpelier, Vermont where he found the money he needed. On August 23, with his plane renamed, "The Green Mountain Boy", he lifted off from Barre on his flight to Norway.

Cruising 2,000 feet over the ocean, the Stinson monoplane gleamed red in the rays of early dawn. It seemed to hang in the translucent air as if pinned to the sky. The sun was rising straight ahead, sending ripples of light across the waves and towards the plane. In the Stinson's wake, Newfoundland jutted out into the North Atlantic.

Taking off from Harbor Grace, pilot and co-pilot had felt a launch of spirit beyond anything they had ever experienced–a feeling close to that of being born again. They were flying where no man had flown. Columbus might have felt this way when he set sail where no one had sailed. But this was 1932, not 1492, and 3,200 miles ahead, a modern Norwegian Navy and thousands of people awaited the aviators.

The two fliers, buoyed by the dream they shared, had come a long way to fulfill it. They had thirty-some more hours to go. The rhythm of the plane's motor provided the drum beat that propelled them forward into history.

Alpha

Hearing the staccato thrum of the engine sent young Clyde Lee running toward the hayfield to meet the flying machine. They arrived at the same time, the tall, gangling fifteen-year-old racing to keep beside the machine as it lumbered and staggered over the bumpy ground before gradually coming to a stop. Roy Larson, the pilot, looked over the side of the cockpit, saw the boy purple-faced from running to catch up.

"Give me a ride, please, Roy," he panted.

"Clyde, what would Grandpa Lea say? Ask him."

"My dad would let me. Please," he entreated.

"I charge $5.00 for a five minute ride," Roy replied, hoping to discourage him. He smiled understandingly at the boy. He had been bitten by the flying bug himself at an equally young age.

Now Roy's brothers–Clarence, Leonard and Newell, whom everyone called "Spo"–had surrounded the flying machine, waiting for Roy to tell them what to do about the crowd mobbing the edge of the field, now breaking down the fence in their eagerness to see the airship.

All his life Roy had been shy and retiring, rarely mixing socially outside his own family. He looked at the crowd and whistled. "Zounds!" he exclaimed. "Hasn't anyone ever seen a flying machine before?"

The number of vehicles jammed along the road and the people spilling into the hayfield were overwhelming. Roy and his brothers spent a few minutes staring at them.

"Ask them if they have $5.00 for a ride," suggested Roy, laughing.

The crowd was a great surprise. He'd started this sunny June day installing a new engine in his flying machine. The Curtis OX5 engine was World War I surplus and had just arrived from New York. The flying machine had arrived in December. It was one of two Standard J-1 Tractor biplanes, Signal Corps Numbers 4524-4628, that Roy had ordered from Aviation General Supply Depot in Houston, Texas, at a cost of $125.00 each plus $425.00 shipping. Leonard had hauled the two machines home from the depot on a sleigh drawn by two horses and the brothers had assembled them.

Roy finished installing the engine by mid-afternoon, June 23, 1923. When he tested it on the ground, the noisy motor hummed perfectly. He was eager to test fly it and, suddenly, he decided it was ready. Taking off from the hayfield, he climbed to 1500 feet and levelled off. As it lifted into the air, the plane sent thrills up and down his spine. This was his first flight over his own farm, over his own airfield. Roy loved the noisy clattering engine, the hum of the propeller and the wind singing through the wire struts between the wings.

It was glorious! He was king of the air, full of the utter joy of flying. Flying over his own and his neighbors' fields was something he had been looking forward to since he was fifteen years old. After all his years of dreaming of his own airfield and of flying, he–Roy Larson–had made it all come true. He was bursting with pride.

Roy looked over the side of the cockpit at the green rug of grass and trees, the red barns and white houses below him. It was a pretty picture–a miniature of a great painting and he loved it. He enjoyed the wind whipping his face and singing through the wires. He looked over the panorama of the fields, seeing the green hay, ripening grain and half-grown corn, with vegetable gardens nestled next to the farm houses. The scene clutched at his heart. And at this moment, it all belonged to him–this magnificent view! His neighbors were raking hay in rows for the loader to pick up and spew on the wagons. He flew over them. He waggled the wings and dipped his flying machine low over the wagons. The farmers froze. All work ceased. Open-mouthed and immobile, the men stared at the airship. Roy waved, arm straight out from the cockpit. No one waved in return. They were fixed as statues.

"Oh, well," Roy told himself, "I should have expected I would shock the neighborhood, bringing a flying machine in so unexpectedly. They probably won't like the idea. They'll have to get used to it, that's all. The world isn't going to stand still for them to catch up. At least my world isn't. I intend to be flying the rest of my life."

Three years ago, walking down the road from Medina Junction, he had fantasized himself flying over that very road. And now he really was.

It was a balmy day with a slight breeze–a day for dreaming–and, for someone who had a flying machine, it was a day for cruising far above the earth. Roy was enjoying himself. He had left his everyday troubles and woes on the ground. This was a new beginning–a new life. Today he had a new business–a flying service and an airfield. Next year he would have a hangar. He dreamed on, cruised on, over the nearby towns of Winchester and Larsen.

The machine functioned well. He circled the small towns once again and headed towards Neenah. Absentmindedly, he noted the people standing around looking up. How small they looked!

In the distance, he could see the smoke stacks of the paper mills at Neenah. It reminded him of flying in Duluth and Minneapolis a year ago. An idea occurred to him. He would persuade businessmen in the twin cities of Neenah and Menasha to buy aerial photographs of their mills, homes and nearby scenery, just as he had in Duluth.

Circling Neenah and Menasha, he considered the picturesque locations–factories, residences, beautifully landscaped estates, mansions. The idea grew to take in the parks, the lakes, even farms. Scenic pictures would sell to tourists, as well. He wondered if he could interest a photographer in taking aerial photos. One who wouldn't be afraid to fly with him, perhaps a newspaper photographer.

He needed money to build a hangar. Selling pictures would help earn it. Circling Neenah a few times, he felt the idea grow into a definite strategy.

He cruised back over Larsen and Winchester, luxuriating, congratulating himself on how well his newly assembled machine was functioning. He continued testing as he turned west toward home. There was a lot more traffic than usual for a Sunday afternoon. Cars, horse drawn carriages, buggies, even a lone horseman, all seemed to be headed in the same direction that Roy was flying.

He banked his machine towards Larsen. The traffic turned down the nearest road to Larsen.

"What's going on at Larsen?" he wondered.

When he banked to the right again, towards his farm, the traffic all turned right, but it still hadn't occurred to him that they were following him.

He put the machine down in the hayfield back of the house. The wheels hit the ground, the plane bounced slightly, hit the ground again and, slowing, rolled to a halt. He was astounded to see cars, buggies and horsemen converging on his farm, some driving right over the fence and into the hayfield. He thought, "Am I a Pied Piper? All these people following me home?"

11

Not many people living near sleepy little Larsen had ever seen a flying machine at close range, only pictures in newspapers and newsreels at the theater. They were dumbfounded to see a genuine airplane in a neighbor's field.

It was exciting, a really big thrill, but fearsome, too. Roy's neighbors knew young Clyde Lee's father, Ham, had flown and repaired flying machines in France during World War I, but to think that the Larsons–boys from the farm just down the road–were flying a machine over their land and homes was frightening. Thunderstorms crashing and lightning striking were frightening enough, but this was asking God's wrath to descend upon them, as one patriot firmly stated.

At the theater, during the war, they had seen newsreels of flying machines streaking down in flames, exploding on the ground, spreading fire in all directions, burning homes and barns. Thoughts of that happening in their community struck fear into their hearts.

But it was exciting to watch Roy flying, sensational to see him flying overhead and landing in their fields. It was much more exciting than watching newsreels and they stayed all afternoon to watch.

Roy had no idea of the terrific impact his flying over the countryside would have on his neighbors. From the comments he was hearing now, he realized just how astounded people had been at suddenly hearing the loud clattering engine in the sky.

Roy gauged the mood of the spectators and decided to put on a show. He hadn't expected it to happen, wasn't prepared for it. Nevertheless he told his brothers, "I guess I'd better continue flying. I was just trying out the motor, but I think I'll take a few people for a ride."

Clarence, Spo and Leonard were his first passengers. To give the neighbors a real show and his brothers some thrills, he did a few loops and barrel rolls. The crowd was enthralled. After their rides the brothers walked through the crowd asking if anyone would like a ride. The usual response was a shake of the head and a sheepish look.

Most of the onlookers were of two minds. They imagined the fiery crash of a plummeting machine, countered by the reality of the jubilant passengers returning after each ride. It was a picture of pure pleasure on the laughing happy faces, with hair whipped about in the wind, as they jumped down from the wing of the airship.

Retired farmers sitting on the bench in front of the country store, basking in the sun, resented it. Their reminiscences of their own past glories would dwindle to nothing.

"Those crazy Larsons," one man was heard to say, as he shook his head.

"Those dum fools," answered his companion. "Squandering all their parents' hard-earned money on a toy to ride around in and show off, just like kids."

"Mark my words," retorted another oldtimer. "They'll all die now. Crash and all die together!"

"Someone ought to start a petition to have a judge appoint a guardian before they spend all their money on flying machines and lose the farm."

Suddenly, silence descended over the crowd. They watched in amazement as Theodore Larson walked over to the machine, stepped onto the wing, and climbed into the passenger seat. Despite his name, Ted was not related to the Larson boys. He was their nearest neighbor, a highly respected member of the community, and the last person anyone expected to ride in a flying machine. A hard-headed business man, a successful farmer, an active member of the church, Theodore Larson was a pillar of the community. His neighbors admired his courage, but thought him foolhardy for taking his life in his hands by flying in that flimsy machine.

Loyall Larson, Ted's only son, stood back and watched as Roy stepped on the wing, lifted himself over the rim of the cockpit, stepped on the flyboy's seat, then slid in.

"I never would have believed it!" said one spectator. "You wouldn't get me in that flimsy thing, wood slats and paper, that's all it is!"

"That's progress," responded a less skeptical one. "What about sending words across the Atlantic ocean by cable? If we can do that, we can think about flying, too. We wouldn't have won the war against Germany if we hadn't had our flying boys and their flying machines. The enemy had them too. They were shooting our ground troops from the air. Our flyers had daily dog fights over France. They kept the German pilots from attacking our troops."

The silent crowd watched while Roy prepared to take off. They couldn't understand very much of what they were seeing. Many had only recently purchased their first automobile, the status symbol of 1923.

Leonard raised the tail of the machine, moved it in a half circle to point the nose into the wind. Walking to the front, he pulled the propeller to suck gas into the engine. Looking at Roy, he said, "Contact."

With the switch on, the spark and throttle ready, Roy answered, "Contact."

Leonard pulled the propeller again. The engine gasped, hesitated, stuttered, faltered, caught and came to life. Briefly idling the engine, Roy eased the levers forward. The spitting engine settled down to a steady, ear-splitting rhythm. Leonard removed the chocks and stepped back quickly to avoid the

13

blades as the propeller spun faster and faster, eventually spinning into a large golden ball.

Mesmerized and silent, the bystanders watched the machine slowly taxi along the grassy runway. They watched it stagger as the wheels bounced into pot-holes and over rocks. Children spread their arms, swooped like birds and shouted, "Vroom, Vroom, look at me. Look at me. I'm flying, too."

Three-quarters of the way down the field, Roy slowly pushed the throttle to the halfway point. As the motor rushed to respond, he gunned it for take off. Obedient to command, it responded with a deafening roar. Fuselage shivering like jello, it rose slowly and gracefully into the air.

Sighs of relief sounded from the crowd, all desperately willing the flying machine to make it safely over the fence. They watched it soar over the top wire with at least ten feet to spare. Ripples of excitement fluttered in their hearts, bursts of conversation began.

"Well. I never."...said one.

"I swear...did you see that?" exclaimed another.

"Ted's got more guts than I have," stated a third.

When he returned, the expression on Ted's face dispelled their fears. As he stepped off the wing, he smiled and declared "Go on, take a ride! It's great! Greatest thrill I ever had!"

A hardy few began to volunteer, including Ted's son Loyall, but before they had time to digest the other Larson's feat of bravery, they experienced a much greater shock. A young woman stepped forward and walked towards the airship.

The spectators were aghast.

A woman!

Loyall's wife!

Georgina Larson!

A woman was the last person they expected to step forward for a ride in a flying machine. Even Georgina couldn't have said what made her volunteer. There were so many fears holding her back. Half wishing she wasn't so brave, she took the arm Clarence offered and let him guide her over the rough field.

Disapproving, but grudgingly admiring her courage, onlookers began to express their fears for her safety.

"Don't do it, Georgie! Think of Loyall! What if you crash?" one called out.

"Good for you, Georgina, go ahead, be a sport," said her next door neighbor and friend.

For the most part, the women encouraged Georgina more than the men. She turned a smiling face towards them all. Holding up her hand, she made a circle with her thumb and index finger, telling them it was OK. Perhaps she didn't hear anyone because of the noisy motor. Perhaps she didn't want to. She kept on.

Clarence helped her step up onto the wing, step over the side of the cockpit, and slip into her seat. She hoped she wouldn't regret it. Pushing such thoughts out of her mind, she kept her anxious eyes on Roy. She watched him, hand on the side of the cockpit, leap quickly onto the wing, swing over the side and slide into his seat.

Grinning at Georgina, he asked, "Saying your prayers, are you?"

A momentary shudder of panic chilled down her spine. Inwardly shivering, she shook her head.

Roy beamed his approval, chuckling to himself, "That will break the ice," he thought. "What man could watch a woman outdo him in courage? I'm sure there will be more men wanting a ride when we get back."

Leonard had placed the machine to face the wind again. At a wave from Roy, he pulled the propeller, said "Contact," and waited for Roy to set the switches. When Roy was ready to start the engine he echoed, "Contact." Leonard pulled the propeller. The engine gasped, hesitated, stuttered, faltered, caught, held and clattered steadily.

Glancing at Georgina, again, Roy saw her wave to the onlookers, a happy smile quivering on her lips. Her golden hair was blowing in all directions, tangling into a windswept shambles.

Again, Roy listened to the idling engine for a minute, revved it, then eased the lever slightly forward. The onlookers were mostly silent now, except for the children, who didn't realize what a momentous occasion this was. Mesmerized, the crowd watched again as Roy slowly taxied along the bumpy grass runway.

Loyall had watched with mixed emotions as Roy slid into his seat. Although he'd just finished his own thrilling ride, he wished his wife hadn't volunteered to go. Then, a reasonable man, he asked himself, "Why not? It should be as safe for her as for me." Suddenly he felt proud of her and smiled.

Three quarters of the way down the field, Roy pushed the throttle halfway and the motor roared thunderously. He put it at full throttle, and pulled the stick back. Shaking mightily, the flying machine rose gracefully in the air and over the fence. Sighs of relief rose from the crowd as once again they watched it soar.

As he watched the take off, young Clyde Lee's face glowed with excitement. Undaunted by Roy's refusal to let him fly, he ran over to Clarence. "Would you ask Roy if I can have a ride? I don't have $5, but I'll save my money."

"You can't..." Clarence began.

"I'll pay you back. I can work for you evenings after chores at Uncle Ted's. Grandpa Lea says flying is foolishness. He won't give me the money."

"No, Clyde..." said Clarence, "Not if your Grandpa says...."

"I can drive a car, change spark plugs, adjust timers. I can help on the planes. My Dad can fly. He told me how great it is. He maintained flying machines. He tested and flew them in the war in France."

"I know he did," said Clarence, "And when you grow up, I am sure you will fly, but not today. Roy is only testing the engine. Save your money and come back another day."

"Someday, I'm going to fly around the world. I'll be the first one," the kid confidently stated.

Roy began the landing, turning into the wind and veering towards the runway. After the machine touched down, Clarence hastened to the landing site and grabbed a wing to stop the "Jenny," which was not equipped with brakes.

To his amazement, he saw Clyde holding the wing on the opposite side, bracing himself just like Clarence.

"My dad told me about the brakes, too," he said.

"I hope he doesn't get to be a nuisance, hanging around all the time," thought Clarence.

"He's got the flying bug as bad as Roy. Maybe a ride will cure him of it."

Everyone was happy to see Roy return to the hayfield with Georgina intact. Face flushed, eyes sparkling, hair a bush, she stepped out of the cockpit onto the wing. As she slid off the wing into the arms of her husband, she exclaimed, "Glorious! glorious! You should all have a flight. It's like nothing you have ever done. Go on, go up with Roy. You'll never regret it. It's truly great fun and a real thrill. You feel so free. It's magnificent! What more can I say? Try it. You'll know how I feel."

Friends crowded around, asking, "Weren't you frightened? What did it look like up there?" "What does it feel like?" "Did you look over the side?"

A few more of the spectators decided to try. All who dared came back enthusiastic. "Go on up, it's great. Greatest thing I ever did," said a proud Ted Larson again and again.

It was getting late in the afternoon and chore time was approaching. The farmers went home to feed the animals and milk the cows, the Larsons included. Despite their dreams about flying, they were still farmers.

Roy taxied across the field to the fence corner. He roped the wings of the Jenny to the fence posts and placed chocks behind and in front of each wheel. He drove a post in the ground to rope down the tail. The Jenny had to be carefully secured. A strong wind could bounce the plane around, smash the wings and damage the fragile fabric covering the fuselage.

Until they could build a hangar, the Larsons would have to keep their planes outdoors. They planned to sink large concrete blocks in the ground, four for each machine, with heavy iron rings embedded in their tops. Anchor lines would be fastened to the wings, one over each top wing, and one over the sides, with a separate line for the tail.

Still trailing Roy as he secured the plane for the night, his face glum with disappointment over not have flown that day, Clyde asked, "Tomorrow, Roy, are you taking her up again tomorrow?"

Roy thought for a minute, then replied, "If the weather is nice, I might."

"Oh, good," Clyde said, his face clearing into a hopeful smile. "I'll be here for sure."

A bemused expression on his face, Roy watched the boy run down the road home. He knew Clyde Lee would come back again to fly. He knew for sure.

Roy Larson Comes Home From The War

It was just after two o'clock in the morning of June 6, 1919, when the interurban train drew to a stop at Medina Junction and Roy Larson stepped off. He had a small suitcase in his hand, his khaki coat over his arm. He stood quietly watching the train's tail light dwindle in the distance as it gathered speed to head north towards Neenah and Appleton.

Medina Junction was not a regular station, and the interurban would not be expected to make a stop there at 2:00 A.M. unless a passenger were getting off or on. This passenger wore tight khaki soldier pants and puttees on his long, well-shaped legs. In the pale moonlight his features showed regular and clear cut, giving the distinct impression that he was a good-looking youth. Roy was not quite six feet tall, but he appeared to be taller and was lithe and graceful. His eyes were a hazel brown and his hair a rich dark brown. His restless hands were long and thin. His left eyebrow had an upward turn at the end–a natural quirk which gave him a look of perpetual questioning–a quizzical expression.

After the train disappeared in the distance, Roy looked around and thought it was as if he had stepped back two years in time. The bench for passengers waiting for the train was still there, the green-leaved maple trees lined both sides of the graveled road as far as he could see. It was the same time of night as when he left home for the war with a moon just past full. Here things appeared much the same, but he knew he was not the same. So many things had happened since then, some horrible, some beautiful, some exciting, some things he wished he could forget.

The young soldier looked long at the countryside. It lay pale and shadowy in the moonlight. He looked with a farmer's eye at the field of newly sprouted corn and saw pale moonbeams reflected in the puddles caused by the recent rain. Looking along the road, he saw again the well-leaved trees, tops almost touching, forming a near perfect arch over the gravel road, the boughs moving with the gentle breeze. He stared at the sky. It was a magnificent night! The stars glowed large and twinkling. Even the Milky Way, with its closely woven mesh of stars, seemed only just out of reach. And over all, the moon furnished a bright light to escort him on his way.

Roy took a deep breath and an exultant feeling of just pure joy of living flowed through him. This was one of those delightfully lovely June nights he had missed so when he was in France. A soul-stirring emotion thrilled through him. He felt a fullness in his heart that had never been there before. He let it wash over him.

The night air was still warm and scented with the new growth and lush blooms of spring. As Roy noticed the strong smell of wet black earth where the sun had shone after the rain, he knew it must have been a very humid day. The dewy night was warm and had a steamy feel, even though the cool raindrops had quenched the thirst of the hot earth. He inhaled deep breaths of the clean washed air. Diamonds of rain drops lingering on the leaves glistened in the moonlight. Tall grass beside the road sparkled with dew and he felt the lushness of spring at its tide surround him. He savored its freshness. It smelled of the farm in June as he remembered it and the happy times with his family before he had gone to war.

The slightest of breezes rustled the leaves mysteriously. They tinkled together, whispering silvery tones of soft music. Brought back to the present by the soft, warm breeze on his cheeks, he felt the excitement of homecoming arise in his breast again and began walking briskly north along the gravel road. His footsteps echoed in the quiet of the night. Roy was good at walking. He had marched endless miles in France in the "war to end all wars." This was the last and best walk of that trip. He smiled slightly as he hurried along, thinking about the surprise he was going to be to his family. A surge of exaltation welled up inside him. He wanted to shout, to yell for joy, to someone–anyone! "Roy Larson is home! Roy Larson is home from the war!"

The weather, the almost full moon, the stars so bright, the very air he breathed, everything had contrived on this night to make his homecoming perfect. HOME! He hadn't seen it for two years. Now all the longing, the homesickness would be over. HOME! He would be home.

He had been homesick over there. He had tried to hide it from the others in his outfit. They were a brash troop, his buddies, a devil-may-care, what-the-hell group. A young farm boy away from home and family for the first time, he had been fair game for the city boys. They had teased him, made him the butt of their "rube" jokes without realizing the cruelty of their fun. He could forget all that now. That was behind him and in a few hours he'd be home.

The Larson home was a farm in the midst of the Norwegian-American community of Winchester. These Norse-Americans were home-loving, family-loving, and food-loving people who rarely missed church on Sunday.

They kept the coffee pot full and hot on the back burner of the wood-burning kitchen stove all day. The stove heated the kitchen, cooked and baked food and served as the focal point of family life. Offering a cup of coffee and a piece of cake or cookies was like a handshake of greeting to friends and strangers. Upon leaving their hospitality, visitors carried with them a feeling of warmth and love.

Now Roy was coming home to again enjoy this warmth and love, but life in the army had changed him. Who could live through a war with its violence and gory happenings and not change? He just hoped his family hadn't changed. He knew they wouldn't all be there. His grandfather Larson, who had taken the place of Roy's father after he had died, had himself recently passed away. Now Roy would be the head of his family.

In the background, he heard the click and snick of his shoes on the small gravel stones as he walked along the road. They sounded the same as they had on the dusty roads of France. Here the ground was firm. Every step was firm, not like in France, where sometimes for days, the ground had shivered under the earthquake-like barrage of the big guns. Only sheer exhaustion had allowed Roy to sleep, though the earth continued to shake. He still had nightmares in which he relived it all. The worst was the horror of watching his comrades falling, struck down by enemy fire.

He brought his thoughts back to the present, saw where he was and continued walking. Again, he relived some of the scenes from the war, until he impatiently shook himself.

"That's over," he told himself. "This ground doesn't shake and I must get on with this life."

In fact, it was so quiet the only noise he heard was that of his own feet on the road and the occasional cheep of a sleepy bird aroused by the sound of his footsteps.

This walking back from something he had done because it had to be done was the best walking he had ever done. He hadn't been sure he would ever return. His survival uninjured had been a miracle. He had been in the thick of the fighting for a very long time. Yes, this road home was the best road on which he had ever walked.

A chorus of bull frogs croaking their brash mating call reminded him that he had reached the marsh about a mile away from the Junction. He stopped and watched the frogs, listening to another happily-remembered sound. Boyishly, he skipped stones into the marshy water and laughed as he heard the plop, plop, plop of the frogs leaping off their lily pads into the water. Then only silence greeted his ears, and he walked on towards home.

He thought of his family–his brother George first–and felt sad and bitter. His sister, Zola, had written that George had tuberculosis and wasn't expected to live. He had survived the flu, but had been weakened by it and had contracted tuberculosis. It turned into what was called "Quick Consumption" and the doctor told Zola that he didn't have long to live.

Roy's mother was quite ill, too. During the past year several small strokes had permanently weakened her and worrying over her two eldest sons in the war had worsened her condition. Thoughts of his mother brought her image into his mind. She was pretty with black, curly hair and laughing eyes. She had always laughed a lot.

He sighed as he thought of again taking over all the responsibilities of farm work. His thoughts dwelt on the fact that–at twenty-four–he was the eldest, strongest and healthiest. He realized he was the natural head of the family and should see to it that the work was made easier for his mother. He had been doing it since he was seventeen when, after the death of his father, he and grandfather had taken over all the responsibilities on the farm. Roy had more or less become the head of the house of Larson.

The Larsons had always been an affectionate, close-knit family. Roy loved all of them very much. He prayed in his heart that George would get well. Poor George, to survive the hell of war only to come home and cough his guts out with tuberculosis. He hadn't even been able to die for his country. What a travesty. Perhaps, since he had contracted the disease during his service in the army, he would, in a way, die for his country.

Life is illusory, Roy decided. You did what you thought was right, lived life as you thought it should be lived and then suddenly life was gone, you were gone! George would soon be gone. George was only twenty-two and that was all he would ever have – twenty-two years and a savage and bestial war.

An owl hooted eerily nearby. Roy, startled, shook himself mentally and physically. The hoot was also welcome music to his ears. He remembered shivering in his bed at night and pulling the covers over his head when, as a child, he heard an owl hooting from atop the big oak tree next to the house. Then he'd been terrified. Now, it was another good homey sound. He'd been a happy child and the owl, no matter how terrifying then, had been a part of his happy childhood. He welcomed the owl's sound as part of his homecoming.

Roy looked ahead and recognized the farm buildings of Soren Hanson. He glanced at the sides of the road, high with uncut hay. The bucolic peacefulness of the night stirred his thoughts, "This is all illusory, too. It is so peaceful and serene and yet that owl is preying on some unsuspecting bird sleeping in the tree. Death stalks us all, but mostly we are unaware. The beginning of life seeks the beginning of death. In the womb, the cradle, youth, or old age, death is not far off for any of us. But in each of us is the firm conviction that it can't happen to me, only to another person.

"I wonder if George knows?" Roy reflected, "and if he does what must he be thinking? When we were little he tagged after me and did everything I did no matter how difficult it was for his little legs. Climbing trees much too tall for him, swimming where it was too deep, even following me to the war, which was too much for him. For the past two years, I have been constantly living with death. But how can I face it here at home when it is my own brother?"

A small rock caught his toe and he stumbled. Glancing back as he caught his balance, he discovered he had passed the Charlie Ziem farm and was approaching the Olson farm. The scenery looked even more familiar to him. The Olsons were friends. They were the people with whom he had exchanged farm work. They were sleeping now and didn't know that Roy Larson was walking along the road in front of their farm. It would be good to see them and work with them again.

He felt sure life would be good. Even the hard, sweaty farm work would be good, just because it was on his home farm.

In spite of himself, his thoughts kept returning to the army overseas. He hadn't liked any part of the war except watching the flying, and he had only seen that from the distance separating a marching doughboy from the planes flying a thousand feet overhead. He pictured the fly boys, fantasizing himself one of them, wearing helmet and white scarf. They wore goggles to protect their eyes from the bright sun. Scarves flying in the wind, they flew overhead towards the front lines to complete their missions. He made up his mind then that he would fly too. "Yes, sir, I am going to take flying lessons and buy a flying machine as soon as I can. That would be good for George, too, good for his morale, to fly."

He reverted to thoughts of flying, which had possessed him since he was twelve years old. A flying machine had landed in Neenah and his father had taken him to see it. That day the flying fever set in and watching fly boys in France had only set it aflame again. "Flying! that's the life," he exulted. "And I am going to fly or bust!" He lifted his chin in determination and, remembering those marching days in France, he marched along the gravel road in army step. The marching he had done over there! Sometimes it had been hot and

23

dusty. He would look up and see them flying overhead in the clear blue sky. He had thought, "That's the way to fight a war! Not marching along on the ground with blistered feet and parched, gritty mouth, weary to death and suffocating from the dust. Mile after mile of that, all in step, raising more and more dust."

In France, watching the flying machines overhead, Roy often thought of the chicken hawk back home. The hawk, wings stretched wide, would soar high over the chicken yard around and up and over, up and over, without ever flapping its wings. Just like the flying machines. Roy often imagined himself soaring over his company of marching men, free as that hawk. Then in his fantasy, he was in a flying machine, banking to the right, banking to the left and making long figure eights in the sky. He would mentally soar in the sky for endless hours as he marched along. In fantasy, he felt the propeller-driven wind lifting his hair from his sweaty, dusty brow and cooling his hot face as if he were really flying.

It was uplifting just to think about it. The propeller wash blasting his face with its wind pressure, pinning his eyelashes to his nearly closed lids as it did the real fly boys. He saw himself wearing a pilot's helmet, chin strap fastened. He pictured his eyes with that special piercing look flyers had. It came from looking off in the distance, they said. Looking ahead, watching for ground guides to follow to their target. There were no air maps. They were guided by lakes, streams, water towers, railroad tracks, church towers, villages and farms. Often they flew looking into the sun and had to keep their eyes slit-lidded for long periods of time.

Roy Larson, holding his eyes slit-lidded, marching along in the predawn, said to himself, "It won't be long now before I become a flyboy. I will be a farmer, too. I will have to be the man of the house, same as before, and help the boys keep the farm going, but I'll find time to fly." Recalling the white scarves waving in the wind as the flyboys flew overhead, he thought ruefully, "More likely when I fly I'll be wearing a red bandanna."

He recalled the trip to Neenah with his father in 1910. His father drove the horse and buggy. There had been speeches by the mayor, the councilmen and a few local businessmen. They lauded the birth of aviation and the miracles to be expected from it. Roy listened attentively, captivated. He wondered if he might be a part of that future. The flyboy, Charles Niles from Rochester, New York, made a speech explaining the significance of the new mode of transportation. Flying machines would carry mail and freight. In the future, they would fly across the ocean and take the place of ships. As many as fifty people might be expected to fly in one machine.

Much impressed, Roy thought about flying across the ocean. "When I am grown up, I could fly to Norway. Take you and Mom back for a visit," he told his dad. Roy's dad placed his hand on his son's shoulder and smiled indulgently.

Presently, the flyboy finished his speech. Dressed in puttees and tight-fitting pants with a white scarf around his neck and a helmet on his head, he donned his goggles, fastened his chin strap and strutted proudly out to his machine.

All afternoon, people had been milling around the machine, touching and leaning on the wings, attempting to see inside. The flyer stepped on the wing. Roy and his dad stepped back. The flyer turned to the crowd and thanked them for coming to his exhibition. They waved and cheered animatedly. He stepped into the cockpit. On-lookers jockeyed for the best vantage point to watch him fly away. The flyboy requested the police to clear the area of spectators so he could taxi down the field.

One of the spectators cranked the propeller. The engine came to life, the flyer adjusted the throttle, the plane moved slowly ahead, about one-hundred feet. He gave it a burst of gas, the motor thundered mightily and the machine began to lift off. Thrilled at the sight, fascinated onlookers watched, "O-o-o-h-ing" and "A-a-a-h-ing," excitedly.

It rose slowly about twenty feet, then, to the accompaniment of horrified gasps from the crowd, it gave a muffled creak as one wing folded and the machine nosed down, crashing into a patch of weeds.

Roy remembered running forward with his dad and some of the people to rescue the flyboy. They feared the engine would explode in flames. Some spectators were in shock. Some ran to call the fire engine. Roy, shocked at his hero's downfall, watched the flyboy, not too badly bruised, walk away subdued and frustrated.

Roy hoped that would never happen to him when he became a flyboy. Stunned, along with everyone who had seen the crash, Roy and his dad stayed and talked over the accident with friends and neighbors.

"That just proves it, man wasn't meant to fly. If he was, God would have given him wings," one neighbor declared.

Roy's father, a more reasonable man, didn't comment on that, but quietly suggested that so many people had pressed and pushed on the machine that they might have damaged the wing.

"Those wings are very fragile," he said, although not many of the listeners looked convinced.

Coming out of his memories, Roy thought of his long-ago plans. Before he had been drafted, he had wanted to enlist in the Canadian Air Force. Since he was the eldest and his mother depended on him to take charge at home, he had bowed to her wishes and refrained from enlisting.

"I'll teach the boys to fly. We'll be the Flying Larsons..." he now thought. Then ruefully he said to himself, "Folks around here will more likely call us the 'Crazy Larsons' or the 'Flying Fools.' Mom won't like the idea of our flying either. I will have to bring her around to accepting the way I feel about it."

These fanciful musings and dreams were brought to an abrupt halt by a barking dog racing down the lane from the McKinley farm house. Roy remembered the dog and called him by name. He spoke to it in his usual soft voice. The dog sniffed Roy over carefully, walked stiff-legged behind him for a few feet and reluctantly, slowly began wagging his tail. After following along for a few minutes, he gave a final 'woof' of acceptance and trotted back to his own home.

The barking dog had startled Roy from his dreaming and he realized he was well over three quarters of the way home. He must have been walking and thinking for over two hours, or else it was the army training in marching that had made him cover the ground so swiftly.

The moon was going down over the horizon and the luminous darkness of the pre-dawn turned the road into a ghostly wraith leading him on. Now, there was only pale starlight as he walked and the dawn was rapidly breaking, lightening the sky. The stars were fading. Soon he watched the pink and yellow pincers of dawn, forerunners of the coming of the sun, streaking down the horizon and up into the sky, piercing the night, lightening the darkness. He heard the roosters crowing raucously all around him, the birds twittering in the trees. He wondered how long they had been welcoming the dawn while he had been woolgathering, talking to himself, seeing visions of his past and his fantastic future.

He gave a shake of his head and said to himself, "Oh, this will be a good day. It is a beautiful dawn. My first day home! It will be the best day, yet, of my life."

The pace of his walking quickened and before he was aware of it he was running. Minutes later he looked ahead and saw the roof of his home and his breath caught. He hadn't really thought the sight of home would hit him so hard. It wasn't a mansion, not even a very large farm house. In fact, it was a small house where his mom, his sister, and all his brothers were sleeping. He took a deep breath and his heart swelled within him. Then he heard Dick bark and saw the dog running to meet him, barking joyously as he came across the field. Dick was leaping, legs-stretched as he ran, his belly almost on the ground as he raced towards the road.

Roy laughed. The dog went crazy! He leaped on Roy with hysterical yelps trying to lick his face, falling backwards and dashing about, leaping again and again. "Here, here, old fellow," Roy laughed, "Calm down or you'll kill yourself." The dog just couldn't stop dashing here and there and around, running circles around Roy. He finally knelt and, taking Dick's paw, held it gently as he talked soothingly to the dog. After a few minutes, Dick calmed down, but kept on licking Roy's hands enthusiastically. Roy did have a way with animals and he could understand them better than most. His mother frequently said, "Roy talks to animals as if they understand him."

Roy and Dick ran swiftly across the fields. He was afraid the boys would be up and out doing chores before he would get there for the big surprise act he had planned. As Roy approached the house he pictured his surprise to his family. "They will still be in bed, and I'll just walk in and wake them all up." He pictured himself pulling the covers off the beds of his brothers. "Oh, what groaning and griping there will be until they see who is doing it."

Minutes later, he crossed the front yard and he was home. The door was locked. How frustrating. He tried the windows–locked, too. Disgusted, he picked up some small stones and threw them against the upstairs window. When this failed to arouse anyone, he took an old fishing pole out of the shed and tapped a tune on an upper window. Someone came to the window and opened it. Excitedly, Roy watched as a tousle-headed boy rubbing the sleep out of his unseeing eyes, leaned out the window and said "Who's there?"

"Unlock the door, sleepyhead, and let me in quick. or I'll huff and I'll puff and I'll blow your house in," called Roy.

"It's Roy! It's Roy! Roy's home," yelled an excited voice in the upstairs rooms. Within seconds the door flew open, and they all came tumbling out: Clarence, Spo, Leonard, Zola and their mother. George stood in the doorway grinning from ear to ear. Clothed in a variety of night-gear, the boys threw themselves at Roy. All were entangled in a batch of arms and legs which soon collapsed and landed on the ground.

Roy emerged from these overpowering greetings with his cap missing, his suitcase knocked open across the walkway, and his clothes on the ground. His fine khaki coat was a disaster at his feet. Even after they had pulled him upright, the boys couldn't stop pummelling him. His mother hurried to him. Roy grabbed her around the waist in a crushing bearhug that made her gasp. With tears of joy sliding down her face, she kept saying, "Oh, Roy, it's you at last," over and over. Then talking on uninterruptedly: "I was so afraid. I prayed so often for you," she said, "all the time you were gone. You look well, how are you? At least you're not skinny like George. Come into the house and I'll make a fresh pot of coffee and cut a piece of cake for you."

She talked on and on breathlessly, trying to regain her composure and come to grips with the fact that her long-absent son was actually home at last. Holding Roy's arm, his mother pushed at the brothers saying, "Move into the house so Roy can sit down. He has had such a long walk, and I want to give him some coffee and cake."

If Roy had wondered whether or not his family had missed him while he was overseas, that question had been quickly answered. He was their "brother hero" returned from the war. The soft Scandinavian accent of his family speaking to him was delightful music to his ears. He was home. Their broad smiles, bright eyes and excited voices moved him deeply. Roy had always been the quiet one of his family. He never spoke much and then very softly. Now, he was the center of all their attention, and he didn't quite know how to cope. He just grinned widely as he sat in the chair at the head of the kitchen table and let all this excitement wash over and through him, enjoying it to the fullest, but yet a little embarrassed. As he watched, one of the boys put the kindling in the kitchen stove for his mother. She was putting water and coffee in the pot to percolate. The match flamed as his mother touched the kindling with it. Setting the coffee pot on the burner she turned to the boys and told them to get dressed while she fixed a little snack for all of them. "Roy is hungry after his long walk," she said. The boys left the room laughing and talking among themselves. Roy stayed in the kitchen and talked to his mother and George and Zola while the women prepared a snack.

There would be a regular breakfast for all as soon as the chores were finished and before they left to work in the fields. Roy watched his sister set the cups, saucers and plates on the table. Sugar and thick cream followed. The spoon dish–a glass actually, four inches round and tall as a spoon–sat on the table. Each person took a spoon to help himself to sugar or stir the cream in his coffee.

Soon the brothers, dressed in their clean Oshkosh B'Gosh overalls and ready for the day's work, trooped into the kitchen. Broad grins on their faces showed their happiness at having their eldest brother home. As they sat down at the table, Roy reached over and poked Clarence in the ribs, then turned to his other side and slid Spo's chair back. As Spo was falling, Roy caught him and pushed his chair in place where it belonged. This kind of horse-play was their way of showing their happiness. Roy couldn't say anything. His throat was tight with emotion as this homely ritual of his family life took place. It was the same as before he had left home. The boys sat around the table talking and laughing joyously as they waited for Zola and their mother to put the coffee and cake on the table.

28

Zola cut the cake. When the boys and her mother were seated at the table, she poured the coffee into the cups. She reached into the cookie jar and filled a large plate with lemon-raisin and spicy molasses cookies. They were Roy's favorites and a special bonus for today. She put these goodies on the table and sat down to eat. Quietly, she listened to her brothers talking to Roy.

The kitchen was the most popular spot in their home and always had been. This was true of most of the farmers in the neighborhood. Usually, they used the parlor only when there were guests. Roy lounged in his kitchen chair and spoke in his soft-voiced way. Although he was very happy to be the center of all this attention, he was also overwhelmed by it. He wished he could disappear out in the barn for a while. His eyes were bright, and if some of the brightness was due to moisture, he wouldn't have admitted it.

Leonard asked, "Why didn't you let us know you were coming?"

"I wanted to surprise you."

"Surprise us?" they chorused, "Well, you certainly did!"

Roy's eyes lighted with laughter and glowed with happiness. This was his family and his home, and it was all that he had remembered it to be. To hide his strong emotions he reverted to more childhood tricks. Reaching out he gathered all the food at his end of the table, saying, "You can't have any of my cookies and cake. You didn't just come home from the war."

"George just did," Leonard spoke up. "He can have a treat, too."

Everyone laughed at this foolishness, and their mother passed around the cake. After finishing, the three younger boys grabbed their milk pails from the rack outside the door and raced for the barn to do the morning chores. Roy, relaxed and full of food, sat on watching his mother and sister clearing the table. He was smiling to himself, seemingly unaware of the dishes being washed and wiped, and the table reset for the real breakfast they would enjoy as soon as the chores were finished.

He watched Zola disappear down the steps into the root cellar. It was her job to bring the ham and bacon and eggs upstairs to be prepared for the very special breakfast for this very special day of celebration. The steps led to a dug out dirt-floored cellar under the house where fresh meat hung and dried smoked meats and cheeses were stored.

Roy asked about the neighbors and what they had been doing while he was away. His mother answered his questions as she prepared the rest of the meal. Roy noticed his mother had a secret little smile on her face as if she didn't want him to notice what she was doing. Roy threw a keen, quick glance at her and saw she was stirring a thick batter. "Hmm," he said to himself, "She is making my favorite breakfast...panneycakes for me especially. All my

29

favorites...ham, eggs, bacon and griddle cakes smothered with golden butter, maple syrup and honey, from our own bees." Despite the snack, his mouth watered. He pretended he hadn't noticed. He would be very surprised later.

Roy noticed a change in Zola. He was amazed at how she had grown. Where there had been a tangle-haired, long-legged bundle of hoydenish tomboy when he left home, today was a young lady on the brink of womanhood. Today, she was shy of him because he was strange to her after two years away, but other than that he saw a young lady of budding womanhood, on the threshold of life and love. Lovely, sweet and sensitive, Zola was ripe for a first crush on some local lad. Roy spoke directly to her and she blushed adorably as she looked up and smiled. Her eyes lit up as she laughed and deep dimples appeared on either side of her face. Tiny pearl-like teeth peeped between her lips.

"So, Missy," Roy said, in his soft voice, "You've grown up since I've been away. Ma, where did my kid sister go while I was away?"

His mother laughed as she said, "You'll know soon enough. And right when you don't expect it. Still full of tricks, that one."

"Full of tricks, eh? Still think you can out shoot me?"

"I hit the bull's eye dead center." she said somewhat defiantly as the color rose again in her cheeks. I've been practicing a lot. Just last week, I shot a rabbit in the carrot patch. I used the rifle and only one shell."

"Who held you up?" laughed Roy remembering the first time she had fired a gun and been knocked flat by the jolt of the gun against her shoulder.

"Wait and see," answered Zola, piqued at the memory. Her dignity affronted, she flounced out of her chair, turned her back on Roy, and walked to the window.

"Didn't I shoot a rabbit last week, Ma?"

"Yes, she surely did, Roy, and we had rabbit pie. Shot right in the head, too. You'll have to look to your laurels when you compete with her, now." Zola looked sideways at Roy, laughed quietly and left the room to do the morning household tasks. Aside from her shyness, she was a captivating girl with an engaging personality.

Pushing back his chair, Roy stood up, walked to the door and said, "I don't think I am very popular in here just now, Ma. I'd better go out to the barn and see what I can do to set the boys on end. I'll leave you girls to get the breakfast."

Head down, Roy walked thoughtfully towards the barn. His thoughts were of how frail his mother had become... so thin. There were grey hairs in her curly dark locks now. There hadn't been any when he left home.

He vowed to himself he would see that things were made easier for her from now on. No more worries for his mom. He realized that although he had not watched his mother this closely before, now he saw pain lines in her face. Pain lines of suffering, both mental and physical, deeply etched around her nose and mouth. She had always been a very pleasant and good-natured woman, and even those lines were shaped by her character. They didn't droop, just deepened into lines of smiling optimism. You felt the depth of her faith, and the abundance of her love. It was all as much a part of her as breathing. He had noticed that her movements were slower than before. Slower, as if she were very, very weary. Her once beautiful eyes, her most outstanding feature, were now sunken into her head and listless.

"I am lucky she is still here to welcome me home," he thought.

The Dream

As he entered the barn, Roy heard the swish, swish, swish of the milk striking inside the pails as the boys milked the cows. Clarence and Spo were milking, Leonard was pitching hay into the mangers and graining the horses. Roy saw the row of cats lined up in the cow barn beneath the milk pail shelf eagerly awaiting their turn to have their breakfast of fresh, warm foaming milk. Reaching for his three-legged milk stool, he felt something brush against his leg. Looking down, he saw old 'Goolie' the calico cat, rubbing against him. He could tell she had a new litter of kittens by the way her belly was dragging. She was full of milk for those little blind balls of multicolored fur in the corner of the manger. Roy scooped her up in one hand and carried her to the manger to visit her kittens. While he walked over, he talked to her and rubbed her head against his cheek, "You're a good cat, 'Goolie,' he murmured into her soft hairy ear. "You are going to keep us free of rats and mice aren't you, old girl? And when that family of yours grows up, who will feed them, huh?"

The other cats, jealous of Goolie, surrounded Roy and meowed their disapproval of his partiality. Disdainful of the others, Old Goolie laid her cheek against Roy's and purred her welcome home to him. Setting Goolie down, Roy gently prodded a finger into the circlet of fur deep in the hay. Muted mewling sounds began to erupt from the wriggling pile of fur. With an anxious "miaow," Goolie moved over, stretched out on her side and purred for the kittens to "come and get it." They began creeping blindly towards their breakfast. Laughing quietly to himself, Roy turned back to the cow barn to talk to his brothers.

Putting his milk stool on the floor next to the wall, Roy sat down. He leaned back on one leg of the stool and braced his back against the wall. He watched the boys milking the cows. He heard the steady, stoical chewing of the horses, their teeth grinding hay and oats, jaws moving rhythmically from side to side. This was his home as he remembered it. He was satisfied.

The boys told him, as if bestowing great largesse upon him, that, since it was his first day home, he needn't help with the chores or haying today.

"A kind of hero's treat," they said.

"If that's the case," Roy said quietly, "what's planned for me tomorrow? Will I still be a hero?"

"More haying," they chorused laughing. "We saved it for you."

This was a joke. They hadn't known when he was coming and hay was cut, raked and put in the barn when it ripened.

When Roy and later George left for the military service, it had been expected that Clarence, Newell and Leonard, with the help of Grandpa, would take care of the farm. Clarence, the eldest of the three teenagers, had been nineteen at that time. But shortly after Roy left, first Clarence and then Newell, came down with rheumatic fever and had to stay in bed for months. There were twenty-five milking cows on the farm. With Grandpa's help, fourteen-year-old Leonard did all the work. Grandpa helped as much as he was able, but he was eighty-six and he could not do any heavy work. Grandpa could show and tell Leonard how the farming should be done and when, but young Leonard had to actually do it. As a result, Leonard had developed a set of powerfully muscled shoulders, more than equal to many full-grown men.

Besides the cows Leonard had to care for the horses, pigs and poultry. He also planted, tilled and harvested the crops. Shortly before Roy returned, Clarence and Newell had begun to recuperate and were able to help Leonard. However, the fever had left each of them with a serious heart condition. Heavy or strenuous work was out of the question.

Leonard finished feeding the horses and joined his brothers at the milking. Roy knew Leonard had done all the farm work while he was in the army. He asked him how he had managed. Leonard told him about the first time he had made hay alone.

He told Roy it had been very difficult in the beginning. It had taken him half a day to lift the hay rack onto the wagon bed before he could bring in the hay. The wagon bed consisted of the wheels and axles joined by a flat bed of boards. The hay rack was used in summer for hauling hay, corn stalks and straw. In winter, the hay rack was taken off the wagon bed and the wagon box replaced it. In the wagon box they hauled stove wood, potatoes, ear corn, apples and vegetables from the garden and stored them in the root cellar for

34

winter use. It was also used to haul coal, barrels of sugar, flour and salt from the store. When it was necessary, Grandpa would walk to the store in Winneconne, nine miles distant, for odd items. In winter, he pulled them home on a bobsled.

Leonard told Roy he had used every type of wedging device he and grandpa could think of. Finally he had succeeded in raising the wagon box off and replacing it with the wagon rack. He knew he was the only one to do it and he had stayed with it until it was done. Roy could picture this as he knew when Leonard began something, he never quit until it was finished.

Leonard had to quit school to keep up with all the farm work. In Roy's absence, he had become the man of the family.

Looking at Leonard anew and approvingly, Roy saw a handsome youth and realized he would someday be a very handsome man. Leonard was a darkly-tanned, blonde youth. He had hazel eyes sparkling with life and vitality. He thought, too, of Leonard's bashfulness and hoped he had gotten over it. It had been embarrassing to find Leonard hiding in the barn or behind a tree or the house whenever visitors came.

Regardless of his bashfulness, Leonard had always known exactly what was going on and everything that had been said. Roy remembered how much Leonard had loved sports. Skiing and ice skating were his favorites. He asked him if he had participated in any sports lately.

"Yes." replied Leonard, "Some, but mostly hunting rabbits. They were circling the bark on the fruit trees in the orchard. The snow was deep and the rabbits were hungry. We had many delicious rabbit stews."

"So," laughed Roy, "That's where Zola has been practicing with a gun. She told me she could shoot as well as I, even if I had been hunting larger game... Huns."

Not being able to wait any longer to broach his pet project for the future, Roy took his courage in hand and asked if they knew of anyone around there who owned a flying machine. "Do you know anyone who pilots flying machines, or gives flying instructions?"

"There is a Mr. Lee, " Clarence answered. "He was an inspector of flying machines in the war and flew them. He tested them after they had been repaired. He is just back from France and the war. He was visiting at Theodore's across the road last week. Alice is his sister. He knew Eddie Rickenbacker and Quentin Roosevelt. They were in his division. He was in charge of maintenance for their planes. Viola will be over later today to help Ma pick strawberries. Talk to her about it. Why do you ask?"

"So you and Viola are still sweethearts, are you? Well, well, what do you know? Hasn't anyone cut you out?"

"No, and they had better not," Clarence grinned boldly at Roy, "Just let them try."

"Any day now," said Newell, to heckle Clarence.

"Anyway," began Roy. He spoke seriously and quietly. "I have something important to tell you, but it must be kept secret. It has been bouncing around in my head for several years. In fact, ever since Pa took me to see the flying machine in Neenah when I was just a kid. I wanted to enlist in the Canadian Air Force when the war first began, before the U.S. was in it. Ma was adamant against it. I didn't want her to worry so I didn't enlist.

"After harvest this summer, I am going to the State Fair in Milwaukee for one day. From there I'm going to Diggins Aviation School in Chicago and take flying lessons. I don't want Ma to know about it yet. She will worry and I don't want that. Just keep it under your hats until I tell her, understand? After I finish my lessons and get my certificate, I am going to buy a flying machine, turn the hayfield into an aviation field and go into the flying business for money."

The milking abruptly ceased. At once, three pair of astounded eyes were turned on him.

"Flying!" they chorused. Clarence, the first to regain his speech, said, "You must have been shell-shocked over there? You can't be serious!" After a pause he asked, "You mean we'll be flying farmers?"

"You betcha," Roy answered, "after I finish my flying lessons, I'll teach all of you to fly. Then we'll be the 'Flying Larson Brothers'. We'll fly all over the state. We'll be stunt flyers, and put on exhibitions. We'll have a flying school of our own, we'll teach flying. We'll build an aviation field north of the house, where the hayfield is now. I plan on buying Charlie Lea's timber marsh and cutting the trees for lumber to build a hangar. I'll do all that, just as soon as I can talk Ma into letting me have some flying machines here." Roy's usually quiet, soft voice was excited and quite determined.

"A hangar?" questioned Clarence, "What's that?"

"A hangar is a barn or garage for flying machines. It's where you store them to keep them out of the weather. It's also a machine shed for repairing and building flying machines, where you do repairs and mechanical work. I also have plans for building and remodelling flying machines. All these ideas have been on my mind for a couple of years. It all depends on Ma."

"Yippee!" shouted Leonard excitedly, "We're going to fly." His loud yell made the cows jump and throw their tails in the air.

"Quiet." Roy said, "and calm down or Ma'll hear you and put the kibosh on everything before we even get started."

Roy had to laugh at Leonard. He suddenly realized what a bombshell he had sprung on the boys. He had been envisioning his aviation field and planning it, in detail, for years. For enough years, in fact, that it seemed entirely sensible to him. No one knew his plans. Like most things, he had kept them strictly to himself. Looking back, to the beginning "over there," when the idea to become a flyboy had first occurred, it had seemed as incredible to him, an impossible dream. He realized that it was now as incredible for his brothers. Sometimes, even now, it seemed to be an impossible dream but he knew he would never quit until he made it come true.

"Whoever heard of flying farmers?" asked Clarence, laughing, eyes crinkled in amusement.

"Well," Roy answered, "If they never heard of them before, they soon will."

With those seemingly prophetic words hanging in the air, Roy stood up, and replaced the stool on its nail in the wall. He turned and walked toward the barn door, leaving the mewling cats and his astounded, skeptical and incredulous brothers milking the cows.

Head bent, Roy walked slowly toward the house, shadowed by Dick the dog. His thoughts were mixed. What I told the boys, he thought, is what I intend to do. I must convince Ma how important flying is to me–the be all and end all. She must understand. I was born for this. I had to be or it wouldn't be so extremely important to me. Nothing else in the world matters. I have to fly. The only drawback is Ma's fear that I might crash. He pondered how to tell her, to get her to agree with his plans. Pausing, as he approached the kitchen door...he veered towards the north corner of the house and leaned back against it. From there he looked out over the hayfield, half of the hay was cut, winnowed and ready to haul into the barn for next winter's feed for the horses and cows.

His gaze moved further afield. He saw a field of young corn, newly-sprouted. It was growing straight and firm, some showing the light color of its new, healthy sprouts. It was a field to be proud of, but the corn was not of much concern to him. His eyes fastened again on the hay field, where the sweet soft smell of clover blossoms filled the air with scent pleasing to Roy's nostrils as he stood dreaming in the morning sun.

"It all begins here," Roy said to himself as he mentally paced off rods of land for the runway. He was seeing it as it would be when the haying was over, the field cleared of stones, the pot holes filled. A perfect landing field for flying machines was what his mind's eye saw. And over there, a hangar with a wind sock waving in the breeze, a garage for airplanes. He smiled, remembering Clarence's excited voice. Roy continued to imagine his aviation field. The hangar will be built rugged and strong to withstand any storm. It will be built on the lines of a very large barn. Large enough to hold six flying machines. We shall each have our own plane and this will be a 'flying family' business, with exhibitions, passengers, as well as commercial and training school. Maybe even take that trip to Norway that I promised my dad years ago."

In his fantasy, flying machines were landing and taking off. Clattering engines noisily building up to a roar for the moment of take off. He saw himself in the next machine coming in for a landing. Gliding, down toward the end of the field and his new hangar. He felt a bubble of pride pressing his throat. Now he was the one flying that mythical machine. He, Roy Larson, was the flyboy. Roy Larson, himself, the owner of that flying machine and that new flying field. With grit and faithfulness to his dream he knew it could come true. Dreaming on, he envisioned the crowds buying tickets to fly with him. Deeply engrossed in his fantasies, he was quite unaware of his surroundings. He never noticed the buzzing bees industriously flitting from delicately colored flowers to vividly colored flowers. He never noticed the twittering or singing birds, flying here and there seeking food for the clamoring young in their nests. A mother squirrel, high up in a towering oak tree regarded Roy with fearful and questioning eyes. She continued to watch until feeling all was safe, then she fed her young bits of newly unearthed nuts that she had carefully buried last October for her winter food supply.

Insensible to this scurrying life around him, Roy dreamed on. Flying machines were stunting and the flying circus was there, zooming up, over and down, as the huge audience screamed and gasped at the daring stunts. Then the clang of the milk pails as his brothers emerged from the barn startled him out of his bold dreams. Turning back to the kitchen door, he entered the house with the boys. They were a merry group as they gathered around the table.

"Well," said Roy, feigning great surprise, as he looked over the table and saw ham, bacon, fried potatoes, pancakes, as well as honey and syrup on the table. "You must have killed two fatted calves, Ma. You are serving me a grand feast."

With that they all sat down and, with the gusto of five hungry young men, proceeded to eat all the food on the table.

Welcome Home

Otto Nelson was the first of his neighbors to welcome Roy home, followed closely by the McKinleys, who had learned he had returned via the party telephone line. After the evening chores that night, the Theodore Larson family heartily greeted the returned doughboy.

In 1913, Theodore Larson had purchased the Charles Lea farm, which was almost directly across the road from the Larson brothers' farm. Ted Larson's wife was Alice Lea, the niece of Charles Lea. Although spelled Norwegian-style, the name *Lea* was pronounced *Lee*. Ted and Alice Larson had two children, Loyall, a son; and Viola, a daughter. Loyall grew to be a tall, well-built, blonde, handsome young man, a credit to his Norwegian forebears.

From her earliest childhood Viola held the promise of real beauty. A wealth of lustrous, warm, brown hair framed an oval face of perfect features. Her small, straight nose, uptilted lips and firm chin molded a lovely face. Vivid blue eyes, shining with the joy of living, were accented by thick dark lashes and delicate, dark crescent eyebrows. She could have been a model for any artist with an eye for perfection. Viola's face exhibited love, dignity and courage. Her beauty was accentuated by the willowy grace of a tall, shapely young woman.

Viola began admiring Clarence Larson in their one-room school days. In 1916, Viola was 13 and Clarence was 20. They were not too young to appreciate a mutual attraction. They fell in love and, except to deepen and grow, their feelings never changed. In 1928, after a long courtship, Viola and

Clarence married. Clarence passed away shortly after, but Viola remained a part of Larson aviation. Pilots could always find coffee brewing, homemade cookies fresh-baked, and good conversation centered on flying.

Sitting across the parlor from Roy on his first night home, Viola was an enchanting picture in plum-colored silk. Her full-skirted dress fell about her in graceful folds. Long-fingered, her hands were folded quietly together in her lap. Her hair, for the first time worn up, was in a tight chignon, replacing the usual long, tidy braid. Captivatingly, curly wisps fell around her small pink ears and pale-pink cheeks.

Verging on sixteen and feeling budding womanhood upon her, she exuded femininity in a charming manner. Her wandering eyes betrayed her love for Clarence, the target of her girlish admiration. He was sitting near her mother, Alice, a comely woman, kindly and intelligent.

Viola and Zola, Clarence's sister, chatted in low tones. Although two years apart they were close friends. Zola, the only sister, was the youngest of the six children and the family pet. She was the only true blonde in the family. Her manners were simple, kind and gracious except when the brothers teased her into forgetfulness and she regressed into their little tomboy sister. In summer, she acquired a warm tan that, with her blondness, was startlingly attractive. Her mother had taught her to change from a tomboy into a demure young lady. With her brothers she was mischievous, impish and hoydenish. How could she help it? She was the only girl with five older brothers.

She had been petted, abetted, and greatly beloved all her life. Her mother's gentle strength and loving, strict discipline had not allowed her to be spoiled, despite a fond father and indulgent grandparents. She had a natural love of fun and quickness of spirit.

Shy, Leonard sat in the corner as inconspicuously as he possibly could. The youngest of the five boys, he was very alert to everything going on. He was a handsome young fellow with a different look than the other brothers. All were good-looking young men, but Leonard had a clean-cut, well-brushed, strikingly mannish look for a young fellow. It was a look of great strength of character as well as muscle.

Newell, nicknamed "Spo" in early childhood, was a witty and outspoken jokester. He had special names–not always flattering, but appropriate–for many of the family's acquaintances. Born on Christmas Day, 1900, Spo liked cats, cooking and kidding around. Tall, lanky, and loosely built, he had a long back and a shirt tail that usually hung out of his pants.

George, born October 13, 1896, died March 24, 1920. He did not live long enough to take part in Larson aviation.

Roy, the hero of the evening, had hazel eyes. He was darker than the others, a little less than six feet tall and squarely built. Roy had a childishness in his humor and a love of acrobatics that contrasted with his quiet manner and cautious good sense when it came to flying.

This was the cast of characters–all family, all solid Norwegian-American farmers–who would make aviation history in the next few years.

Interim

By the middle of July, the hay was cut, cured and in the barn, with the overflow in a stack in the field nearby. By the middle of August, the grain was harvested, threshed and stored in bins, with the straw stacked outside. The corn was cultivated and would mature in early autumn. With the four young men working together, farming was a breeze. On the night the threshers left, Clarence asked Roy when he was planning on leaving for Milwaukee and the State Fair.

"I plan on breaking the news to Ma tomorrow," Roy replied. "About the State Fair, that is. Nothing more and don't even think about the other. She might read your mind."

When Roy told his mother he was going to the State Fair and might be gone a couple weeks, visiting friends and travelling some, she stopped preparing the evening meal and said, "Roy, I have been aware for some time that you're not yourself since you came back from the service. You are no longer content to be the farmer boy you were before you went to France. Something is bothering you. You are so restless. Did you meet a pretty French girl and fall in love and don't want to tell me?"

"No." said Roy. "Now that you have asked me I will tell you that I fell in love, but not with a girl."

"What do you mean, you fell in love, but not with a girl...what else is there?"

"I fell in love with flying, Ma, and I can't live without it."

"You might not live with it, either, Roy." she said. "No Roy! no! no! I

43

don't ever want to see you fly. You know that George is dying of the quick consumption. The doctor thinks our Zola may have it, too. I don't know how I can stand it to lose him and my only daughter. And such a lovely girl, too. Dr. Hendrickson thinks she may have caught it from George. If I have to lose them, it will be all I can stand. If I had to live in fear of losing you, too, I just couldn't bear it. Especially from crashing in an airplane. It is just silly to think of you flying. Your father would tell you that if God meant for people to fly, he would have given them wings. Promise me, Roy, promise me that you will forget this absurd notion and be a good farmer boy and help the boys and me."

Roy swallowed painfully. How could he give up flying? Most reluctantly, he gave her his promise that she would never see him fly. "I promise, Ma, I will help you on the farm and you will never see me fly." Roy answered her.

Roy had never been one to chatter about his thoughts. He talked little and thought a lot. He was still determined to fly and he would work it out somehow, but he would never worry his mother with his plans. She would never see him fly.

Roy was very unhappy and frustrated after that conversation with his mother. He loved her dearly and did not want to give her a moment's worry. She was frail and sickly and might go at any time. He also knew George's condition was worsening. He had heard Zola coughing, too, and noticed she was growing thin and pale. He felt frustrated and angry because there was nothing he could do to help them, to make his family well again.

"No!" he thought, "Zola is our only sister, something must be done for her right away before it is too late."

Later that day he went to Larsen to see Dr. Hendricksen but Mrs. Hendricksen told Roy the Doctor was ill and couldn't see anyone. Roy knew that meant he was on one of his drinking sprees and that made the young farmer very angry.

"Why does such a brilliant and gifted doctor have to be drunk when he is needed so much?" he asked himself, and got no answer.

When he returned home, Roy was very angry. He told his mother where he had been and why. He also told her that Doc was on another drunk. His mother told him the doctor had recently lost another case of consumption–a young fellow at Zittau–and he just couldn't face it when a young patient died. When that happened the only way he could keep on practicing was to get dead drunk for a while. It lessened the agony of remembering.

"And before that he lost Clarissa Cross with pneumonia. She was a young mother of four children. That was really sad. Poor motherless children, the eldest was seven years old."

"Forget they died, Ma, why should he? Why doesn't he go out and try that much harder to save the rest of us instead of being in bed dead drunk when he is needed by others who are seriously sick. Besides, he is the only doctor within thirteen miles of Larsen. What do the rest of us do? If we need a doctor, who will be there when we call him?"

With those angry words, Roy stormed out of the house. He closed the screen door very quietly behind him. It was an indication that his usually gentle disposition was greatly disturbed. All the boys usually shoved the door open and let it bang behind them. If one of them was gentle with the door, it meant he was being rough on himself.

Not long after he spoke with his mother, Roy went to the State Fair. He had been going to the Winnebago County Fair–one of Wisconsin's largest–for as long as he could remember and had always enjoyed it. The State Fair was many times larger, with exhibits that would interest him as a farmer and plenty of entertainment, but this year everything–from the blue-ribbon cattle to the freaks in the sideshows–was boring.

He was anxious to go to the Diggins Flying School in Chicago. No matter how long it took, Roy Larson was going to be a flyboy. He was going to have his own flying machine and his own aviation field. Roy reasoned that if he went to the Diggins Flying School right away, his mother wouldn't have to know or worry about it. She would think he was enjoying the State Fair in Milwaukee.

Roy had been raised in the faith of the Lutheran Church in Winchester, and he knew that what he was planning was, in a way, lying to her. On the other hand, he felt confident that nothing would happen to him and as long as he kept to his word that she would never *see* him fly, or even know about it, it wouldn't be hurtful to her health and he wouldn't be breaking the letter of his promise.

"I didn't say, I wouldn't fly," he rationalized. "I promised her she would never see me fly."

Diggins

On the train from Milwaukee to Chicago, Roy met a young Chinese man named Chung. The two travelers soon discovered they had much in common. Like Roy, a veteran of the war in France, Chung was on his way to the Diggins School of Aviation to take flying lessons. He had no prior flying experience, only a determination to learn, just like Roy. When each learned why the other was going to Chicago, they laughed over the coincidence of a fair-haired farmer, war veteran and would-be flyboy from Wisconsin sharing a seat on a train with an equally young war veteran and would-be flyboy from China.

By the time they arrived in Chicago, they had decided to become partners in their great adventure. They would room and train together, two young men in love with flying. Their heads were already in the air. All they needed was to get their feet off the ground.

From the North Western railroad depot in Chicago, the two would-be aviators hurried to a streetcar. They gave no thought to finding rooms or a hotel. The Ashburn Park office of Ralph G. Diggins was their destination and that was where they went. Mr. Diggins met them at the door of a large building that looked like a storage shed. He invited them into his office and asked them what they wanted.

"To learn to fly," said Roy and Chung, in almost the same breath. Mr. Diggins smiled at them and then brought them down to earth quite quickly when he explained that flying lessons were $50.00 an hour and they would need ten hours of instruction before they could solo. If they wanted to learn aerobatics they would have to have an additional two hours of instruction. It would be a total of $500.00 to solo and $600.00 for the full course if they wanted to become a stunt pilot and put on exhibitions. It was $25.00 for a ride, he added. If they decided to take lessons he would apply the $25.00 towards the total.

Their decision was unanimous, "Yes."

Mr. Diggins sent them away to find rooms and a place to eat. "Come back tomorrow and I'll take you for a ten minute ride over the city and Lake Michigan. Then we'll talk about the flying lessons," he said.

They found a room three blocks from the airfield near a grocery store. They bought cheese, a long loaf of bread and a bottle of milk for their supper. Neither cared what they ate or drank that night. Their minds were on flying the next day. Both decided to take their flying lessons at a later date. They agreed on how wonderful it would be to float around in a plane, high in the air. They spent the evening talking about what they were going to do and the wonderful future ahead of them. When Roy was excited or unusually happy about something, he would do some stunt. That night Chung was amused to see Roy walking around the room on his hands while he talked about flying.

The ride over Chicago, above the skyscrapers and over Lake Michigan, was all they had anticipated and more. Neither thought it was nearly long enough to satisfy their appetites for flying. All it did was raise the temperature of their fever to go aloft.

Neither Roy nor Chung had the $500 they would need to start lessons, but they did sign up. They also promised each other to return as soon as possible and train together.

Weeks later, back at Diggins School, both were studying intently, eager to learn all they needed to know.

"*The resistance experienced by the parts of an airplane in flight is due to (a) distortion of the free flow of the air, otherwise streamlined flow,*" read Roy out loud to Chung. This was their third day. Roy had bought a book on airplane mechanics because, as he said, "If I am going to fly it, I'll have to know how to fix it."

Chung answered, "If I am going to fly it in China, I will have to build it." Then he read aloud from his textbook: "*The only road to proficiency is practice.*"

"Oh, listen to this," answered Roy, "*The minimum time a pupil shall be in the air in the aggregate before making the necessary flights for an aviator's certificate shall be five hours, of which at least two shall be solo.* That's the Federal law. Wonder why Diggins makes us take ten hours?

48

"I'll bet I could solo now," said Roy, as he started to recite what he had learned from his book.

"I've memorized the controls. Here is what it says:"

"*The lateral ailerons are on the wing tips: movable surface of the wing on the trailing edge. As the stick is moved, the ailerons move. If the wing on the left is to go down, push the stick towards the left wing. This we do on beginning of the turn and coming out of the turn. After you begin the turn and the stick is pushed over to the left pull the stick back to neutral position.*

"*The rudders are vertical on the plane. They steer the nose to where you want to go. They are operated by the feet. Two foot pedals. When you step on the left pedal it will move the rudder to start the turn, at the same time push the stick way over to the left. When the turn is established, let the pedal up and bring the stick back to neutral. Do the same for the right turn only the opposite.*

"*Starting the airplane: Walk around the airplane and run a line check of all controls. Also water and gas. Check gas and water with sticks (carried in plane). Be sure to chock the wheels, or else the person turning the propeller could be struck down by the plane when the engine engages. When the pilot is alone, fasten ropes on the chocks, then pull them away from the wheels when the plane is idling.*

"*To move out: push the throttle forward, slightly (called, 'crack the throttle'). You can hear it sucking gas when the propeller is turned. Pull the stick back slightly. Otherwise, if the motor comes on too fast, the tail may come up and the propeller will go into the ground and break.*

"*Initiate carburetor flooding by hand, then pull the airscrew...*"

("Did you hear Diggins say they are beginning to call all airscrews propellers, though our book says that only pushing airscrews are propellers and pulling airscrews are tractors?)" ...*through several times in the direction of rotation with the switches set to off to avoid premature starting, then against the usual direction of rotation, in order to distribute lubrication and adjust the amount of gas in the engine. When the person pulling the propeller, or cranker, believes the engine is ready to start, he says* "Contact!". *The pilot sets his switches to on and answers,* "Contact!". *The cranker turns it in the forward direction again and the motor engages.*

"*The cranker steps back quickly when the motor catches, to escape the whirling propeller. At that time the motor should be left idling for a bit to warm it. If the engine doesn't start, turn the switches to 'off' and begin the whole procedure over again.*

"If there is no wind sock in sight, before the propeller is rotating, wet your finger and hold it up to the wind. Wind direction is very important. All take offs should be into the wind. When the motor is warmed, remove the chocks and taxi into takeoff position. Push throttle forward and use rudder for turns to get into position. It is usual to have the stick in neutral position when taxiing for take off. Check to see it is clear ahead of you and nothing coming in behind you. To lift off, put throttle in forward position until going full force. Then put stick forward just enough to get going at a pretty good speed. That speed varies with the velocity of the wind. If the wind is strong, a lower ground speed is sufficient. When you feel you have sufficient speed, pull stick back and that will depress the tail because the elevators raise and the wind pressure on them depresses the tail which will cause the front end to raise off the ground.

"Climb to at least 1,000 feet and neutralize the stick. If the plane is tail heavy, move the stick forward just a little. Make a few gentle turns while climbing so you know the student has learned that. Check your wings to see they are straight with the horizon. Practice with controls at 1,000 feet to keep plane straight and level. The student should make a few turns keeping the plane level.

"As one approaches the field for a landing, he should turn into the wind and pull the throttle way back and usually pull the stick back a little to establish a normal glide.

"A normal glide is when the pilot can glide the farthest as the plane is steadily dropping. The motor is merely idling. Pull the stick back gently as the ground approaches and when touch down is accomplished, pull way back to slow down the plane and maintain control by keeping the tail on the ground. After landing, put the stick in neutral and push the throttle forward so the engine will taxi the plane to the spot where you want it."

"Well," said Chung, "Now it's my turn:

"While gliding, the student should make turns using stick and rudders while in a normal glide. He should practice gliding turns from straight and level positions. Rules: (1) A pilot must never turn down wind at a low altitude when faced with the possibility of a forced landing. A pilot in difficulties after leaving the ground must keep straight on and not attempt to turn back. (2) A pilot must save himself and his passengers first and not the plane. It is better to smash propeller and wheels than to burn a man to death. (3) A pilot must take particular care to maintain flying speed after engine failure."

"Some hints," said Roy, *"The best times for flying are the stillness of very early morning or in the calm of the late afternoon. The wind dies down at sunset. And there is often the least wind at sunrise."*

Later, "Did you read that the windshield is made of isinglass?"

"Yes, and did you know the cover on the wings is put on loosely, sewed like a pair of pants and then the dope is put on? The dope is like lacquer and is made of guncotton, acetate and nitrate, something like fingernail polish. The dope shrinks the slipcovers to fit the frame of the wings like skin."

"Yes," said Roy, "I know all of that, too, and soon I'll be a bird."

And with that he put a broom stick between two chairs and began walking across it and flapping his arms like wings.

"I'll bet I could fly, too," he continued, "I am going through all the motions in my head all the while I'm away from the airfield as well as when I am in the plane with Diggins."

Once again he began walking around the room on his hands.

"We are to concentrate on 'dead-stick' landings tomorrow."

"Yippee," said Roy, "the farm boy showing. Standing upright again, he said, "Let's go have some chow tonight," and they did. It was the Chicago version of Chinese chow mein.

Back in their room the next night, Roy said, "Those dead-stick landings are a real thrill when you know you've got a guy sitting behind you with a stick just like yours in his hand and he knows what to do with it."

"Know what you mean," answered Chung, soberly. "Roy did you ever think before now that we would some day be doing such things? I can't wait to tell my family and friends in China that I can fly and repair airplanes. They will think I have been smoking too much opium."

(Aviation had matured enough to have its own jargon: flying machines were now aeroplanes or airplanes; flyboys were pilots or aviators; and aviation fields had become landing fields or airports).

Finally, they reached the day when they would attempt their first solo flights. Fears the weather might be bad haunted their sleep. In their dreams, they were taking off, flying and landing all night. They were up at the crack of dawn and rushed out to the field, always testing the wind, always fearing that it might be too strong or too weak.

They had to wait nearly an hour for the instructor to prepare for them to take off. They flipped a coin as to which would make the first solo flight. Roy won.

Now the airplane came out of the shed, pushed from behind by one man and pulled from the front by another. It was a "Cannuck", the Canadian made-

Curtiss JN4, universally known as the "Jenny". To Roy and Chung, this homely workhorse of pioneer aviation was the most beautiful sight they had ever seen. With it they would accomplish life's goal of flying solo.

Their stomachs jerked taut at the thought. Presently, the men returned to the shed and brought out another Cannuck. Although there were two planes ready to fly, the field was too small for more than one to take off at a time. The ground crew chocked the wheels and the instructor motioned the boys onto the field.

They ran quickly across to the planes. Each ran a line check of all controls according to instructions. They checked the gas and water with the measuring sticks they were to carry at all times when flying. They checked the motor to be sure nothing had dropped into it to cause trouble when it was in operation. They checked the tires for pressure as Mr. Diggins had advised them. Then Roy stepped onto the wing of his plane and quickly slid into the pilot's seat.

At last he was going to solo. Today, he would be a pilot.

Inside, he tried the rudders and ailerons, pulled on the stick and found all was in order. With the throttle slightly open for flooding to commence, Roy was ready to start. Each of these early airplanes had its own idiosyncracies for starting, and each one required a slightly different mix of forward and reverse pulls on the propeller. The instructor stood in front of Roy's plane and pulled the propeller around to suck gas into the engine. When the engine had flooded, he reversed direction to pump a little out again. Finally, the mixture seemed right.

"Contact," he said.

Roy turned on the switch and replied, "Contact."

The instructor pulled the propeller in the forward direction. The motor caught, coughed, caught again, spinning the propeller more rapidly with each passing moment. The wind from the propeller blew words into space and the loud roar of the motor made conversation impossible. Roy's hair felt like tiny whips as the propwash blew it against his face.

The chocks were pulled and the plane began to move forward. Roy checked the direction he was facing, the direction of the wind and the length of the runway. He checked for any obstruction ahead. His was the only plane. It was his solo and now everything was right for take off.

He looked over the side of the plane at the ground, and smiled. He was exactly where he had always wanted to be – in the pilot's seat of an airplane. He adjusted his goggles and fastened the chin strap of his helmet. Settling down lower into his seat, he took a good grip on the stick, tried the ailerons and rudders. He looked for smoke from chimnies in the city to ascertain the direction of the wind. There wasn't much air moving today.

After he determined the direction for take off, he moved the throttle forward slowly until he felt the plane begin to move. The stick was in neutral and he kicked the pedals to make the rudder move so he could head into the wind and the correct position for take off. Again, he carefully pushed the throttle forward until he felt the engine quicken and the plane begin to move. He pushed the throttle forward until the engine was going full force. The plane roared and Roy pulled the stick back.

The plane taxied over the rough, rutted ground lurching from side to side, reminiscent of a Saturday night drunk. The piano wire supports became taut and loose in turn as the plane lurched on, in and out of pot holes. It gained momentum, clattering loudly, engine roaring, louder and louder. The thunder of the engine was sweet music in his ears. He pulled the stick back, and depressed the tail. The nose gradually lifted. He was airborne and climbing.

He took another look at the ground. The joy of the moment caught in his throat. It pulsed through him and, for a moment, he was emotionally unstrung. Nearly always cool in any situation, Roy now fought his emotions. He was flying at last. Soloing. A dream accomplished.

The wind was getting stronger and he leveled the plane off at about 1,000 feet. "Now, now," Roy told himself. "Now for the figure eights and the three-mile trip back, the landing, and that will be it. I shall be a certified pilot. He checked his wings to be sure they were straight with the horizon.

Mr. Diggins took a personal interest in each of his students and if possible, was always on the field to watch his students solo. It was a new thrill for him each time a pupil soloed successfully. He always caught some of the excitement of the student and remembered his own first flight alone. He watched Roy take off."

"Not bad," he noted. "A little wobbly, but then..."

He watched Roy make the figure eights, the right and left turns. He watched the three mile trip and the turn into the wind for the landing, and he smiled with satisfaction at his student's prowess. He watched Roy come in on a normal glide, with the plane steadily dropping. He was always a little nervous as a student approached touchdown. He felt that was the crucial point of any first flight.

In the plane, Roy concentrated on his landing. He made sure he approached into the wind. He pulled the throttle way back and pulled the stick back a little to establish the glide. He pulled the stick back gently as he approached the ground. When the plane touched down Roy pulled the stick all the way back to slow down, then put the stick in neutral and pushed the throttle forward to regain enough speed to taxi to the spot where he wanted to stop.

Diggins, the assistant and the other students crowded around Roy as he slid off the wing of the plane. It was all congratulations and pats on the back.

It was Chung's turn and he did his flight as well as Roy.

"Good show," the instructors said to the boys.

"Your wings have sprouted, boys," said Mr. Diggins. "From now on they will grow and grow."

Roy returned from Chicago, to remain a most reluctant, but nevertheless capable and industrious farmer. He had tasted the glorious fruit of flying and he didn't want to give it up. He had also kept his promise. He never flew or mentioned flying in his mother's presence. He became the farmer his mother wanted him to be, sharing the farm work with his brothers, each according to his physical ability.

The farming days drifted by, each much like the other. Chores and field work had to be done. In 1921, Roy heard of a school which taught engineering as it applied to automobiles and airplanes. One winter, when the farm work lessened, he took Clarence and enrolled in Sweenie's School of Engineering in Kansas City, Kansas. Both Clarence and Roy were skillful, apt students and they finished the course early.

Roy's mother was very happy to have him home, but she also sensed the banked fires within him longing to be released. She worried about it too, but she couldn't convince herself that she should release him from his promise. Her fear of losing him, too, was constant. She had already lost her husband and then three more deaths came in three years. First Grandpa, then George and beautiful young Zola. She feared that more of her children would die.

In the last months of her life, in the depression of her own mortal illness, she said many times, "We are a doomed family. I wish this old house would burn down and burn all the illnesses we have had along with it."

Julia Larson passed away after a severe stroke on April 22, 1922.

After his mother's funeral, Roy was released from his promise. He felt free to pursue the one love of his life, flying. He began to dream again. He still had his army discharge money. He could use it to buy Charlie Lea's marshland timber and an airplane. Then he would be in business.

A few days later, as the boys were milking, Roy talked again about his dreams. "I have a proposition to make to you. When the estate is settled, we will automatically be co-owners of the farm. Do you think you might want to go in with me on my crazy notion of building an airport here and entering into the aviation business? I, personally, have enough money to buy the marshland. There will be more than enough lumber to build a hangar for the airplanes. The business would entail giving flying lessons, taking passengers for rides around the state, doing exhibition flying, stunting. We could repair our own and other people's airplanes, if there are ever any others around here. We would have our own gas tanks and sell to other aviators.

"We would continue to farm the same as now. The aviation business income would be just an added bonus. We would be co-owners of the farm, the hangar, and any airplanes we buy. Think it over very carefully. You will each have to make up your own mind. If I crash and get killed, you'll have an empty hangar and a lot of debts. None of you are able to fly as yet, and you'll be out of the flying business. Of course, you'll always have the farm income as long as you keep the farm and work it. As soon as I have a plane, I plan to teach all three of you to fly. With two planes we can make more money flying than farming."

"Must we make a choice?" asked Leonard. "We are your brothers, remember?"

Roy laughed, "Want to fly, too, do you, little brother?" his eyes glinted at Leonard with understanding and mirth.

"Well, OK for Leonard. How do you two feel about it or haven't you made up your minds?"

Clarence and Newell each responded with an enthusiastic "yes."

"Naturally, I hoped you would all feel that way," Roy said. "We'll have to move slow at first as it'll probably take a year to settle the estate. We can't do much until we get the money and make a contract to share and share alike to finance this operation. I have heard of an aviator in Duluth named Marvin Northrup. I would like to buy his plane. Next week I'm going there to see him.

"There is something else. We need to keep very quiet about this. The whole neighborhood will be very agitated about our affairs. To save listening to their advice, 'mum' is the word."

Duluth

In May 1922, Roy was one month short of marking the third anniversary of his homecoming from the war. Now he was traveling again, this time to Duluth, Minnesota to buy his first airplane.

Clarence accompanied Roy to the railroad station at Larsen, but the two brothers exchanged few remarks. Both were thinking about their train trip to attend engineering school in Kansas City a year ago. Clarence was thinking, too, that with Roy away, there would be only three Larsons left to do all the farm work, the housework and the cooking. As Roy had pointed out to them, they were grown men and should be able to take on the work that had to be done.

More importantly, Clarence also thought that possibly they were all courting disaster–and not just by eating their own cooking. The papers frequently carried tragic stories of young aviators crippled or killed outright in plane crashes. Clarence didn't want that to happen to his brothers, especially to Roy.

Clarence had never ridden in an airplane, but he understood Roy's enthusiasm for flying. All four of the Larsons were equally imbued with the desire to become aviators. Eldest brother Roy was the role model for the others–the ambitious big brother hot to have his whole family share his passion for flying. The boys accepted his decision with enthusiasm.

Hissing a cloud of steam, the locomotive waited at the depot with its line of passenger cars. A slow runner, familiar to everyone along the route, the train was lovingly called "Old Kate." The conductor with his step stool was ready to help the passengers board the train. Roy hurried toward the passenger car, carrying his battered suitcase and his lunch, since Old Kate did not have a dining car.

Roy nodded to the station master, who said, "Taking a trip, Roy?"

"Yes," was Roy's laconic, noncommittal answer.

The porter took his suitcase, motioned Roy aboard and followed him into the passenger car. He put the case on the overhead rack, above Roy's seat. Roy pulled up the shade, looked out the window and watched with mixed emotions as Clarence drove down the road home.

Roy settled into his seat, relaxed, tie loosened, legs stretched under the seat in front of him. He looked out the window at the bucolic scene surrounding the depot. A weekday in a dull season for travelling, only a few people were on the train. Early spring was the time to work, the season for getting the land ploughed and seeded to grow next autumn's harvest.

Old Kate did herself proud. No one could remember how that particular train became known as Old Kate, so-called with much affection by everyone for hundreds of miles along her route. Every farmer knew her schedule and, when they climbed aboard, her ornate, red plush seats were uncomfortably hard, but gave a feeling of luxury to farm people who seldom experienced it.

On shipping days–Monday of each week–she pulled one or more stock cars. Farmers hauled or walked their old cows–the canners–and their steers, calves or pigs to Larsen to be shipped to the slaughterhouses in Milwaukee or Chicago. On shipping days there would be long lines of farmers, usually with a family member along to prod the old cows or control the frisky month-old calves and load them into the livestock freight car. Once loaded and crowded into the cars, the bawling calves, bellowing cows and squealing pigs rendered the air raucous with their unwelcome noise.

Roy had not left on shipping day, so the train he boarded had only passengers and freight cars. Two local women he recognized and a man who was a stranger to Roy had hurriedly entered his car shortly before the train pulled out. He greeted the women, but wondered who the man was.

With a sudden jerk and jolt, Old Kate slowly moved forward. Another cloud of steam arose and the whistle blew a warning for kids, dogs and cows to move off the tracks. Roy watched the farmland slide by, with farmers plowing, raking, seeding. It was early in the morning, the air was fresh and shiny eyelets of dew lay on the grass.

Roy had lots of time not only to dwell on the past, but also to dream of his gloriously thrilling future as a flyer. The train accelerated and the farm boy on his way to a flying career and fame, dreamed on. He was beginning a journey that would change the course not only of his life, but also that of his brothers and many of their young friends.

Roy remembered a tale he had heard in his youth. In the 1890s, an elderly couple known to everyone as Grandma and Grandpa Clark lived about six miles from the Larson home.

They were born in a different age–Grandma Clark in 1837, and Grandpa Lewis Clark in 1833–where even the railroad was new-fangled, strange. They had lived at Clark's Point on Lake Winneconne, about 15 miles from Oshkosh for most of their lives when a new rail line was laid nearby. Whenever they traveled to shop in Oshkosh, the Clarks had to steer their horse and buggy across the railroad tracks. Cautious and careful whenever they approached the tracks, Grandpa would stop the horse about 50 feet in front of the train tracks. Grandma would step down from the buggy, walk up to the tracks and lay her ear on the rail, listening for the humming that would tell her a train was approaching.

The Clarks never quite understood how fast, or slow, a train could move. They figured that just because they couldn't see a train, it didn't mean that a train wouldn't streak up on them before they could cross the line.

So Grandma always laid her ear on the track. If she didn't hear it humming, she quickly returned to the buggy and hopped in as fast as she could. Grandpa would then crack his whip in the air over the horse's head and the Clarks would hurry over the tracks.

On their return home, they went through the same procedure. They had a fairly fast trotting horse. It only took them about an hour to travel the fifteen miles to Oshkosh, but they were never in so great a hurry that they didn't check the tracks before they crossed them.

Grandma Clark lived to be 102 years old. She never saw nor heard a train on that railway track, but she never crossed it without laying her ear on it to listen for the humming.

Leaning his head back and closing his eyes, Roy thought that when it came to aviation, a lot of his neighbors were just like the Clarks–afraid of something new they didn't even try to understand.

As Old Kate rolled on through the Wisconsin countryside, he snoozed. The steady pulse of the engine and the rhythm of the wheels seemed to say, "I'm going to fly, I'm going to fly, I'm going to fly, I'm going to fly..."

His thoughts travelled back over the recent past, over the happenings since he had returned from the war. He thought about the past three years, and how difficult they had been. Losing his mother greatly saddened him. She had so bravely worked at keeping the family together despite losing her husband and coping with all the illnesses of her children. She had given so much love and hope to all of them. Putting aside her own grief, she had maintained a cheerful mien for her family. He shook his head and his eyes were moist as he thought of the hardships his mother had endured. Losing George to tuberculosis had broken her up, but the death of her beloved, only daughter just a year later had nearly destroyed her. She had never regained her strength after Zola passed away. Roy nearly broke down and sobbed remembering his lovely and vivacious sister. Only seventeen years old. Her gradual decline had been painfully distressing. She had wanted desperately to live.

He thought about the present too, and leaving the boys behind to do all the farm and house work. "I don't think they were very happy, but I'll make it up to them. Wait until I teach them to fly."

For Roy, flying would be the greatest gift of all, the ultimate reward anyone could possibly receive. This train trip spelled Duluth and his own airplane. That was his first goal. It would be the best future for him and his brothers. He envisioned the sign on the road that would read, "The Larson Brothers Flying School".

The Flying Larson Brothers. He saw it all again—the airport with planes flying in and taking off, and the crowds of people. No more tiresome train rides, he decided. Hereafter, in my plane, I shall soar like a bird, hither and yon. No more sitting in a train with hard seats. I'll fly to Duluth in a couple of hours. The train rolled on, he continued to dream.

When he arrived in Duluth the next day, Roy was elated to learn that its owner, a man named Northrup, had not sold the plane. He wanted to yell a loud "Whoopty-do-o-o" but, being Roy, he was quiet and outwardly self-controlled, with only a large smile on his face.

The plane for sale was a Cannuck, a Canadian-built model of the American JN4. Roy stood and looked at it and saw all his dreams coming true at last. "Oh, you beautiful bird," he thought. Joy choked his throat, then trickled down his spine. His legs were weak, his thoughts chaotic. He couldn't think of a thing to say. Soon, practicality set in and realistic questions arose in his mind. Where was he going to keep it? Should he fly home with it? Now? Where would he keep it on the farm? How could he protect it from the weather?

Northrup asked him those very questions.

"No," said Roy. "I hadn't really believed I would be able to get it right away. I haven't made any arrangements. Just thought I would fly it home. Couldn't I just tie it to a tree? or two? Would that hold it?"

No, said Northrup, "that wouldn't hold it unless you had three or four trees in just the right position and with enough room in between for the plane to go through. You have to tie it to pull from the front and the tail and both sides. You don't know from which direction the wind will blow. It can come suddenly in very strong gusts. It could rip the wing fabric. If the wind were strong enough it might even tear the wings off the fuselage."

While Roy and Northrup talked, another young man approached. He too had admired the plane. Northrup turned to the man and said, "Hello, Seevers, this young man is Roy Larson from Larsen, Wisconsin. Mr. Larson, this is Ray Seevers of Duluth. He was a Captain in the Air Force in the war. He flew with Eddie Rickenbacker. Mr. Seevers would like to buy my plane, too, but he will have to wait a while to raise the money. He can't afford it now."

Roy and Mr. Seevers shook hands. Roy's eyes shone appreciatively as he looked at the captain and realized Seevers had probably been a leader of one of the squadrons of fighter planes he had so enviously watched flying over his infantry company in France.

"What would you do with the plane if you bought it?" Roy asked Seevers.

"W-e-ll," Seevers replied, "I've been giving it a lot of thought for a long while. I believe I could make it pay for itself doing aerial photography. You see there is a lot of big business in Duluth. The ports and mills are very busy. I think they would pay for pictures, taken from the air, of their places of business. Also, there are several millionaires who have large estates with beautiful, luxurious homes. I believe they would like to have aerial photographs of their property. Picture cards could be made from the photographs and sold to use in advertising.

"We might sell scenic picture cards to tourists. After a while the people will become used to seeing us flying and realize it is safe. It may be possible later on to make money carrying passengers at $5.00 for a 5-minute ride.

"Businessmen like to fly to other cities–Minneapolis, Chicago, Milwaukee. I believe it would pay, be a good investment. That's what I would do."

Roy liked what he was hearing and, thinking it over, he said, "Mr. Seevers, if you were to buy this plane where would you store it?"

"I wondered about that, too. A few days ago, I heard there was a place to store a plane at the Tri-State Fairgrounds. There would be plenty of space and a good lift off area. You could head into the wind in any direction. I don't think they would charge a lot because the fairgrounds is not used most of the year."

Roy stood in deep thought for a few minutes while Northrup and Seevers walked around the plane admiring its sturdiness and extolling its maneuverability in the air.

The two men returned but Roy had yet to make his decision. He was stymied by the difficulties of remaining in Duluth, of storing the plane, and of making enough money to cover his expenses.

Sensing his dilemma, Seevers spoke, "I have an idea. If you haven't made any plans in regard to the plane after you buy it, I have a proposition to make to you. Fly it to the Fairgrounds, store it there and stay with me. We will see if we can get some flying contracts with Portland Cement and other businesses in Duluth. We could hire photographers to take pictures of their buildings from the air. Also, there is the *Duluth Herald*, the local newspaper. They like to get close-up pictures of disasters and public events. Also, I think we could sell pictures of the Aerial Bridge.

"If it didn't work out in Duluth, we could fly to Minneapolis and try there on the weekends, when I am not on my regular job."

"Mr. Seevers," Roy said, "Would you call the manager of the Tri-State Fairgrounds and ask him how much he wants to store my plane for a month?"

"Right away," Seevers replied.

By the time Seevers had returned with a favorable answer, Roy had decided to give it a month's try. He would stay with Seevers, and they would try all the money making ideas he had suggested.

Seevers held out his hand to Roy and said, "Is it a bargain, that we will be a flying team for a month?" Roy shook hands with him and said, "My name is Roy."

"Ray is mine," Seevers replied.

"Twins–Ray and Roy," laughed Northrup. "I'm sure you will do well."

Roy thought he should observe while someone else actually piloted his plane. He hadn't been in a plane since that memorable day in Chicago when he had received his pilot's certificate from Mr. Diggins, and he needed a refresher course before he would again feel comfortable in a cockpit.

Roy took the bill of sale from Northrup and walked out of the office with Seevers. As they inspected the Jenny, Roy was walking on air. This was his own plane. He ran his hands along the wings, stooped down and looked at the underside. He climbed on the wing and slipped into the passenger seat. Ray had waited to see which seat Roy would choose before he climbed into the pilot's seat.

"You fly it to the Tri-State Fairgrounds today and put it in storage. I want to see if you are a good pilot," grinned Roy.

They operated a flying business out of Tri-State Fairgrounds for about five months. With no other flyers in town, they had the skies above Duluth all to themselves. Most of the flying work consisted of taking aerial photos of large business places and bridges. They sold lots of pictures. Some were of boat clubs, of elevators, of iron ore docks, and some were of the large flour mills. Business was good for a while. Occasionally they flew passengers, but for the most part, people were afraid to fly. Crowds thrilled to watch Roy and Ray fly and stunt–Roy even did some wingwalking–but few of the spectators wanted to take a ride.

Several young teenage boys hung around the Tri-State Fairgrounds watching the pilots take off and land. It was a real thrill for the kids and they would swarm over the plane, but they were rough on the wings and Roy noticed that they were damaging the delicate fabric. He remembered what had happened to the wing on Charles Niles's plane back in Neenah and decided to find another place to store his machine. He moved the Jenny out of Duluth to Pike Lake, on Miller Trunk Highway.

Later in the summer, the pilots heard that two government planes were being auctioned in Texas and they thought they had made enough money to submit bids on them. Both Seevers and Roy bid with the idea that Roy would buy the planes if either bid were accepted. Seevers' bid was accepted and the planes were sent to the Larson Brothers farm, where they arrived December 22, 1922. These were the Standard J-1's, the first of which Roy assembled and used to astound his neighbors back in Larsen.

The Standard J-1 biplane was a "Tractor" model, which meant it had the propeller facing front, unlike many of the pioneer flying machines which were pushed along with the prop facing the rear. It differed from the JN4 in that it was built for a Hall-Scott engine and had more square feet supporting the surface of the wings, which were farther apart and swept back instead of mounted at a right angle to the fuselage. In the Jenny, the radiator was on the nose, while on the Standard it was mounted above the engine.

Between the wings, both the Standard and the Jenny were strung with piano type wire, unlike many other planes, where cable was used. It didn't make a difference to the pilot, but the wingwalkers complained that cable wires cut their hands. The Standard also had an altimeter and tachometer, but like most other planes in 1922, it did not have a compass.

While he waited for the Standards to be shipped to Wisconsin, Roy flew the Jenny and lived with Seevers and his wife. Mrs. Seevers said later he was a very quiet person. He rarely had anything to say except to praise her for her good cooking. One day he looked up at her and said "It helps to have a wife who works." It shocked her to hear him say something to her, as he rarely spoke.

By late autumn, the flyers had taken all the pictures they had contracted for and their income had all but disappeared. Even if they had work, flying in winter in Duluth was not practical. The Jenny was an open cockpit airplane, and the weather of northern Minnesota would freeze the pilot to his seat. The engine would not run properly; oil would thicken and clog the pump instead of circulating through the engine, which would soon burn dry and crack. As if to reinforce the point, the winter of 1922 was exceptionally cold and the winds very strong.

Roy and Ray had no choice but to take the wings off the Jenny and put it in storage. Roy left Duluth to find seasonal work and wait out the winter. At first he worked for Caribou Farms sawing railway ties, but that didn't pay enough. Then he went to the Wisconsin northwoods at Draper in Sawyer County, where the Hines Lumber Company was conducting one of the state's last great logging operations.

He was there a short time when he received word to come home at once. The family home at Larsen had been destroyed by fire.

The Fire

After their mother passed away, Clarence had taken to sleeping downstairs in a small room off the kitchen. It was his job to build a fire in the kitchen stove early every morning to warm the house before the other boys awoke.

There was a flat-topped, wood-burning stove in the kitchen. It had a warming oven over the back and top which jutted out over the burners on the flat top. After the food was cooked it was placed in the warming oven where it stayed warm until the men came in the house to eat. The chimney passed from the back of the stove through the ceiling, and into the attic to the brick chimney that ran through the roof. The stove was old. It had been in the kitchen when their father bought the house in 1900.

The kitchen stove was the only heat in the house for cooking. In the wintertime, it supplied all the heat for the house. A very large coal stove stood in the middle of the parlor, but it was used only when guests came on Sunday. It had isinglass windows on its sides so everyone could watch the fire, and threw out a tremendous amount of heat, at least for those who sat nearby. Anyone unlucky enough to sit away from the stove shivered in the cold.

The duties of the farmer's wife kept her in the kitchen most of every day. Monday was wash day with a tub of water in the kitchen for washing and another for rinsing. Tuesday was for ironing the clothes washed on Monday. Wednesday was baking day. Besides the cakes, pies and doughnuts, she baked bread for the entire week. On most days, all the heat needed in the house was supplied by the wood burning cook stove in the kitchen.

At night, the stove was stoked with wood until it was full of bright red smoldering coals. At that time the coals were lightly covered with ashes. That was called 'banking the fire'. It burned slowly and the banked coals provided heat most of the night. An open register in the kitchen ceiling allowed some heat to rise into the upstairs rooms. Usually, it was comfortably warm at bedtime and throughout the early part of the night.

The fire would burn itself out towards morning and Clarence would build a new one each day. It was bitter cold throughout the house in zero or below weather. In winter, the boys waited in bed for Clarence to rise and build the fire. Then they climbed out of their warm beds, grabbed their clothes and dashed downstairs to dress comfortably in the heated kitchen.

It was fortunate Clarence was a light sleeper and awakened at the slightest sound. On this freezingly cold winter morning in December he woke up suddenly from a deep sleep and wondered what had awakened him. He could hardly believe his ears when he heard the crackling of fire. Had he overslept? Had his brothers awakened early and built the fire for him?

He ran quickly to the kitchen. The stove was cold. No fire in the grate. As he listened, he still heard the crackling noise. He looked at the ceiling. There was no visible fire. He smelled no smoke.

"It must be in the attic," he thought. Rushing up the stairs, he called out to his brothers, "Fire! Fire! Get up! The house is on fire!"

He snatched open the attic door. An inferno met his eyes, a sheet of white hot flames. The heat singed his face. He saw that all within was destroyed. The 50 pound bag of millet seed—worth $500.00 and which he was to sell in Neenah that very morning—was incinerated.

Although he had slammed the door as soon as he could, Clarence hadn't noticed that a burning coal had flown out the doorway and landed on the steps. When he turned and dashed downstairs, again calling out to his brothers, he didn't notice the smoldering red hot coal until he stepped on it. It stuck to the sole of his foot. When he stopped to pull it off, the skin came with it, but in his urgency to alarm his brothers, he didn't feel the pain.

He dashed downstairs, calling out repeatedly to his brothers, "Fire! Get up, the house is on fire!" He ran outside and began pulling the bell rope to sound a call for help. Nearly all farmers had such a bell. It was mostly used to call the men from the field for a meal or a message. When it rang at that time of night, all who heard, realized the bell was signaling a major disaster.

Aroused from the deepest sleep of the night, the neighbors were slow to respond to the outdoor bell. Some, deep in sleep, didn't hear the tolling, but all who had telephones heard the single long ring of the emergency call. Both bells carried the same urgent message. "Disaster has struck. There is an immediate need for help."

The alarm bell and the phone signal were the only methods the farmers had of calling for help in a crisis. At the first sound all who could hear dropped whatever they were doing and swiftly answered the call. Like nearly all rural areas, Larsen had no fire department, and the nearest village fire station was ten miles away in Winneconne. The neighbors helped each other like a local volunteer fire department, but all they could do was try to save some of the furniture in the house and prevent the fire from spreading to the barn. Their hastily-filled buckets of water would not put out the fire.

Upon hearing Clarence yell, "Fire!" the boys didn't wait to dress. They moved fast. Spo ran across the road to get help from the Theodore Larsons. Viola began ringing the telephone, sounding the long single ring that would send the emergency signal down the party line. When someone picked up the phone, Viola told them, "The Larson brothers house is on fire, they need help!" She continued ringing until her arm ached from turning the hand crank and the fire had completly gutted the house.

Viola's parents and brother had grabbed water pails and rushed across the road to help. Neighbors dressed in the first thing they could grab, hurried into their winter boots, and rushed down the road to Larsons', pails banging against their knees, as they ran.

The smoke and red glowing flames were a beacon, plainly visible in the dark of the early dawn. It guided the would-be fire fighters to the burning house.

Hearts fell, as they saw the large red column in the sky. It appeared to be too late to save anything. Now, their hearts went out to the brothers. "Those poor boys! Three years ago they lost a brother, two years ago they lost their only sister and seven months ago it had been their mother. Now they were losing their home."

By the time the neighbors arrived, the house was completely engulfed in flames. Clarence stood in the snow in a stupor of utter disbelief, still pulling the bell rope. Shivering in his night shirt, his feet bare, toes numb, nose purple, he kept the farm bell ringing, hoping vainly, help would arrive in time to stop the fire. "The fire has to be put out," was a refrain running around and around in his head.

Even after all the neighbors arrived and the fire had destroyed the house, Clarence stood there tolling the bell, refusing to accept the fact the family home was in ruins. He told himself, "It is all a horrible nightmare," sure he would soon wake up. He had watched his brothers carrying out the piano, an old kitchen table and a chair, before the fire drove them out of the house. Shivering, he had huddled within himself, still vigorously pulling the bell rope.

Stunned, the three brothers stood around the piano in their night clothes, bare-footed in the cold. The piano, an old rickety kitchen table and chair plus a few family treasures painfully collected in a lifetime of struggle were their only possessions. These were pitiful mementoes that meant more to their now dead mother, but had lost any identity for the Larson boys.

The piano was covered by insurance but they had struggled to save it and had lost valuable time in carrying it out. None of the boys played the piano, but their mother had loved it. The dining room table was on its last legs but had been saved at the loss of a very valuable antique table in excellent condition that was uninsured. The few of their other humble belongings they had been able to save had been dumped in a heap on the ground.

When catastrophe falls in this manner compassionate people in the neighborhood stay close, extending sympathy for a while, wishing they could do something, anything. The neighbors began to approach the brothers offering sympathy, clothing, food and any other help they could extend. Still in shock, the boys spoke automatically, thanking them.

The brothers couldn't realize their home was gone, couldn't realize yet that it meant they had no place to go and no clothes to wear. Still in their night clothes, they walked around the now smoldering ruins, slowly, not talking, too stupefied to realize they had no home. Clarence had finally stopped pulling on the bell rope and had joined his brothers. They stood in a small circle, speechless in sympathetic silence.

The neighbors, as the sky lightened and dawn broke, slowly left to go home and tend to their farm chores. Their muted voices drifted back faintly as they walked slowly back down the road over which they had so recently raced to reach the fire.

Ted Larson, their nearest neighbor, approached the boys and told them to come home with him. "You boys can stay with us until your home is rebuilt," he told them.

Dragging their numbed, bare feet, the boys slowly followed their benefactor across the road. They slept upstairs in Ted's house. The next morning, Clarence discovered a blister the size of an apple on the sole of his foot.

It was not a complete catastrophe. The insurance premiums on the house had been paid. It was insured for $500.00, enough to build a modest, but new house. Roy arrived home on December 16 and they began planning to rebuild as soon as spring arrived.

In the meantime, the brothers stayed with the Ted Larson family. One day a traveling salesman stopped in at meal time and, as was the custom in farm homes, the Larsons invited him to dinner. During the mealtime conversation, Clarence happened to mention that they were moving that afternoon into their new home.

The salesman looked at him in amazement. "Man, your're moving in half-a-day? Have you ever moved before?"

"Yes," Clarence answered, "We moved out in twenty minutes."

The First Airport In Wisconsin

The ringing of the axes resounded throughout the countryside when the Larson brothers began cutting trees for lumber to build their new home. They decided to log trees for their airplane hangar at the same time. After drying for a year or so, the logs would make fine timber frames for the first structure in Wisconsin built specifically to house aircraft.

It was a month after Roy arrived home from the north woods, before the weather was mild enough to commence clearing the area for their new home. The remains of their former home had to be removed and dug out before the new foundation could be laid. It was not until January 23, 1923, that the first axe blade struck the first tree.

The brothers spent long hours getting the preliminary work finished so the carpenters and masons could begin. They also worked steadily at logging the trees. The rumble of the lumber wagons, over the rough trail on their way to the forest-swamp to bring home the new cut logs could be heard from dawn to late in the night.

"Timber," shouted the axeman as a tall tree began to sway and fall. Then he ran for his life in the opposite direction from which he had chopped the tree. The large branches had to be avoided. There would be no sound from the tree until it hit the ground. In the early days, many a pioneer father, intent on building a log home for his family, was caught by a falling tree and either killed outright or maimed for life.

In spring the crew came with their large gasoline-powered sawmill. As almost every farmer had a woodlot and all of them used lumber and firewood, the sawyers were in great demand. The limbs were chopped off, and the logs and larger limbs were sawn into lumber. Some limbs were cut to fence post lengths and sharpened on one end. The rest were cut into 15-18 inch lengths for stove wood.

Work on the hangar, with space for six planes, began in the spring of 1924. The site was a short distance north of their new home, just where Roy had dreamed it would be. The boys chose that site because it was higher than the surrounding land, just right for the planes to land and take off in any direction. In 1924, there was no other hangar in the state of Wisconsin, no place where space could be rented to store airplanes, and Roy Larson, entrepreneur, pilot and dreamer had the idea to build it.

They needed a work shop–other than the house–in which to repair and construct planes in all kinds of weather and the hangar would supply it. They had the money, partly from farming, partly from their small inheritance, and partly from barnstorming in 1923. The main frame was raised with a Fordson Tractor, a Dodge touring car, and a hoist and tackle. At times, the up-to-date flyboys had to rely on some old-fashioned help. Sometimes the heavy hauling could only be completed with aid from the strong shoulders of the oxen from the neighboring Gore brothers. A significant sign of progress–from oxen to flying machines in the same place at the same time.

The Gore brothers were two bachelor farmers. Considerably older than the Larsons, they were card-playing, deer-hunting friends. The Gore brothers went everywhere together. One had a bad knee and the other couldn't see very well, which made driving a car a source of amusement for the neighbors. One manipulated the foot pedals and the other steered. They sat so close, it looked as though one sat on the other's lap. They had many exciting experiences behind the wheel. They drove into their house a couple of times, once taking off the front porch. A few times they drove into the ditch.

People meeting the Gores as they wove down the road, pulled onto the right side of the road and stopped, breathing a sigh of relief after the brothers passed. Occasionally, they flew with the Larson boys. Brother Art Gore had a long white beard which billowed out behind him in the plane. It was a sight to behold, surpassing Santa Claus and his reindeer.

Even before the oxen, the tractor or the auto could help build the hangar, the ground for it and the airfield had to be clearedand made reasonably level. Dirt fill was shoveled by hand from the basement excavation to fill the pot holes and make a smoother runway. Fencing had to be taken up and hardwood trees—hickory, maple and oak—cut. Live stumps from freshly cut trees were difficult to remove and often had to be blasted out. The goal was to make the field large enough for the planes to land and take off from any direction.

Then the masons–Louis Fenner, Harry Hanson, Leander Young–began work on the foundation. Louis Fenner was a German immigrant and World War I veteran who lived in the German settlement west of Winchester, Harry Hanson a neighbor of Norwegian heritage. Leander Young was short, bald headed, not very handsome, but nice. His father was English and his mother Norwegian.

The carpenters were the Johnson brothers–Bud, Knute and John Johnson. Bud Johnson, christened Berdell, was the youngest of the Johnsons. He and his wife, Bessie, were the proud parents of fourteen children. Bud was a jovial fellow, but enjoyed a little too much of the juice of the vine to please Bessie. However, she was a good sort and took it in stride. He fiddled a wicked wing ding on occasion and played for many dances when he wasn't busy farming and carpentering.

Knute Johnson never married. He was the boss of the builders, and a careful inspector of all the work. He could fiddle a wild square dance and make the fiddle talk. He was so good at telling whoppers that he would have taken first prize as a member of the Burlington Liars Club. Not only could he tell a whopper, he could make you believe it.

John Johnson, the third brother, did not drink. He was a very quiet person, well liked, married and had seven children.

During construction, one of the neighbors threw a party. The masons attended and unfortunately one imbibed a little too freely of the liquid grape. On his way home he was arrested for drunk driving. He was put in prison to await trial. His special skills were desperately needed to build the hangar, and the Larsons couldn't wait for him to stand trial and be sentenced. They sent Clarence to pay his bail and bring him back. Clarence didn't have quite enough money for the bail and he went to the bank to borrow it.

The banker told Clarence, "I will let you have the money to bail him out of jail, but don't ever ask me to lend you money to buy any airplanes. Banks can't lend money for such foolishness."

The building of the hangar was the main topic of conversation throughout the community. Advice and criticism abounded. Arguments, pro and con, raged constantly. The party line buzzed. Most neighbors were critical of the amount of money the boys were sinking in a foolish business.

"How could they earn enough money to pay back what they had spent?" asked one. "When everyone had a ride where would any other money come from? It would take a lot of rides to repay it. It was too much money to spend for a building to house airplanes."

"They don't need a storage building," declared another. "The planes can be anchored to those cement blocks and covered over with canvas."

73

One dairy farmer was indignant because, "That building is better than the barn they have for their cows!"

Others, with more vision, thought it a great enterprise and lauded the boys for being so far-seeing. Many farmers on their way home from their daily trip to the nearby cheese factory would stop a few minutes to check on the progress of the work. They would comment and agree or disagree according to their viewpoint. Undaunted and undeterred by the negative advice of the older generation, the boys continued building their hangar and saw it to completion.

In their first winter–1923-24–the Larsons had their first customer. Barnstormer Elwyn West stored his airplane in the Larson Brothers hangar. Roy stored his two Standards plus a third machine he was assembling there. It was a simple building, easier to build than a typical Wisconsin dairy barn. Instead of cows, it was full of promise for aviation's future and the birthplace of more than one aviation legend.

Clyde Lee Flies – Up and Down

In the spring and summer after the Larson hangar was completed, and Wisconsin's first airport was operational, Roy Larson taught Clyde Lee how to fly. Clyde was a natural. He had the right instincts, a sense of wind and weather, an ear for the engine and—most importantly—a burning desire to be the best pilot in the world. He was also 16 years old, and possessed of all the impetuosity of a teenage boy.

After five hours of instruction both on the ground and in the air, the long-awaited moment arrived.

"That's it," said Roy, "Take it up. Solo!"

"Do you mean it, Roy?" said Clyde.

He couldn't believe it. He had only had five lessons! Oh boy! Oh joy! His moment in history was here. He would be a pilot right now! He jumped back into the plane so quickly, his feet barely touched the wing.

Almost simultaneously, he put the plane in motion. The motor already warm, he took off fast. He soared. Heart filled with joyous emotion, around and around he circled the air field. Tiring of that, "Where shall I go now," he asked himself. "I'll fly over Clark's and show my sister, Bernice, she will be thrilled, too, for me! Her big brother flying an airplane!"

He piloted the plane over Lake Winneconne and approached Clark's Point from the west. He had buzzed over Clark's three times before he saw Bernice come running out of the house and waving at him. He held his arm straight out over the side of the plane so she would see him waving to her. She told him later she had known it was him.

That, in itself, was a great boost to his self esteem but, as he was heading back to Larson's field–oh, bitter, bitter, horror! The engine had begun to cough, sputter and die out. He realized immediately that he was going to have to make a dead stick landing. "Thanks, Roy, for all that practice," he muttered to himself.

He looked for a long field with no trees, flat land smooth enough to land on without damaging the plane. He saw the hay field on the Miller farm and began his descent. He was flying into what little breeze there was to help stop the plane after it landed.

"What will Roy say to me, when I come walking back? What a stupid thing not to check the gas, after all the times he told me it was a must before every flight!" At least the plane was not damaged.

In fact, he was proud of the three point landing he had made without any power. But that pride didn't last long after John Miller got through letting him know how mad he was at the swath of flattened hay he had had left behind the plane.

He plodded along the gravel road towards Roy's, thinking, "I have never experienced such a powerful emotion. I may have pulled a stupid stunt, forgetting to check the gas, but I've soloed. The successful 'end all' of months of working and saving my money for lessons, I finally made it. I shall never forget the joy of it. Nothing will ever take away the intense emotions of rapture and exhilaration, the complete freedom, utter spacelessness! How I had always envied birds."

The next night, Clyde borrowed Roy's car, took gas to the plane and flew it back to the airport. Just for fun, he invited two neighbor girls, Jane Labudde and Gwennie Gunz, to ride along. Just before they reached the Miller farm, it began to rain, pouring rain and didn't stop. The girls were good sports and despite the rain, climbed into the open cockpit plane with Clyde. When the propeller started, it spewed the rain into their faces. It felt like sleet pellets drilling into them. Crowded into a seat meant for two people, the three of them made a miserable wet flight to the Larson Brothers Airport. The two girls never forgot their first airplane ride, and neither did Clyde.

But merely learning to fly was not enough for Clyde Lee. He wanted to be a wingwalker. Watching others climbing around on an airplane while it was in the air, only stimulated him to do the same. He had always wanted to do high wire acts. Spellbound, he had watched circus acrobats and aerialists balancing on the high wire.

His desire was so great that one time when we were children Clyde and I were visiting our grandparents–the Leas–we climbed to the top of the windmill. While I stood at the top of the tall, flimsy tower, Clyde grasped a blade of the windmill and rode it as it whirled around and around. When Grandma Lea came out to see what we were doing, she threw her apron over her face and hurried back into the house. She couldn't bear the sight.

For Clyde it was only a small step from windmill riding to wingwalking. When one of Roy's planes was on the ground he spent hours walking and climbing around on the wings, getting the feel of it and fitting his 6-foot-plus-tall-body between the upper and lower wings.

In the beginning he practiced sliding from a sitting position in the cockpit to standing on the wing. That accomplished, he began climbing to the upper wing. One stunt learned led to another. Climbing to the upper wing led to practicing standing on top of it.

He wore a strong belt–known as a tumbling belt–around his waist. It had a large buckle with a two-inch ring interlocked into it. A two-inch snap fastener attached to about a four-foot wire was snapped into the two-inch ring on the tumbling belt. Another two-inch snap fastener was attached to the other end of the wire and snapped into a ring in the center section of the wing. There was a front and a back part fastened to the center section of the plane over the fuselage. The wire was fastened to the ring in the front center section and to the buckle on the chutist's belt.

Two leather, half-loop stirrups were attached behind the wire fastener on the center section of the top wing. When the stunt man placed his feet in these half-loops, they were held firmly in place so he did not slip.

As the stunt man stood on the top wing and leaned slightly back, the wire tightened and secured him there. With his feet firmly in place, and his arms free, he stood tall and waved at the crowd. When the pilot looped the plane, the stunt man was held in the same position on top of the plane. Later some stunt men had side braces also, but Clyde used only the single front bracing wire.

Winds of 75 miles per hour are considered to be hurricane force. A stunt man standing on the top wing of an airplane with a wire connected to the top wing was being flown at a minimum of 65 miles per hour. Only daredevils attempted to stand up to these winds.

If the wire was too long and the stunt man couldn't hold his stance firmly enough and fell, he would land on the wing and remain there until the pilot landed the plane. This rarely happened, but on at least one occasion, a stunt man who fell received a severe back injury. The danger extended to the pilot, for it was very difficult to maintain the balance of the plane with someone laying on the wing especially while attempting to land.

The parachute was–of course–a new invention in the early 1920s. Jumping out of an airplane, falling free through the air then pulling the ripcord to open the silken parasol and floating to the earth without harm was still a flying circus stunt in these days. Clyde Lee couldn't wait to jump as soon as his cautious cousin Roy would let him. Instead Roy insisted that Clyde practice folding and packing his parachute so it would open properly. Like most 16-year old boys, Clyde believed he would live forever, but Roy knew the teenager's life depended on cautious good judgment–and did his best to provide it.

The day came when Clyde's impetuosity overcame the sense of caution that Roy had tried to instill in him. One Sunday afternoon, Speed Holman, an experienced flier and stunt man himself, had an exhibition contract to fill in Manitowoc, Wisconsin. He needed someone to stunt and make a parachute drop. Clyde heard about it and applied for the job. After watching Clyde climb around on the plane as if it were his second home, Holman accepted him to be his stunt man for the day. It was 1924 and Clyde was 16 years old.

The teenage stunt man was in his glory. He had flashed to stardom and his excitement was contagious. All the Larson brothers, plus Clarence's wife, Viola, accompanied him to Manitowoc and stayed to watch. Holman and Clyde were to stunt over the city, followed by the parachute jump with Clyde landing in a parking lot.

The crowd went wild when Clyde climbed on the upper wing and stood straight and tall. Holman looped the loop several times and flew some barrel rolls. The spectators were always thrilled to see the stunt man remain on the plane even when it flew upside down.

After the rolls were done, Clyde climbed down on the lower wing and, walking hunched over to fit his tall body between the wings, moved to the edge of the right wing. His parachute was hanging there and–2,500 feet above the ground–he slipped into it and readied himself to make his first parachute jump.

Exhilarated by the success of his initial stunt flying, the screaming of the crowd and his own emotional "high", he looked toward the ground and for the first time realized it was a long way down.

In his own words, he later described this thrilling episode: "With a feeling words cannot express, I stepped out upon the edge of the wing and stood looking below me. Imagine yourself standing on the wing of an airplane, 2,500 feet above the earth, looking down upon a group of moving dots which you know to be people clapping and cheering as they see you preparing to jump. The ear-splitting roaring of the engine, and the force of the wind from the propeller stream nearly carries you away before you are ready.

"Allowing a brief second for judging the wind and locating the center spot [landing place] I threw my arm upward, a signal to the pilot, and stepped over the side. Whereupon the pilot kicked the rudder, skidding the ship sideways to prevent me from getting caught in the tail group.

"In stories they tell of counting before pulling the cord, but in real jumps by the time you have turned to take one look at the plane it is already growing small. My hand which has been on the rip cord for some time, automatically pulled it so hard that it released the chute immediately, and a huge mushroom hung over my head. That rip cord was the only thing I had to hang on to. I hung tight!

"All is quiet. There is no sound of the roaring engine. You are all alone in vast space. The people are not making a sound. They watch in breathless suspense. A death-like silence prevails. There is the slight sound of the wind rustling through the silk of the parachute. Oh, to always be like this! What a glorious sensation tingles through me. Troubles disappear. They are too minute for consideration in this atmosphere.

"But in two or three minutes this is over. Now I must concentrate all my attention on reaching the center spot on the ground.

"A great jolt, and I had landed. I was laying on the hood of an automobile in the parking lot. Immediately, I slid to the ground and pulled the lower cords of the chute to spill the wind and keep the parachute from dragging me. That could be painful. It didn't take much wind for that to happen.

"All this time there has not been a sound from the crowd of people. Suddenly they break forth in a great shouting, cheering and screaming. They make a great hullabaloo about it and swarm around me. But the thrill is all over for this time. Not even this thunderous accolade could create that sensation of awe which I had...of absolute aloneness. I had left everything behind me. I had left the roaring engine and whistling wind and entered into a space and time of ultimate quietness and peace."

In later years, he was heard to say, "No matter how seasoned a jumper one may be, there is always the same thrill before and during every jump. The uncertainty of the outcome furnishes that."

Larson's Flying Circus

$\mathbf{Y}$oung flyers returning home from WWI were hungry for excitement and thrills such as they had experienced in dog fights with German fighter planes. They needed a way to sate that appetite.

Without a doubt they were happy to be home. Friends and relatives listened with awe and gazed with worshipful eyes at the returned heroes, hanging on their every word as they recounted their fighting experiences.

The flyers' eyes sparkled, their voices raised to fever pitch in remembrance of sensations and emotions they described as they entertained their local audiences with stories of the thrilling antics "Over there."

The enthusiastic spectators were held spellbound by these hair-raising tales of glory. Teenagers greeted them on the street with demands for more tales of daring-do. They listened in awe and idolized the flyers. They, too, desired the thrills and excitement of flying. But eventually, it all paled, grew boring, and "old hat". Twice told tales became flat and the eager teenagers drifted away.

The future beckoned. What could these pilots do? They could go back to school, get an education, learn a skill, become an executive, but a sedentary life did not appeal to these volatile young men. They craved excitement, the thrills of the death defying chase after, and escape from, the enemy planes and bullets.

Flying was in their blood and that was all they wanted to do. Some used their discharge money to buy government surplus Jennies and entertained themselves and their friends. Others experienced the sentiment expressed in the song popular at the time. They couldn't be kept "down on the farm" after they'd seen the bright lights of Paris. For the flyers, they couldn't be kept away from the airfield, after they'd experienced the joy and excitement of flight.

Soon they were demonstrating stunts and staging air combat maneuvers for the thrill seekers desiring cliff-hanging flutters of excitement. As the crowds of spectators grew, the pilots were encouraged to put on shows and charge admission. Entrepreneurs realized money was to be made from these flying exhibitions and approached the flyers, with contracts for a day of publicized flying.

They needed a large vacant field–a fairgrounds, park, pasture or hayfield–and advertising to bring out large crowds. Someone remarked, "It's like a circus," and the words stuck. Thus the expression, "Flying Circus" evolved and the show became very popular entertainment for the next ten to fifteen years.

The Larson Brothers, with Clyde Lee as stunt man and wingwalker had their own flying circus, which was very popular throughout Wisconsin. The whole family worked to make each event a sell-out. Clarence and Viola Larson, who were married in September, 1928, were the advance team.

Roy would choose an event at which a large crowd was expected to attend. Clarence and Viola would drive or fly there and put notices in windows and advertisements in the newspaper. They would also arrange to rent a field. The farmers were usually very obliging. For a free ride or a small fee of $5.00 they would keep the cows out of the pasture or make available a field of the right size.

If it was necessary to be away from home overnight, they carried a tent along and slept next to the plane. The day of the event, Roy would fly over a wide area around the city, several times, to attract the people. He charged $5.00 a ride whether he carried one or two passengers.

Roy flew his dependable old JN4 Jenny, putting the plane through impossible maneuvers. He spun a plane that shouldn't be spun, did barrel rolls with a plane that shouldn't have rolled. When he did a ground loop, he flew only a few feet above the ground with the plane upside-down and waved at the crowd.

Roy and Clyde had contracted to do an exhibition flying show at the county fairgrounds one Sunday afternoon. The day had started out beautifully, bright and sunny with a slight breeze. Shortly before the exhibition began, the sun faded under thin clouds and the slight breeze turned into a strong wind which began to blow in sudden gusts. Sudden gusts of wind were particularly dangerous for open cockpit planes. They blew under, between and over the wings and could pitch the plane into a spin. Few stunting pilots were able to pull a Jenny out of a spin in a strong blustery, gusty wind.

Roy considered cancelling the show, but the grandstands were packed with excited people anxiously awaiting the performance, so he continued with the program. Roy flew the plane over the fairgrounds in front of the grandstand and saw that the wind was gusting dangerously. Added to the hazardous gusts, the engine started to run sluggish and didn't respond well to Roy's commands.

"Oh, no," he thought. "The carburetor must be clogged."

The engine was losing power and the plane was having difficulty climbing. What to do? If the situation worsened they would have to discontinue the exhibition and give the money back to the people. Because of the contract, they decided to continue, with caution, and be mindful of any change in conditions.

Roy flew in front of the crowd, climbed as high as the Jenny would take him and looped the plane. It was difficult to reach the height necessary to loop and spin, but he continued stunting as best he could. He flew in front of the crowd coming from the right and from the left, performing a different stunt during each fly-by. He looped the plane high in the air and near the ground. He climbed as high as the Jenny would go then flew straight down, spinning it. The dive ended in a low swoop less than a hundred feet above the ground. His last fly-by was with the plane upside down in front of the grandstand with Roy waving at the crowd. It was something to see and the crowd was entranced.

Each time he passed in front of the grandstand the people would cry out in exultant fear. "Oh's" and "Ah's" would continue until he circled back for the next fly-by. His daring, hair-raising stunts prompted excited screams from the women. They loved it.

His part of the show finished, Roy banked in and landed in the farmer's field adjacent to the fairgrounds. The Jenny didn't need a paved runway, just a fairly level farm field, with as few potholes as possible.

Clyde jumped on the wing and fastened the parachute onto the strut between the wings. Laying flat on the lower wing, he tied a four-rung rope ladder onto the under carriage and set the folded ladder on the wing. The stunting equipment in place, he climbed into the cockpit with Roy. They were ready for take off and Clyde's daredevil stunts.

Before lift off, Roy expressed his concern about the gusting wind and the sluggish engine. "Maybe we should call it off for today," he suggested.

"No." Clyde answered. He had noticed the gusts of wind becoming stronger and that the plane had been slow to respond. "I didn't think you would do the spin today, " he countered. "That was too dangerous, Roy."

"I know it and that is the reason I am suggesting we call off the rest of the show and do it another time. We might crash while you are doing your stunts."

Clyde disagreed. "If you could do the spin under these conditions, then I can do my part." he said.

They circled the field several times to gain altitude. The Jenny wasn't cooperating very well. Clyde climbed onto the center of the top wing. He clasped the balancing wire buckle into the ring of the buckle of his special stunting belt. He placed his feet into the leather shoe straps which fitted around and over his instep. Standing tall, he braced back to pull the rope taut. With arms outspread, he waved and bowed to the crowd as Roy flew the plane in front of the grandstand.

With Clyde standing on the top wing, Roy looped the plane and executed barrel rolls. Wingwalkers always fascinated the crowds at airshows and the excitement built every time Roy and Clyde flew past the grandstand. It would climax with Clyde's parachute jump.

But there were problems. Over the roaring engine and the shrieking wind, Roy yelled to Clyde, "In this wind, the parachute drop would be next to suicidal. We'll have to skip it."

Dropping the parachutre jump from the show would disappoint the crowd. At a bull-fight, there are always those who would rather see the matador gored than the bull vanquished. At a stock car race many fans wait only to see a crash. At the air shows in the 1920s, where accidents were frequent, there were many who waited with bated breath for the plane to crash or the parachute to fail.

If the chute failed to open, some jumpers had the presence of mind to turn around and pull the chute out of its pack, hoping that it would open in time to cushion the fall. Many didn't make it and went to their death minus fingernails ripped off when they desperately tried to open the chute by hand.

Despite Roy's reluctance, they decided to continue the show. Before Clyde's parachute jump came the last of his daredevil stunts. He moved down on the lower wing and climbed onto the ladder which was underhung from the airplane. The plane flew past the stands with him hanging by his hands and one elbow over the second rung of the four-rung rope ladder. The next fly-by he was hanging by his knees from the bottom rung. Roars and cheers and foot-stamping by the spectators greeted him as they flew by.

Waiting expectantly for the next event, the people were startled to see the small plane roaring toward them with someone apparently floating through the air just below it. Motor chattering loudly, the plane flew down to within a hundred feet of the ground and passed in front of the viewing grandstand. Waving to the crowd, both arms outstretched, Daredevil Lee was dangling under the plane at the end of a slim rope clenched tightly in his teeth. The other end of the slim rope was tied to the bottom rung of the ladder.

As the plane flew by, some of the audience were struck speechless at this daring feat. Some women awestruck, screamed in fright, while the rest, breathless...frozen in astonishment, felt their hearts stopped in their throats.

It seemed only an instant before the plane passed by the stunned audience and disappeared over the fairgrounds. The people sat silently, bound to their seats, watching the plane carrying the young daredevil back to the field. He swung his long legs up, caught on the lower rung of the ladder and climbed back onto the plane. Laying flat on the wing, he reached underneath, groped at the undercarriage where the ladder had been tied and dropped it to the ground.

Roy landed the plane. Clyde jumped to the ground, ran back to retrieve the ladder and threw it into the back of the cockpit. He climbed into the seat beside Roy.

The shocked viewers suddenly realized what they had been watching. The stunt man daring to hang by a slim rope with only the strength of his teeth to hold him aloft. He had hung below the rope ladder, dangling there, beneath the plane flying at ninety miles an hour. Now he would come back and end the show with the most spectacular stunt of all–the parachute jump.

The wind had been gaining in velocity all afternoon and buffeted the plane with gale-like gusts. As the air roughened, the wooden and paper bird fluttered and pitched temperamentally.

For a safe parachute drop, Roy would have to reach an altitude of 1500 to 2000 feet. When he attempted to reach that height, the Jenny coughed, spit, missed and caught, coughed a few more times, climbed sluggishly, and refused to gain over a thousand feet.

"Dirty fuel," yelled Roy, the wind whipping away his words. "I have it on full throttle and it won't go any higher. You can't jump at a thousand feet, you'll be killed. Jenny can't do any more than that and in this wind, you need more altitude, two thousand feet, at least."

Clyde kept making signs he was ready to jump. Roy kept shaking his head, "No." He was certain it wasn't safe. He made a sharp turn, a quick descent, and landed the plane. He flatly refused to take Clyde up for the jump.

Clyde argued. He had contracted to make the jump and was determined to do it. After Roy adamantly refused him again, Clyde suggested they test the drop with a bag of sand that weighed 140 pounds, as much as Clyde. If the chute with the sack attached didn't open at 1,000 feet, he wouldn't jump. If it did, they would end the show in the regular way with Clyde parachuting down.

With the bag of sand laying on the wing next to Clyde, they took off again. The engine was still accelerating sluggishly. The plane rose slowly and reluctantly to 1,000 feet but couldn't do any more. The stiff wind battering the frail craft caused it to dip and side slip dangerously. To make a safe jump, the pilot had to hold the plane steady as the chutist went over the side.

If Clyde jumped with the plane in an incorrect position, the tail might hit him and possibly cut off his head. It would at least knock him unconscious. With the plane unstable and a strong wind gusting, even standing on the wing was exceedingly dangerous.

They circled and circled the fairgrounds attempting to reach 2,000 feet but the Jenny couldn't do it. Clyde was growing more impatient by the minute and yelled at Roy, "Lets just do it." In a slight lull in the wind, Roy was able to tilt the plane in the correct position to drop the sandbag and Clyde heaved the bag over the side. Staying with it long enough to pull the ripcord on the parachute, he was almost overpowered and pulled off the plane. Roy, realizing his predicament, tilted the plane in the opposite direction, Clyde caught his balance and pulled himself back into the cockpit.

The chute never opened.

Closed, it fell, streaming, a long ribbon, a very long necktie, following the sack down.

The spectators thought Clyde was falling to certain death. In silent fear, their eyes followed him down as he fell and fell with the parachute failing to open. In fascinated horror, they watched him dropping nearer and nearer the ground. With bated breath, hypnotized by fear, they saw the sack hit the ground, bounce six feet in the air and lay motionless.

Women screamed, some fainted, men wept. They were sure Clyde had been killed. Momentarily, they sat, stunned at what they had seen. Then almost as of one mind, they swarmed out of their seats and onto the field.

They raced across the field to see the mangled boy. To their angry astonishment, they found a ruptured, half-empty bag of sand. When they realized that what they had thought was Clyde falling to his death was in fact only a sandbag dummy, they were furious.

The anguished mood quickly changed to one of outrage. They were irate. They had been duped. They were surely Hell-bent-for-election MAD!

Watching the jump, their emotions had been roused to fever pitch, their adrenalin elevated, their fear for Clyde so intense, they had to vent their "let down" emotions in great anger. They demanded their money be returned.

An announcement was made over the loud speaker, "Windy weather conditions and engine trouble with the plane forced us to make a test drop with a sandbag instead of risking Clyde's life, recklessly. Obviously, you can see what would have happened to Clyde.

"Weather permitting, the show will go on next Sunday in the same place at the same time. Your admission tickets will be returned to you. See you then."

Free tickets were handed out at the gate as the disgruntled, grumbling people left the Fairgrounds.

The next day when Clyde read the newspaper article, "Where was Daredevil Lee last Sunday when the Parachute Dropped?" he remarked wryly, "Who says people are civilized? They'd rather have me dead!"

The following Sunday was windy, but it was a steady wind and less powerful. Roy and Clyde—pride piqued—did the whole show for the same ticket holders. Its engine running smoothly, the Jenny climbed easily to 2,000 feet and Clyde slipped swiftly off the wing. The parachute opened quickly and fully, blossoming out into a beautiful mushroom.

An unexpected gusty, blustering blast of air caught it and tossed it. Clyde fought vigorously and skillfully with the chute lines, twisting and whirling downward as he struggled to direct the landing. A crosswind tipped the chute, spilling too much air too fast. He couldn't pull the shroud lines in rapidly enough. Still grappling with the lines, he was able to guide the chute just inside the farthest end of the fairgrounds, scarcely missing the power lines.

He attempted to set it down in front of the grandstand, but at the last minute, another gust of wind caught the chute, lifted it, and threw Clyde against a barbed wire fence. The sharp barbs ripped a half-foot long, half-inch deep gash in his left thigh, tore his leather jacket and scratched his face and arms. The wind held the chute taut in the air. Unable to free himself from the shroud lines, he hung on the fence.

The thrill-maddened-crowd, adrenalin high, poured out of the grandstand and ran screaming across the fairgrounds to swarm around the badly battered and bloody boy. Some embraced him, some grabbed at his clothing, tearing his jacket and shirt to shreds in their excited frenzy. They were happy. He had made the jump. They had their money's worth. Clyde Lee had given his pound of flesh.

Flying For The Klan

The Klu Klux Klan became publicly active throughout Wisconsin in 1923 and reached the Oshkosh area early in 1924. Daniel Woodward, the National Grand Dragon, visited Oshkosh to stimulate the movement. He ordered a tabernacle to be built on Jackson Drive Road, north of the city, ready to host a convention that thousands of people would attend.

The first general public meeting of the organization was to be held on April 19, 1924. Its stated purpose was to advise the community that the Klan was about to eliminate all corruption in Winnebago County and to enforce prohibition. In fact, the Klan was racist, anti-Semitic and–since African-Americans and Jews were scarce in Wisconsin–blatantly anti-Catholic.

Crosses would be burned at the close of the meetings, to supposedly alert the immoral and corrupt citizens of Oshkosh that they were going to be punished. "The Klan will expose the bootleggers and moonshiners as well as the corrupt politicians," stated Pat Malone, the spokesman who was called the Klan's "Billy Sunday."

On May 13, 1924, a fiery cross was burned at the World War I veterans plot in the Evergreen Addition of Riverside Cemetery, just north of the city. As the Grand Dragon said, the crosses were burned because the Klan membership had surpassed 4,000 and to give another warning to all bootleggers and moonshiners to cease their immoral business.

On May 27, 1924, shortly before 11:00 PM, another, larger cross was set on fire near the North Western Railroad tracks off 18th and Doty streets in the southern section of Oshkosh. The entire nine foot pole and eight foot cross arm had been wrapped in kerosene-soaked burlap. The burning of the cross was preceded by a blinding flash of exploding dynamite. A spark from the dynamite caused a whump of air which exploded into a blazing ball of flame streaking to the top of the cross. It burned fiercely for about a half hour. People were attracted to the scene. Some very angry at the Klan, and some who just liked to see a fire burn.

In 1924, prohibition was only four years old and quite difficult to enforce. People were as accustomed to their drinks as their food. Lots of basements were stocked with home brew, some people made bath tub gin–and it was just that–made in the bath tub. Whiskey was smuggled over the border from Canada. Even the Jenny was called into service to fly Canadian whiskey to people living in Winnebago County. The pilots laughingly called that operation, "Moose Hunting in Canada."

One Sunday, Roy was flying passengers out of a hay field near the KKK tabernacle. A convention was slated for the weekend and he hoped some of the Klansmen would be interested in taking a ride with him.

"Maybe I can find ten brave souls out of 8,000 people who would like to have a ride in an airplane," he told his brothers before leaving home.

On these business trips, one of the brothers or a friend always accompanied Roy. Someone had to sell the tickets while Roy was flying passengers. On a good day there would be as many as twenty people standing in line waiting for a ride.

The Grand Dragon approached Roy with a different proposition. He asked him if during the convention, Roy would consider attaching a lighted cross to the undercarriage of his plane and flying over the city after dark.

Roy begged off. He told the Grand Dragon he would ask around among his flying pals. "Perhaps I could interest someone," he said. None of his brothers was interested. The Klan was too controversial and feelings in Oshkosh too high.

Elwyn West, a close friend and pilot extraordinaire from Waupaca, agreed to fly for the Klan. The terms were excellent. "Quite a generous remuneration for the job," West said afterwards. "It was pretty scary. People, especially people of the Catholic faith, were very angry and up in arms that the city had allowed the Klan to rent the meeting space."

The burning of the cross was especially upsetting, especially to Catholics. They remembered what the Klan had done to freed slaves in the south after the Civil War and the lynchings it had been responsible for in the years since. Emotions were running high. Some feared flying the lighted cross over the city might foster a riot.

Elwyn flew over the city two times with the lighted cross attached to the under carriage of his plane before fear got the best of him. He feared that an anti-Klan person might take a shot at his plane and blow him out of the sky.

This atmosphere of fear and anger made May 30, 1924 a momentous night for the residents of the hamlet of Larsen, Wisconsin. It had perhaps no more than 10 homes and a population of less than 50 people. The business district consisted of a blacksmith shop, lumber yard, telephone company office, grocery store, bank and barbershop. It was a source of supplies and services for the farmers in the area.

The women were a close knit group. One could hardly sneeze without everyone in the town knowing about it. Gossip and their card clubs were a large part of the ladies' entertainment.

On Sunday evening, May 30, Uncle Ted and Aunt Alice Larson, who lived about three miles from Larsen, went to a meeting at the Grange Hall. They left their son Loyall and nephew Clyde Lee home to do the chores.

Wilbur Zehner walked into the barn as they were finishing the milking. Wilbur's nickname was "Wib." He and Clyde were close friends, a couple of pranksters who had many a lark together.

"Oh, Oh!" muttered Loyall under his breath, "mischief is brewing tonight!"

"Tonight," Wib said, "What can we do tonight to kick up some excitement. We need something to liven things for the neighborhood. It's getting too quiet around here."

"Well you find the dynamite and I'll set off a few bombs for you. That will liven things for the neighborhood," Clyde volunteered.

"Takes too long. Where would I find dynamite around here? Anyway I don't want to wait. It has to be tonight." Wib said. "I've got that devilish feeling. It has to be tonight."

"I hear the Klan set off a few bombs in Oshkosh," said Clyde. "That really stirred things up. I could always set some off in your backyard."

"Dynamite! Just the thing," Wib agreed, "but who has some? But not in my backyard."

"You could burn a cross," Loyall volunteered jokingly, entering into the fun.

"That's it." exclaimed Wib and Clyde in chorus. "We'll burn a cross."

"But where?" asked Wib, "Neenah? They haven't had one yet. They need a treat, too."

"I don't know of any illegal taverns, there," Clyde replied. "How about Butte des Morts? They have two. Everyone knows that."

"Too far to go. Let's do Larsen. I hear the barber sells moonshine. Let's burn a cross in front of his place. Scare the bejassus out of him."

"That's right." Loyall agreed. "The barber hides it, but he sells moonshine."

"Perfect," the boys chorused. "Let's do it." Wib said. Clyde nodded, yes, and Loyall agreed.

"You're right. That will certainly liven up Larsen. Like a hornet's next," Loyall agreed.

"It will be a great mystery! Those upstanding, law-abiding citizens are in for a real shock. It'll be a seven days wonder. A 'who done it!'" exclaimed Clyde.

"Let's get started, we will need 2 x 4's, burlap sacking, nails and kerosene." Clyde said, "Do you have all of that, Loyall?"

"I will furnish all the supplies you need, but I am not going to be involved." Loyall informed them.

"No, not much," laughed the boys, "just furnishing all the combustibles for us to create mayhem...fraidy cat," they said.

They finished the milking in record time. To speed things along, Wib grabbed a milk pail and milked the last cow.

First, they blackened their faces with soot so they could sneak around in the dark, then laughed at each other's new image. Next they wrapped the kerosene-soaked burlap sacks around the 2 x 4's, and nailed the two poles together to form a cross. One pole was eight feet tall, the crossarm, five feet. They had an open-topped Ford car and had no problem fitting the cross into the car. Then they took off for Larsen, but parked about a half-mile from the barbershop. What a rare, exciting and fun time they were having.

"We'll drive out those crooked politicians," chuckled Wib. "Don't forget the bootleggers", Clyde laughed.

"And at least one moonshiner", Wib laughed. Then soberly he said, "Maybe we will frighten the barber out of town. That'll make the residents happy."

Armed with matches, kerosene, and the cross, they slunk across the field toward Larsen.

"We'll certainly cause a stir and a lot of excitement if nothing else in Larsen. We'll have all those bootleggers quaking in their boots," quipped Wib. "I hope the folks haven't all gone to the Grange meeting. Our little hoax would fall flat if they have."

The people residing in Larsen, except for the barber, were very circumspect, law-abiding citizens. That is why it struck the boys as being highly amusing that they were "clearing out the corruption" in the town.

Unknown to the boys was that Larsen had a moonshine still in a vacant two-story house. The vat filled the upper story and copper tubes ran down from the top of the still to the first floor, where they emptied into large jars. The actual owner was never apprehended and the still was only discovered by children playing hide and seek who broke into the house one day. They were not supposed to play there so they had been afraid to tell about it until many years later.

Since they didn't know about Larsen's real bootlegger, Wib and Clyde made the barber the target of their prank. They had soaked the cross with kerosene before they left home, and breathed the pungent odor all the way to Larsen. They were glad it wasn't any farther. Bracing the cross with rocks, they were able to make it stand erect in front of the barber shop. They poured the rest of the kerosene on it. One lighted match was all it needed. The fire exploded in a flash of flames, fast and hot. It nearly caught them in its blast. In seconds a ball of fire raced the length of the pole.

The boys left Larsen, running as if all the hounds of hell were after them.

The first person aware of the fire was Eva Hallock, the twelve-year-old daughter of the grocer. She happened to walk into the front room of her house, glance out the window and scream. Terrified, she ran to the phone and rang the one long ring, the neighborhood warning of disaster. The Hallock home was just across the road from the barbershop and Eva was home alone. People dashed out into the street and ran towards the burning cross. They hadn't far to go. Soon, all the residents were gathered around the fire. Caught in the "Come as you were" at 11:00 P.M., it was a motley group, men in long nightshirts, women in high-ruffled-neck, ankle-length gowns, with a flimsy shortie a small minority. The fire burned fiercely for about thirty minutes.

Gasping in indignation, one woman exclaimed, "Who did this? Why? We don't have any Catholics living here."

"I'll bet the Klan did it because they heard the barber sells moonshine." A prominent lady exclaimed.

"The barber sells moonshine?" asked a young woman in disbelief.

"Do you really believe he does?" asked another lady. She was a rabid prohibitionist, and became very angry, saying, "We have got to get rid of him. If you'll go with me, we'll invite the others and raid his place tomorrow."

The next day, Mabel Hallock and Ada Hough decided to find out once and for all if the barber was selling intoxicants. They riled up the whole populace, about 40 people, and marched on the barber shop. They found several gallon jugs of liquor hanging hidden in the rain water cistern. They poured the liquor away and smashed the containers.

Greatly incensed at the discovery, Grandpa Hallock went stomping angrily down the street. He spied a drunk sleeping it off in the back seat of a car, and grabbing him by the throat, began choking him. He nearly choked him to death and only his son Herb could pull him away.

The drunk, driving recklessly, took off for Winneconne where he found an illegal tavern. He warned the bartender, "Never go near Larsen. Those people...!" he said.

The next night after chores, Wib was back to ask Clyde and Loyall if they had heard anything.

"Haven't heard a thing," they said. "No one went to Larsen today. Aunt Alice heard about it on the phone, but she didn't say much. I could tell she didn't suspect." The boys chuckled slyly.

The next day they read about it in the Oshkosh paper. "We've made the newspaper. We're famous." laughed Wib.

"More likely 'infamous,'" retorted Clyde.

Days later, the three boys were talking about their Klan warning and Clyde said, "They suspect we were the culprits. Aunt Mable and Uncle Charlie Cross visited at Clark's Point where my sister lives.

"Bernice told me Aunt Mabel had heard a whisper that we probably were the pranksters and not the Klan. She is very straight laced, and was quite perturbed about it. But she did chuckle a little. She was more perturbed at finding out about the moonshine at the barbershop. She hadn't known anything about that.

"'At least burning the cross did warn that moonshiner to get out of our town. He's gone. He left, bag and baggage the next day,'" she said. "'Good riddance!'"

The Flying Snake

Ray Isodorek frequently accompanied Roy on his barnstorming trips. He sold tickets and assisted passengers to climb on the wing and into the cockpit. In the 1920s, all aviators, especially barnstormers, had to get used to unexpected hazards, but few ever had a more surprising and dangerous experience than Ray Isodorek. He tells the story.

"Roy had been flying passengers for five-minute rides at Weyauwega, Wisconsin since ten o'clock Sunday morning. It was a blisteringly hot day and I had not enjoyed my job, selling tickets, as much as usual. The field was dusty. The propeller wash raised a cloud of dust each time the plane landed or took off. Dust carried on the breeze made one's mouth gritty and eyes teary. Between the unusual heat and dust I was most uncomfortable. Because of the heat, business had been booming. Airplane rides were very popular."

"'It was heavenly'," passengers said. They not only enjoyed a thrilling ride, but also the cool wind whistling through the cockpit and over their sweaty bodies.

"There was no shade on the fairgrounds. While I suffered, Roy enjoyed himself. Piloting his JN plane was his idea of the best way to keep cool on a hot day. Even though the customers had to stand around in the sun waiting for their ride, I was having no problem selling tickets. My sales pitch was encouraging them to have a ride to cool off. The more gutsy ones were sold on the idea of telling their grandchildren how brave they had been.

"Toward evening the crowd thinned and the day cooled. We flew for home. It was late in the day. I was tired. The wind whipping my hair and drying my perspiring face was a welcome relief. My back burned. I felt it through my shirt. Even in the cool wind, I still hurt.

"Roy was jubilant. We had had a very prosperous day.

"Flying toward home, the continuous monotonous drone of the clattering engine, together with heat exhaustion, made me sleepy. Sitting in the co-pilot's seat next to Roy, fatigued and drowsily thinking over the events of the day, I wasn't doing my usual superior co-pilot job. In fact I was near sleep with thoughts and images circulating in my brain.

"I remembered meeting the Larson brothers at the wedding of a friend. I was a member of the band, the singer, besides playing instruments. I drank a little too much beer and don't remember much more than meeting them. I liked the looks of the boys, and their being flyers excited me. I decided to join them. I left the dance and went home with them. That was several months ago. I had been accompanying them to the barnstorming events, selling tickets and being a general handyman ever since. Thoughts of that past period flashed through my mind.

"Something hung on the edge of that drowsiness and just as I was dozing into real sleep, an inner impulse urged me awake.

"As I opened my eyes, I thought, 'I'm having a nightmare! or delirium tremens! Incredulous!' I saw something move...slither and wriggle out from the cowling. Dumb struck, I watched a very large rattlesnake writhing and squirming sinuously, floundering out and attempting to climb up the side. Then slithering and wriggling it saw me and stopped.

"Stunned...voiceless, I gasped...and lightening fast shoved myself back and over to the right hand seat corner so hard and fast I nearly went over the side of the cockpit. At that point I wished very much I could continue on over and down.

"It was across and in front of me. And it was horrible to see.

"Flattened against the side and back of the plane, glued to my seat, I was terrified! How had a such a very large rattlesnake made its way into the airplane? Impossible! A prankster? But this was no prank! That snake was deadly serious, and deadly poisonous. Sinuously, twisting and turning, it swayed back and forth, each time edging, it seemed, a little nearer.

"The shift in weight in the plane when I lunged toward the back and side of my seat, had tipped the Jenny slightly and Roy gave me a dirty look as he levelled off again. When he glanced at me, I motioned him to land and I pointed toward the snake, making slithering motions with my arm. Roy looked below at the ground, he didn't see anything unusual. I motioned again to land the plane. Roy looked at the plane's controls, nothing wrong and the motor was ticking over perfectly. He looked questioningly at me. But he never saw the snake.

"Levelled off again and back on course, he continued looking straight ahead completely unconscious of the fact we had a stowaway on board. His usual thing when flying was complete absorption in the plane, the weather, and his whereabouts.

"Regaining my voice, at last, I yelled, 'Snake, Roy, SNAKE,' at the top of my lungs, at the same time pointing at the snake. I might as well have saved my breath. The clattering of the engine, together with the propeller wash blew my words away.

"Unaware of my situation, Roy flew on. The snake must have heard me yell as it seemed to upset him. It tried more desperately to move nearer, wriggling closer until it was directly across and in front of my face. Being in such close quarters was upsetting my nervous system. I had never had a snake for a cabin mate before and I was very apprehensive. What could I do? I couldn't get Roy's attention to warn him. The snake seemed to be targeting on me. Apparently he blamed me for his untenable predicament. I had no weapon to protect myself. There seemed no way out of my dire plight.

"Once more I looked over the side at the ground. No, it was too far to jump. Anyway, I couldn't jump without a parachute. It must have been over 1,000 feet. I had never dropped in a parachute. I wouldn't have been able or brave enough to jump if I had one. I was definitely not one of those reckless young barnstormers, but I think I would have felt reckless enough to use a parachute if I could have gotten my hands on one at that moment.

"Looking back at the snake, eyes glaring in that vicious head, mouth open, tongue flickering in and out, it seemed nearer and inching along...

"I couldn't hear its rattles nor its hissing, but there was no doubt in my mind that it was happening.

"Realizing the only thing I could do was convince Roy to land the plane, I tried again to get his attention. I kept trying to make him look toward me by jabbing him in the ribs with my elbow. Roy was used to our tricks...horsing around, really kid stuff. He didn't usually pay much attention. When he only gave me a dirty look as a result of the jab in the ribs, I knew he was thinking, it was just another prank.

"Things were getting pretty desperate in the cockpit between me and the snake. Fear, shivered up and down my spine. I realized I had to make Roy understand this was serious and not just another silly trick. I gave him a terrific jab in the ribs.

"Roy's disposition was that of a very mild person except when he was flying. Then he would stand for no foolishness. So although I gave him a really hard jab, he just shrugged it off and kept his eyes on the horizon. Roy had always taken flying and its dangers very seriously. I knew that distracting him would not be easy.

97

"Another look at that snake made me more determined to get Roy's attention.

"Squirming and writhing, it had moved further and higher on the cowling and was stretching, reaching out directly in front of my face. While it kept its malevolent eyes intent on me, its tongue flicked lightning-fast. That was the first time I had ever had a close-up look into the eyes of a snake and I hoped it would be the last. Especially as they were staring directly into mine, eyeball to eyeball, cold, weird, and angry. Panicking and hard pressed, I gave Roy such a jolt he couldn't possibly ignore it any longer, and I kept on jabbing him.

"Roy looked at me then. Grim of face and shaking his head angrily, he opened his mouth to yell at me, when... mouth hanging open ... his eyes noted the flickering motion of my tongue and the slithering snake-like gestures I was imitating as I pointed at the snake.

"It seemed forever before his eyes, following my arm pointed at that swaying head, took in what he was looking at. Luckily for me, just at that moment the snake lurched frenziedly toward my hand. Roy saw it.

"The amazed, incredulous look on his face was gratifying to see. I kept my eyes on Roy because the way he looked at that snake I wasn't sure he wouldn't go right over the side of the plane and leave me with the stowaway.

"The snake becoming aware he had two targets instead of one, began sinuously swaying his body and head like a pendulum between the two of us, moving dangerously nearer to both.

"Roy didn't take kindly to this and began looking around for a place to land the plane.

"Airfields were few and far between in those early days of flying. A cow pasture or hayfield was the best we could hope for. Roy's airport was one of the few in the state and it was at least a half-hour's flight time away.

"Shortly, we saw a farmer's hayfield. The hay had recently been cut and winnowed in neat rows. Roy swiftly circled the field for a landing, a fast landing. I had never known the overly cautious Roy to come in so fast or to land at such speed. The field was not prepared to be an airfield and it was a very bumpy set-down as the plane bounced from pot hole to pot hole. The snake wasn't happy either as it was jounced around as much as we were. There were no brakes on airplanes in those days and as soon as it came to a natural stop, we both leaped out in record time, leaving the snake in charge.

"The snake was every bit as anxious as we to leave his unusual environment. It tried vainly to slither over the cowling and onto a seat. Its desperate efforts to climb the side of the plane proved how much it wanted to get out. Since snakes have no feet or legs, the side proved too slippery. It coiled itself on the seat swinging and swaying its body protectively, rattles at full sound, mouth hissing and tongue flicking.

"I had never seen such horrific anger on Roy's face. He wasted no time in searching for a large club. There was no doubt in my mind as to the fate of that snake once Roy found what he was looking for. It had frightened me so badly, I was in complete accord with Roy's thinking. I had never felt so near death in my life. Never, as long as I lived, would I be able to forget that awful menacing head, tongue flickering in and out as those weirdly cold angry eyes glared into mine. Malevolently aimed straight at me, slowly moving nearer and nearer, and I a captive audience.

"As soon as Roy found a long thick limb, he headed back to the plane with murder on his mind. I held the stick while Roy climbed onto the wing. Just before Roy was set in place, club in hand, the snake made another desperate effort to get over the cowling and leave the plane. As its head came out in the open, Roy, clinging to the overhead wing with one hand, swung the club viciously at the snake's head and missed. Roy had not been ready and the snake moved too fast. He hit the cowling a mighty blow.

"There wasn't room to swing the stick inside the cockpit. He waited for the snake to make another attempt to get out. This caused the usually gentle dispositioned Roy to become very irritated. The next move was up to the snake.

"Roy was surprised to see his victim's head appear over the opposite side of the plane. When it had jerked back to avoid Roy's stick, it had fallen on the floor and had to slither up on the seat. It was again trying vainly to get over the side of the cockpit.

"Roy had to reposition himself and at the same time keep his head and shoulders bent forward to avoid the top wing of the plane. It was difficult to hold on to the wing, swing the club and still be out of reach of that shifting head and flicking tongue.

"He saw his chance as his doomed victim, in dire straits, once more raised its head over the rim of the cockpit. Swiftly swinging the club, he caught it.

"Watching from a distance, I saw Roy's successful strike. The snake dropped instantly to the floor of the plane and Roy leaning over the side of the cockpit hammered it to a pulp. I saw him lift a bloody lifeless mass on the end of his club. He threw it as far as he could across the farmer's hayfield.

"The hay was heavy to move, nevertheless we had to do it if we expected to lift off from the field. It was alfalfa hay which is especially apt to cling and wind around the undercarriage of a plane. It was a long field. We needed every inch of it.

"Airborne again, neither of us were the least bit drowsy nor spoke of the thing uppermost on our mind. How did that snake get into our plane?"

Roy Larson Crashes

Leonard, Newell and Roy Larson were cutting trees along the fence row for their winter wood supply. The limbs were chopped off and the logs were hauled as soon as they were felled. They were using the horses and sleigh to move the limbs to a stack to be corded ready for sawing into stove lengths. It was a cold day. Snow blanketed the ground.

Late morning they heard a plane approaching and watched as it landed in their airfield. They recognized the Swallow plane of William Weid, of Menasha, who Roy had recently been instructing in flying. They watched the would-be-pilot as he approached and then asked Roy to teach him aerobatics. Cautious as usual, Roy was reluctant. He told him he didn't think it was a good idea that day and that he didn't have a plane of his own in condition to do that kind of flying.

"If you'll wait a few days, we can use one of my Wacos," Roy said.

Bill was most insistent they fly that day, and right away. He said, "I flew here in my Swallow. It has dual controls, and if I can't pull it out of a tail-spin, you can take over. I can't come here again for quite a while. You promised me yesterday, Roy, so let's go."

Very reluctantly Roy agreed. "I haven't flown the Swallow very much, and it is difficult to get it out of a tail-spin. I'm afraid we might spin in. Maybe if we get up high enough, we will be all right," Roy conceded.

He smiled at young Weid and said, "I know just how anxious you are to get your aerobatics license. You need more instruction and more practice time flying and doing spins, stalls, rolls. W-e-l-l. We can try a few today."

Roy walked to the house to change his clothes. Later, Leonard and Newell watched them take off in the Swallow. "From time to time while we were working, we heard them as they flew near our house. I would glance at them occasionally when they were near us." Leonard said.

"All at once," Leonard went on, "I noticed a difference in the sound of the motor... a whine..."

Flyers themselves, the brothers knew that whine spelled trouble. Leonard and Newell watched apprehensively as the plane began to go into a spin. At first they didn't worry, they knew Roy was instructing Weid in how to bring the plane out of a spin. Still they felt anxious. They stopped working and watched. They noted the flyers were about five miles from the airport and at about 5,000 feet altitude.

Leonard began to feel anxious as they didn't come out of the maneuver. He knew it was taking too long to straighten out. He and Newell began to worry as they waited and waited for the nose to come up. It kept on dropping lower and lower. Once it seemed to make an effort to come out, but went back in again. Uneasy and extremely fearful as they saw the plane was not responding, Leonard exclaimed, "They can't come out of it. It's taking too long. It's too late! They are going to spin in." He had flown a lot. He knew what a plane had to do and the timing. He knew it was too late.

Frozen in horrified anticipation, they watched the plane continue to fall. They couldn't see through the trees when the plane nosed into the ground, but they saw it bounce back up about twenty feet and go down again.

Although it had appeared to be closer, the site of the crash was over five miles from the home airfield. The crash had appeared to be closer to them than it was. They took a wrong turn on a nearer side road and lost valuable time turning around on the narrow gravel road. In his haste and distraught condition, Leonard nearly ditched the car.

Many thoughts were racing through Leonard's mind as they sped to the crash scene. Mostly the question was, "What could have gone wrong? It was a new plane, it should have responded." He remembered Roy telling them the one time he had been flying a Swallow he had spun it and it didn't respond well at all. He had to use the motor to get it out of the spin. Blast it out!

Neither spoke. They were frightened nearly out of their wits with worry over the fate of the two pilots. With great anxiety and little hope, faces pale, jaws clenched, they arrived at the crash site. They were too late.

Others seeing the plane crash had rushed to call an ambulance and hastened to the scene. They had already put Roy in someone's car and headed for the hospital in Neenah.

Leonard and Newell looked blankly at each other. "What to do?" The people who were gathered around the shattered airplane told them Roy was alive when he left for the hospital, but they didn't think young Weid was.

Realizing they couldn't do anything to help Roy, Leonard and Newell began looking over the scene of the crash. They walked over to the largest heap of twisted metal. It was complete wreckage. The impact was so intense, the nose had dived six feet into the ground and telescoped back into the forward cabin.

In a state of shock, the brothers remained at the site for a while. They stared at the crackup but did not really see it. Over and over in their minds was the question, "What could have gone wrong? Roy never made mistakes. He could have pulled the plane out of that spin, he had done it before. Weid must have frozen to the stick almost as soon as the tail spin began." Leonard noticed that Roy's stick was in the correct position to pull the plane out of the spin. Weid's was in the opposite position.

"Yes," Leonard declared, "Young Weid must have panicked and frozen to the stick, making it impossible for Roy to move his stick to pull them out of the dive."

"Roy had the presence of mind to turn the key 'off' so the engine wouldn't explode," Leonard pointed out.

"Yes," Newell agreed, "and he unfastened his seat belt so he would be thrown clear and have a chance to survive." Newell remarked, woodenly.

Dazed, too shocked to realize the fruitlessness of their actions, they walked around the crash site for a while picking up pieces of the wreckage and dropping them back on what was left of the fuselage.

A few days later, William Weid's obituary appeared in the newspaper.

"William Weid, 28, of Lind Center, Wisconsin, a student flyer, was fatally injured when he crashed his airplane shortly before noon on the Frank Porath farm, a half mile west of the Neenah/Menasha Golf Club grounds on Highway 26. A fractured skull was the immediate cause of his death.
"For the past two years, Mr. Weid had lived in Menasha with Mrs. A. M. Winters at 343 Chute Street. Another flying enthusiast, Weid devoted his spare time to studying aviation. He had been employed for the past two years by the Valley Cylinder Regrinding company's plant in Menasha. He was dead on arrival at the hospital."

Roy clung tenaciously to life. Doctor T. B. Smith operated immediately to stop the internal bleeding and restore the chest to a more normal condition.

When Viola answered the telephone at the Larson's home that afternoon, she didn't recognize Leonard's voice. It was so low and husky it was strange to her. And what he said next was stranger. When she heard him say, "Roy crashed with young Weid," she feared the worst.

She cried out, "No, oh, no. Is he alive?"

She felt faint and nausea hit her. She said, "Leonard, I don't have the car. I can't come. Where are you? Is Roy in the hospital? Which one? Maybe Loyall can bring me."

"No, don't come now. There isn't anything we can do. It's all up to the doctors. Newell and I will come home for dinner and milk the cows. You can take our car and stay with Roy until we return. We'll call you to pick us up after chores. We'll stay the night with Roy. We will work it out in shifts...stay with Roy. The doctor hasn't told us anything except that it's serious. We know he has lost too much blood and has a severe concussion. He was unconscious when he arrived here and is still on the operating table. They are patching him up and staunching as much of the internal bleeding as they can and hope they can get it all. He is very weak. They can't do much more.

"The concussion is the most serious and critical injury," the doctor said. "We are at Theda Clark Hospital in Neenah. It would be senseless for you to come. We'll be home around six o'clock. There is nothing any of us can do except wait and pray."

In a state of shock, Viola stood clutching the telephone. She couldn't believe this. Roy was the best. Finally, she began to realize the awful truth. What Leonard had told her. Roy had crashed, was seriously injured and might not live. Minutes later, she hung up the receiver. On rubbery legs, she walked to the davenport and sat down, weak from shock. She was living over again the last days of her young husband, Clarence. Ever since his death the previous June, any other death or violent accident affected her that way. Clarence had been too young to die and so was Roy.

"Oh, no! it can't be...it mustn't happen! He must not die...not Roy, too!" she exclaimed loudly. This was another nightmare! Appalled and shocked, Viola sat staring into space, unaware of the tears sliding down her face. No thoughts of telling her family about the crash entered her mind. She sat immobile, as if paralyzed, her mind stupefied. She couldn't think of anything except Roy–his flying goals, his future as an airmail pilot lost, all lost! His great dreams shattered. It couldn't be, he had too much to live for. He had to live! She prayed with intensity and fervor for his life to be preserved.

After a while, prayer seemed to calm her emotions, she began to realize there were things she needed to do. She realized she owed it to their friends and relatives to tell them what had happened. First she called Verna Erickson, who came immediately to help. She knew Viola would need a friend at this time and she was the closest. Verna was also a close friend of the boys and thought the world of Roy.

Viola's family also came, offering to do the chores so the boys could remain at the hospital. Neighbors were stunned. They brought food, prayers, sympathy and words of hope for his life.

Viola and the brothers spent ceaseless hours at Roy's bedside. At least one of them was there every minute. He moved and made sounds several times, but for the most part was motionless. He lived for three more days without regaining consciousness and died on the morning of Thanksgiving Day.

His obituary read:

"Roy Larson, nearing his thirty-third birthday, the instructor in the passenger seat, observing and teaching, sustained critical and what later proved to be fatal injuries. He lived three days. He sustained two fractured legs, just above the ankle. One broken stump had penetrated the earth, a broken left shoulder, a crushed chest and in addition a broken jaw, and severe face and body lacerations. The most severe of his injuries and most crucial to his recovery was a severe concussion."

No one can ever be sure of the cause of the fatal plunge of the plane. Witnesses near the scene observed the Swallow plane flying at roughly 5,000 feet. The sound of the engine suddenly changed to a whine and its flight became erratic just before the nose dive as it fell into a tail-spin. There was one obvious attempt to come out of the spin, but it went back into it again and never recovered. It was a well-known fact among the airmen that the Swallow was not an easy nor a reliable plane to bring out of a spin. Roy had been most reluctant to teach young Weid to do aerobatics in it.

Leonard remarked that Weid was anxious to learn more than was taught in the usual ten lessons. The first hour of the fatal flight was spent giving instructions in performing rolls, stalls, and spins. The last instructions were in bringing a plane out of a tail-spin. Then Roy turned the flying over to Weid, while he, Roy observed. That was the usual method of teaching aerobatics.

Other flyers hazarded a guess that the student, unaccustomed to being in a spin, 'froze' to the control stick. The plane had dual controls and ordinarily the instructor would have been able to control the plane and bring it out of the spin. Also, still others observing the crashed plane noticed the student's dual control stick was in the wrong position, opposite the direction of Roy's. They all agreed; Larson's stick was in the proper position to bring the plane out of the spin.

This fatal accident robbed the community of its pioneer entrepreneur aviator. Roy was among the first of the commercial flyers and airport managers in Wisconsin. A pioneer in his field, he was rated on a par with the best in the nation.

Hundreds of morbid curiosity seekers drove to the scene of the accident and some friends who couldn't believe what they had heard and had to see it for themselves. Souvenir hunters carried away broken and bent metal and other airplane parts and splinters from the propeller, motor and fuselage. The heavier pieces of the fuselage had been scattered over 50 feet of ground. The broken seats snapped off and were some distance from the crumpled mass of the plane. Any large salvageable parts were hauled to the Whiting Airport north of Menasha.

Roy had over 3,000 flying hours to his credit. He taught over a hundred people to fly. He carried stunt men at exhibitions, flew commercially and was about to realize another dream of becoming an airmail pilot like his friend, Speed Holman. Roy numbered among his more famous friends and students: Major John P. Wood, Noel Wein of Alaskan pilot's fame, Clyde Lee, Elwyn West, Speed Holman, Mel Thompson, Howard Morey, Doc Ross and many others.

When Senator La Follette was running for office, his speaking dates were, at times, scheduled too close for him to fulfill them on time if he used automobile transportation. On those occasions he hired Roy and his plane. Roy and the Governor became friends and Roy often flew him to his speaking engagements.

In 1928, President Calvin Coolidge had a summer home on the Brule. Roy saw an opportunity for business flying tourists over the area and moved temporarily to Ashland, Wisconsin. Tourists, eager to view the presidential dwelling from the air, hired Roy to give them an aerial view. It was 140 miles round trip from Ashland and back. He flew over rugged wooded country with no landing fields. He never had to make an emergency landing. Roy was popular among aviators and many flew in for repairs to their planes or just to visit with him. He sold the new Wacos to other aviators and held the Waco franchise in Wisconsin. When the celebration of Chief Oshkosh day was planned, it was arranged for Roy to drop pamphlets announcing the event and time and place. He flew over city and country dropping pamphlets advertising the event. He gave Princess Alice Oshkosh and her ladies an airplane ride on her special day.

Roy's airport was the only one listed for the state of Wisconsin in aviation magazines for 1922 and 1923. In fact, the Larson Brothers Airport is the first and only airport to open before 1923 and to remain in operation until 1990, when Leonard Larson died.

Roy's commitment to aviation was carried on by his brother Leonard. He was the youngest and strongest of the brothers and an extremely cautious pilot. He never flew stunt men, nor did any stunting himself. He once said the only thing that could get him to jump out of an airplane while flying would be if the plane caught on fire or the engine quit. Neither of those things ever happened.

The five original Larson brothers had been a family unto themselves. They rarely went anywhere except for their flying activities. The world came to them. Through illness and accident they were now a family of two.

On the morning Roy died, Clyde Lee flew out from Oshkosh. Leonard, Viola and Newell had just arrived home from the hospital when he arrived and Leonard met him on the airfield. Clyde asked immediately, "How is Roy, I just heard about the crash."

"Roy is dead, Clyde. Roy died about an hour ago."

The words hung in the air and sounded over and over in his head. He was sure they weren't true, they couldn't be. Numb and miserable, beyond comprehension or thought, he stood there, a statue staring at Leonard. Leonard, equally without words, stared back. Desolated, Clyde realized he had lost his flying pal, his teacher, his friend, the quiet man with big dreams and boyish clowning tricks. His death was inconceivable, frightening. Roy couldn't die like that. He was the best pilot in the world. He often used dual controls and he always remained in control. He could bring any plane out of anything, even with a student piloting. He always maintained control.

Finally, Clyde spoke, his voice low and barely controlled. "Do you know what happened with young Weid? Did Roy regain consciousness, was he able to tell you?"

"No, Leonard said. "Indications are Weid panicked and froze to the stick when the plane went into a nose dive. Apparently, he never eased up. Roy couldn't pull it out, couldn't move Weid's stick. Of course that is pure supposition on our part. We will never know. The answer to that died with them."

The moment when one pilot came face to face with the death of another, and that one an even better pilot than he, was a great shock. Clyde pictured how desperately Roy must have fought with the controls to bring the plane out of the spin. He also knew if Weid's stick was in the wrong position and he froze, nothing Roy could have done would have brought it out of the spin.

Clyde was bitter, greatly agitated, with tears in his eyes, unable to speak, or control his emotions. He turned away from Leonard and walked slowly to the house. Viola was his cousin, the Larson boys his in-laws. He often dropped in to visit with them all. They were his buddies. He just couldn't comprehend what Leonard had told him. Why...? Why...? Why, Roy?

Viola had continued to live in the Larson brothers home after Clarence's death. She had a financial interest in the business and the boys had asked her to stay. "Viola," Clyde thought, "what a cruel blow this is for her. The boys were like so many brothers. She must be in deep grief and shock."

Entering the house, he found no one there. Later he learned she was at her parents, across the road. He waited. When she returned her eyes were red and she was like a zombie. She spoke to Clyde as if he were a stranger. There was no trace of her usual happy smile. Clyde began to speak to her, extend sympathy. "I can't talk now," she said. "I don't want to believe it. I can't! I just want to be alone. We just came home from the hospital and it's horrible, a nightmare!

In tune with and appreciative of her emotional trauma, he walked outside. He walked over to his plane and flew to his home in Oshkosh. He respected their need to be alone. This was Thanksgiving Day. What had any of them to be thankful for?

The next day Clyde flew back to see what he could do. They asked him to be a pall-bearer. He knew it would be difficult to watch his flying buddy, pal, teacher and friend being laid to rest, but this would be the last thing he could do for Roy.

During the services, pilots, friends and flying buddies sat dry-eyed, grim-faced and stunned. They couldn't accept it. To them, it was unbelievable. They were all there. Pilots from far and near, from all over the Midwest, attended. Roy was well known, greatly respected and recognized for his exceptional flying ability. People he had met at flying meets and exhibitions or "Flying Circuses" were at his funeral. The graveside ceremony was brief and highly emotional. There was not a dry eye. Viola stood beside the grave as the ceremony was carried on. The depth of her grief obvious. The two brothers morose, pale and stricken stood beside Viola. They may have been thinking, "We were five and now we are only two."

Later, at the funeral dinner later with the table piled high with food, Leonard, Newell, Viola and Verna Erickson stood tight-lipped and pale, somber with grief. They answered many questions from Roy's friends. All but two questions could be easily answered. They couldn't tell how or why it happened.

Leonard

The unsung hero of the stories of both Roy Larson and Clyde Lee was Leonard Larson. He was the shy blonde teenager who quit school after the fourth grade to keep the family farm solvent while his two older brothers were serving in World War II. He was also the fourteen-year-old who helped grandpa set out an orchard of young apple trees, who watched the swarming of the bees, captured the queen and returned them to the hive; who milked 25 cows night and morning, helped with the calving, plowed the land, seeded and harvested the crops. By the time he was sixteen, Leonard Larson had experienced all the responsibilities known to many a man.

Roy, the boy hero, home from the war with his extravagant and highly improbable dreams, lit a spark in Leonard which never faded during his lifetime. He was born the year of the Wright Brothers' famous flight, soloed in 1923 at age eighteen, and barnstormed the state with his brothers to support their fledgling aviation business years before he was old enough to vote.

A dogsbody for Roy's every wish and request, Leonard–like many others–became caught up in and became a part of Roy's dream. An aviator of excellent prowess, ever cautious, engaged in every aspect, contributing to the profits of farming and furthering the careers of the brothers in maintaining their airport, he was also an able mechanic who repaired and rebuilt planes for the airport and for others who requested help on their own machines. An excellent, reliable pilot, he never cracked up in 52 years of flying.

The quiet teenager whose presence was ever there, often hidden in the background, but always aware of everything said or planned. His demeanor friendly, self assured, but never intrusive. He was a plus to his community.

After the distressing sudden death of his hero brother Roy, all the responsibility of maintaining the farm again fell on his shoulders. Now he also had an airport to run. George died before the airport was established and Clarence and Newell weren't well. Clarence died of heart disease several months prior to Roy. Never faltering, just as in his teen years, Leonard assumed responsibility and carried on.

Much of the history and lore of the pioneering years of aviation in Wisconsin would have been lost were it not for Leonard and the diaries of his wife, Viola. The names of many unrewarded and forgotten flyers of the twenties are recorded in her books together with descriptions, personalities and daring deeds which they performed.

Many of these were students Roy and Leonard had taught to fly, or perhaps had purchased a JN4 Jenny or Waco, or sought parts or services. Others brought their damaged planes for repairs to the Larson Brothers Airport. Many dropped in for a cup of Viola's coffee, ate doughnuts or those famous cookies and to chat about aviation. Many a convivial Saturday night was spent in their home around the piano, with Verna Erickson playing all the latest tunes while many barbershop arias filled the air. The boys and neighbors participated fully if not especially harmoniously.

In 1942, during World War II, Leonard trained glider pilots at Antigo, Wisconsin and in 1943 he trained aviation cadets at McBride, Missouri.

Leonard, truly the entrepreneur of aviation in Wisconsin, had his airport dealt a deadly and unfair blow when the Wisconsin Power and Light Company insisted on running a power line across the middle of his air field. After that it was dangerous to fly out of or land in the Larson Brothers Airport. Moving the power lines 500 feet west or east would not have lessened the capabilities of the Wisconsin Power and Light company. Instead, the power line put Leonard out of business and destroyed the function of the airport. It can only be used to store airplanes in the hangar the brothers built in 1923. Everything still stands as it was then, a memorial to the dreams of a family of aviation pioneers.

On April 5, 1984, the Larson Brothers Airport was listed on the National Register of Historic Places. A large stone monument on Highway 150 west of Neenah marks the spot.

Roy Larson and Ray Seevers working on the airplane Roy purchased in Duluth in 1923.

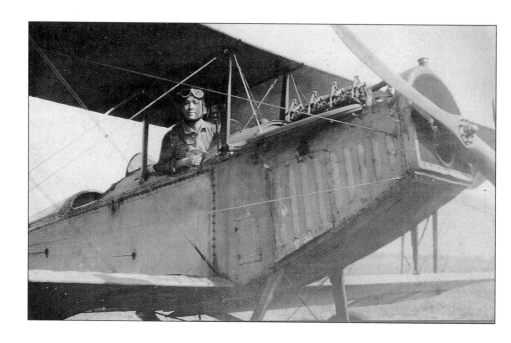

(Top) D. S. Chung, Roy's fellow student pilot at Ashburn Field in Chicago, 1921. (Bottom) Two Jennys at the Larson Airport, 1925.

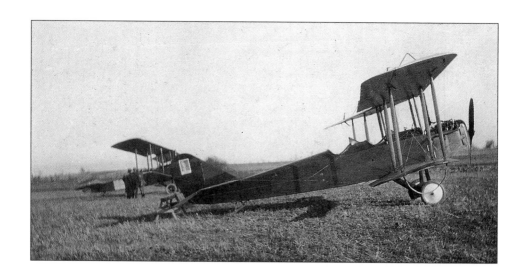

*(Top) The flying, farming Larson brothers, with friend Reuben Bergo.
(Bottom) The Johnson brothers building the hangar of Wisconsin's first
airport.*

Top) Scene at the Larson airport, late 1920s. (Bottom) A re-creation of the Larson's road sign.

LARSON FLYING FIELD

WE TEACH	AND GIVE	FLIGHTS
FLYING	EXHIBITIONS	DAILY

Newell Larson leans on the fuselage and Leonard Larson prepares to spin the prop on an OX Standard.

(Top) Noel Wein's Stinson and (Bottom) a Thomas-Moore Scout at Larson's.

(Top) Roy Larson in his favorite seat, the cockpit of an airplane. (Bottom)
Progress in the 1920s: an oxcart shares the highway with new Ford autos,
with airplanes parked in the field nearby. Elwyn West stands next to the
oxen.

The wreckage of the Swallow airplane after the crash that claimed the life of Roy Larson.

(Left) Leonard Larson in 1930 and (Bottom) with his last plane in the 1970s.

The Beginning

The French-Canadian legacy in northeastern Wisconsin dates back to the 1600s, when missionaries, explorers and fur traders canoed up the Fox River. Many settled among the Indians whose tribes they named "Menominee" and "Winnebago." The presence of both the Indians and the French is found in the names they left behind–Winnebago, Poygan, Neenah, Menasha, Kaukauna, Winneconne and Oshkosh.

The French named Fond du Lac, which is a French phrase meaning foot-of-the-lake. Butte des Morts (pronounced Beaut-a-mor) was a small settlement on the Wolf River named to mark a battle between the French and the Fox Indians. It means, Hill-of-the-Dead. Although the exact meaning of Winneconne is uncertain, it too harkens back to a battle in which many Indians died.

The Wolf River flows from northern Wisconsin into Lake Poygan and then out through the south end of Lake Winneconne, before joining the Fox River near Butte Des Morts. The Winnebago Indians had fished and hunted on these two lakes since the beginning of their time in Wisconsin and many burial mounds are located around them. In some spots plowed ground was white with the shells of clams fished from Lake Winneconne. Occasionally, even a skeleton was unearthed when a farmer was plowing a field.

Succeeding waves of immigrants followed the French and occupied the old Indian ground. In the 1830s and '40s and '50s an influx of Germans and Norwegians took place. Although they migrated for many reasons, economic conditions were the leading factors encouraging Norwegians to move to

America. In the 1850s, Wisconsin was a promising destination for Norwegians. They came first to southern Wisconsin then spread north and west, some to the fertile Winnebago county township of Clayton, north of Oshkosh and west of Neenah-Menasha.

Some Norwegian-Americans held to the old custom of handing down family names. For example, Lars Gjeilo, grandfather of the Larson brothers, and father of Charles, handed down the name of Lars to Charles. Charles had as a last name Lars + son, or Larson. Had Charles–Carl in Norwegian–followed the old country tradition, the last name of his children would have been Carlson. However, he was also an American so he followed the tradition of his new home and his children remained Larsons.

In Winnebago County, summer days are hot, often stifling hot–then cooled by angry thunderstorms accompanied by heavy winds which whip the trees and crops. The lightning zigzags across the sky, slicing erratically through the thick black clouds. The rain can be either a gentle patter or a downpour in driving sheets, flooding the parched earth and laying hay and grain crops flat.

Beautiful autumn, with its trees, dressed in brilliant red, orange, yellow and russet foliage, blends into an unbelievably perfect masterpiece. As the autumn season goes out in a blaze of glorious color, winter swiftly takes over, covering all with a carpet of soft white snow. Although the winter can be bitterly, freezing cold, and blustery with blizzards, the ethereal loveliness of spring erases the memory. Bloodroot and crocus, anxious to be the first heralds announcing the coming of spring, brave the cold of the snow and ice to push their tender shoots through and, standing staunchly, bloom.

There is a certain special fragrance at the bursting of spring in Wisconsin. For anyone who has lived there it will always come hauntingly to mind with mention of the word, "Spring." In the woods are the Jack-in-the-Pulpit, purple violets, white violets, may apples, six-pronged star flowers, squirrels teeth, honeysuckle, with its sweet breath, and many others equally as beautiful. The soil is mostly rich, fertile black loam with some sand and fine gravel. Holding sway in the pastures and wet swamps are cowslips, buttercups and blue flag. All is beautiful, fragrant and lovely. There are many springs and natural fountains. Also, there are some bottomless springs with quicksand which lie in wait for the unwary. For the unwary, there is always the snake in the garden of Eden.

The area around Winchester is flat, fertile farmland interrupted by an occasional small creek. The Rat River and Mud Creek meander around and curve back to make small streams, brooks, and an occasional marshland. To the north of Winchester and slightly east are a few hundred acres of very low land, often marshy. This area is called 'The Island'. In the beginning, it was covered with virgin timber, now all logged off.

Six miles south of Winchester, the settlers were mostly of English descent with one or two German families intermixed. Irish and Germans settled in and near Winneconne. In the early days, visiting in one area and then another was like travelling from one foreign country to another.

It had been a wild, difficult life for the Gjeilo (pronounced Yehlow) family in 1841 when they settled in Muskego, Wisconsin. The immigrant ancestor, Knute Gjeilo, was born in Voss, Norway in 1800. Voss is a village located northeast of Bergen, Norway. In 1840, Knute and his son Lars decided to try for a better life in the United States. They arrived in Milwaukee via ship up the St. Lawrence and across Lake Michigan. Their first home in Wisconsin was with the Norwegian settlement at Muskego, south of Milwaukee. They joined many of their friends and relatives living there and settled among people of their own culture.

In 1850, Lars and his wife, Mary Bakke, seeking greener pastures, moved to another settlement of friends and relatives. The former Perry farm in Winchester, Wisconsin became their new home. Lars was born in Norway and immigrated here with his father, Knute. Later, Lars and Mary purchased the farm on which their grandsons built their airport. There Charles Larson was born, November 27, 1858.

He met and married Julia Espeseth from Blue Mound, Wisconsin. They lived in Poskin, Wisconsin at the time of the birth of their first child, Roy, March 12, 1894. In 1900, Charles moved his family to the farm in Clayton. There they raised their five sons and one daughter.

Leonard, the only family man of the brothers married Viola Larson and they have four daughters: Theda Alice, Zola Gail, Judy and Bernice (Bonnie).

Born near Telemarken, Norway, Halvor Lea with his wife, Kari, and son, Halvor, migrated to the U.S. about 1850. They settled near Winchester. The Andres Boe family arrived from Norway early in the 1800s. Andres' son, as was the custom, took the name of Anderson (andres + son). Signe Boe Anderson, granddaughter of Andres Boe, married Halvor Lea, the son of Halvor and Kari Lea.

Their only son, Hamburg, broke the culture barrier and chose his wife from the English settlement six miles south of Winchester. She was Bessie Cross, daughter of 'Till' (Julius) Cross and Mary Jane Barber Cross. They were married in 1902. Hamburg Lea anglicized his name to 'Lee'. Bessie and Hamburg, better known as H.S. Lee, were the parents of Clyde Allen Lee, and two daughters, Neita Evelyn and Bernice. Edward Doty, a passenger on the Mayflower, was an ancestor of Bessie Cross.

Bessie and Hamburg homesteaded 100 acres of land near Rozelville, Wisconsin, not far from Marshfield. They used a crosscut saw to cut the timber to build their log cabin home. On cold winter nights, as they lay in their bed, they heard the wolves howling.

At 6:00 PM, on the cold night of February 16, 1908 a son was born to H.S. and Bessie Lee. He weighed in at six pounds and they named him Clyde Allen Lee. He was named after Clyde Buckstaff of Oshkosh who was a close friend of Bessie's father. The only assistance at the birth was Clyde's father and his mother's sister, Zella Hough. The Houghs were farming nearby. An older sister, Neita Evelyn was also born in the log cabin. Bernice, his younger sister was born at Larsen two years later.

One year later, March 3, 1909, the parents of Clyde moved to Larsen on the farm of his father, Halvor. They remained there for a couple of years while deciding to buy another farm in that area.

Following the death of his mother in 1913, Clyde lived with his mother's family, the Julius Cross family. His father, H.S. Lee, quit farming and worked at Clintonville, Wisconsin for 4-Wheel Drive until late 1916 when he enlisted for World War I in Canada. The U.S. was not in the war at that time. When the U. S. became involved in World War I, he reenlisted in the Army Air Corps of the American Expeditionary Forces. He became an inspector of airplanes, maintaining and inspecting damaged planes before they were returned to their pilots.

Reading letters from his father during the war triggered Clyde's great interest in airplanes. In 1923 when Clyde was fifteen, he worked on the Theodore Larson farm. With a budding airport across the road, his great enthusiasm was sparked again. That was where he spent his free time. It didn't take him long to talk Roy into giving him a ride followed by flying lessons.

The Gin Bar

During the prohibition era, Oshkosh had a very popular beer and liquor joint in an old home on South Ninth near Oregon Street. It was a speakeasy known to us as the Gin Bar. Clyde and some of his friends, former high school pals, congregated there to conceive and plan their daredevil pranks. Since Clyde and Dave Reed were the only ones who had an airplane and who did exhibition flying, they were very popular. Whenever either one was at the speakeasy so were several of their pals.

One had to be "in the know" in order to gain admittance to the speakeasy. It looked abandoned, dark and deserted, with no house lights shining through the windows. Customers had to be "clued in" as to where and what the house looked like and the ritual for getting through the door.

After knocking or ringing a bell, you stood outside the door and waited. There would be no sound from within. You stood in such a way that someone looking out through a small glass slot could see and identify you.If you were known or with someone who was known by the doorkeeper, the door would open and you would pass inside. There were no lights in the hallway. A first time customer felt a bit eerie walking down the darkened hallway to the next door. It was a little like Halloween in the witch's den. There was another door at the end of the hallway. You knocked again with a special rat-a-tat and faced another small glass slot.

Here, again you were checked, to be sure you were a known customer. Passing through the second door, you walked downstairs into the basement. You had arrived. You were in the bar room. Booths lined the walls. There was no bar as such, and no back bar where bottles were displayed. In the middle of each table was a handbell and each table was set with clean glasses. For service, patrons rang the bell. The bartender entered the room from behind a curtain which closed off another room. It was probably where the beer and liquor was stored. No one was allowed behind the curtain.

After taking the order the bartender disappeared behind the curtain. He would reenter carrying a tray bearing uncapped bottles of beer, or whatever drink you had ordered. He set it down in the middle of the table. You were expected to help yourself. He disappeared behind the curtain again and remained there until someone rang the bell. Except for the muted voices of the customers, it was very quiet in there.

The beer served should have been called "fire water" as it was more potent than any the cowboys and Indians had to drink even in the wildest of the Wild West. The proprietor, using a hypodermic needle, injected a shot of ether in the beer to give it a boost. Before the ether was injected into it, the beer was legal "near-beer", with an alcohol content of 3.5% It didn't have much of a kick, so bartenders gave it a jolt with a shot of ether. If ever there was a drink to make hair grow on your chest, this "needle-beer" would do it.

The owner of the speakeasy had an arrangement with the law enforcement authorities. In return for an under the table payment, the local law enforcement people would tip off the bar owners if they heard that federal prohibition officers were about to make a raid. Whenever a liquor raid was planned, a paid friend in the police department would make a phone call and tell the bar owner that the raiders were coming, "immediately."

Upon receiving such a phone call the bartender would enter the bar room, quickly remove all the drinks while very quietly informing the patrons, "There is going to be a raid. Leave quietly and I'll replace your drinks next time you come in." In fact he was so hurried, he took the glass out of the hand of a person in the act of having a sip.

The patrons hurriedly and quietly let themselves out the back door into a dark back yard. A faint light shone from the nearest street light. Following a well-worn path, they came out on the next block and returned to their cars parked at least 3 blocks away. It was necessary for the cars to be parked at some distance and spaced. It would have appeared suspicious to see a row of cars parked in front of an apparently abandoned house.

On one occasion in 1928, Elmer Clark, Dave Reed, Fritz Pinkerton and Clyde were at the gin bar and all were feeling quite friendly. During the course of the conversation Clyde said to Dave, "My compliments to you, Dave, for getting rid of your wife so deviously, or should I say dramatically"? I hear she has not only left town, but the state as well, and for good."

"Good riddance." said Dave, "Clung to me like a pit to a peach, and I wanted out. She refused, so I had to use desperate measures."

"But she was my second cousin, Dave, and a nice girl. Why did you have to concoct something that brutal? You ruined her reputation and she was almost thrown in jail. The family didn't approve of that."

"I told you, she wouldn't give me a divorce, and I wanted out."

"How much did you pay the bartender to put knockout drops in her drink? Huh? And how much did you pay the 'retarded hunk' to pose naked in bed with her while she was unconscious from the drops? A pretty rotten trick, Dave."

"None of your damn business," said Dave. "And I don't give a goddamn if she is your second cousin. I didn't want her any more. And furthermore you just keep your nose out of my affairs."

Dave was getting surly and, as he was a bit unstable when angry, the matter was dropped.

"Fritz," Dave demanded, "When are you going to let me take you ice skiing behind my plane? I've dared you several times and you declared you weren't a coward, so all right damn it, set a date and we'll do it. Of course if you are too cowardly, I'll drop it. If you are up to it, I'll be waiting down by the river for you tomorrow morning at ten o'clock."

Fritz had done quite a lot of cross country skiing. He was no coward and he was feeling no pain. He assured Dave he wasn't afraid to ski behind his plane on the river ice. The pact was sealed with a toast in ether beer and, in a gloriously adventurous mood, all left the tavern.

According to plan, they met next morning on the ice at the bend of the river just beyond West Algoma. Dave had the plane ready with a fifty foot rope attached to the undercarriage. He told Fritz to put a loop in the end of the rope to grasp it more securely so it wouldn't slip away from him when he was being towed.

Fritz arrived skis in hand plus a leather jacket and helmet he had borrowed from Clyde. It was cold and he needed to dress warmly. After he fastened his ski straps and tested them to be sure they wouldn't slip, he donned the jacket and the helmet. After fastening the chin strap and putting on his fur-lined gloves, he grasped the rope loop and motioned Dave to move out.

As his ex-wife learned, Dave Reed was known to have a cruel streak, especially if he had been crossed or criticized. No one suspected he had anything to feel cruel about that morning, as far as Fritz was concerned. Still Fritz was slightly apprehensive. He hoped Dave didn't have anything unusual in mind other than towing him on the ice.

Dave revved the plane's motor, idled it, and slowly taxied along the ice. Fritz followed along behind at a very fast clip for cross country skiing. There was a peninsula about a half mile up the river, on the right hand side. As they approached opposite it, Dave suddenly accelerated for take off. He lifted off in the direction of Sunset Point and proceeded to fly over it.

Fritz was not prepared for that kind of skiing and was caught completely off guard. Before he knew it, he was off the ground flying through the air above the treetops. He could not drop the rope. If he did, he would crash onto the ice and be severely injured.

Fritz's life depended on his hanging on. He hoped Dave would return to the ice, as soon as they had passed over Sunset Point, so he had to hang on to the rope and keep on flying.

Dave landed as soon as he was over the island. When Fritz touched down on the ice he was traveling so fast, he passed the airplane and kept right on sliding. When the gang finally caught up with him he was halfway to Butte des Morts, and about four miles beyond his starting point.

Visibly shivering from the cold and fear long after he had stopped, Fritz told his friends he was confident he was the first and only person, so far as anyone knew, to have skied over the island. They most heartily agreed with him, but they were shocked at what Dave had done. Had he let go of the tow rope, Fritz could easily have been killed.

As if unaware of how he had risked another man's life, Dave laughed so hard he had to hold his sides. He said, "You should have seen the expression on your face, Fritz, when you were dodging the chimneys on the house tops. 'Shocked' I guess would best describe it," and he kept on laughing as he walked to his plane.

A couple of weeks later, the same four men were at the bar on ninth Street. They were imbibing their needle beer and were half out of their minds when one of them said, "What's this I hear, Clyde, about you rescuing Lutz's wife off an ice floe in Lake Winnebago last week?

"Yeah, Clyde," another friend added, "We heard you rescued a couple who flew out and landed on the ice for a bit of cannoodling, but the ice broke loose and they drifted, in more ways than one."

"Menning was teaching Lola to fly. They were practicing dead stick landings on the ice. They didn't realize the temperature had risen so much above freezing that the ice was melting. After a few landings, the jolt of the plane on the honeycombed ice broke a large block of it loose from the mainland. The current pushed the ice floe away from the shore, with Menning and Lola still on it. Since the floe was too small for a take off, they were stuck.

"Prior to seeing them I had flown over a large patch of blue water in the middle of the lake and as soon as I saw them, I realized they had to get off that ice floe right away. Flying over them, I waved to let them know I would be back. I was afraid to fly low over them. The vibration of the plane might help to break up the rotting ice.

"By the expression on their faces, I guess they thought I was being sociable and abandoning them. Fear, I have never before seen such panic as on their faces. There was nothing I could do by landing, so I kept on flying to the airport. I had to get planks, chains and flat boards to use to haul them over the water. The plane was no good for towing them. I needed a car.

"Dusk was setting in, and they were scared. They thought they would have to spend a very cold winter's night on the ice or worse, drown in the freezing water. They told me afterwards, I had been their only hope of rescue."

"How did you happen to find them?"

"It was happenstance. I was out for a spin over the lake and saw them. The ice was dotted with fishing shanties and I didn't notice them right away. I thought they were ice fishermen. Then I saw the plane and figures jumping and waving. I flew over there and saw they were in a desperate situation. She was jumping up and down, waving and yelling, 'Help'.

"They were two very frightened people. The constant loud "boom.....gaboom," of the ice breaking up all around them was not reassuring and they feared their ice floe might be next."

"What were they doing out there all that time?" asked Dave.

"Don't ask me." Clyde said, with a wide grin on his face.

"How did you rescue them?"

"There were some guys hanging around the airport and I asked them to help. We loaded some boards and a tow rope into my car and went back there and towed them in. I hoped I could tow them in without the ice block breaking. It was all luck. My flying over that way and seeing them, and the ice not breaking before we got them off.

"I threw a stake to Menning to pound in the middle of the ice block. He attached the rope to the stake and we pulled the whole ice floe near to shore with the other end of the tow rope attached to my car. When we could get it near enough to shore we put planks across. We hauled them and the plane over on them. It was a risky time moving the plane. I was afraid moving it around might cause the ice block to break apart."

"What was their excuse?"

"Just that he was teaching her to make dead stick landings..."

Guffaws of laughter greeted this remark. Clyde grinned and said, "You can't prove anything by me. I only rescued them."

Winter turned to spring, then to summer, but the gin bar's atmosphere of risk and danger remained the same. On one warm afternoon, a few of the guys happened into the tavern.

Dave asked Clyde, "What's all the advertizing painted on that old wreck you're driving around town."

"Another money-making scheme for a second-hand car dealer. He took them in trade and can't sell them. He wants to get his money back. The only way is to junk them. I am the answer. He's selling tickets for people to go to High Cliff next Sunday and watch me drive that one over the cliff. He's paying me $35.00.

"You're nicked in the nob," said Dave. "That's at least 30 feet down. Are ya trying to commit suicide? Has life become too much for you?"

"No, I am not trying to commit suicide. I am not going over the cliff. I am going to jump out the last minute before it goes over. When the car goes over the edge, I'll be sprawled on the ground just short of the edge."

"You're a fool," Clyde, "What if the door sticks or you can't get out of the car for one reason or another?"

"Then I'll go over the cliff, too," was Clyde's response. "I need the money."

The Fabulous
Parachute Jump of Elmer Clark

Like many young men in the 1920s, Elmer Clark was interested in aviation. The story he tells about his first and only parachute "jump" reveals much about the atmosphere of the time and place that nurtured Clyde Lee—when both aviation and the men involved in it were usually young and often foolish.

"I am Elmer Clark. In 1926 I made my first and only parachute drop from a plane flown by Elwyn West. At that time, the plane was owned by Dave Reed and Clyde Lee. This all came about when Clyde Lee and Dave Reed had a flying circus. Their plane was an OX5 Jenny.

"Their flying circus consisted of stunting with the plane at the state fairs in the Middle West and Clyde wingwalking, stunting on a rope ladder and jumping with an old muslin parachute. The parachute was stuffed into an old duffle bag that was tied to the strut of the wing of the Jenny. Clyde would get down, place himself in the ring, an iron ring, and then proceed to unravel the parachute out of this bag. It was an old type parachute.

"It was breathtaking to watch the thing fill with air as it came down. They had to come down from quite a height in order to get the parachute to open. In those days he earned the magnificent fee of around $50.00 a jump, and it was something to see.

Clyde and Dave came to me and told me if I wanted to be a member of their Flying Circus, one of the things I could do was to finance them to a Russel Lowe parachute. This was one of the first seat-packed chutes ever developed. It was packed in an arrangement like a seat. You jumped free of the plane, and

131

the pressure of the silk popped the parachute out in the open and you were on your own. This appealed to me because in those days flying was a remarkably romantic thing. You could wear riding boots, a white silk scarf, jodhpurs and all the paraphernalia of an aviator and this appealed to me.

"In raising the money, I discovered the parachute was going to cost me about $350.00, and since I didn't have that kind of credit, I remembered what my father had told me. He said, 'Son, one of the first things you do when you get out of school is to establish your credit and to do that you go to the bank and borrow some money. Do it whether you need the money or not and pay it back over a period of two months and make sure you make these payments promptly. The next time you have to borrow money they will never question you.' He added, 'Probably at your age I will have to co-sign the first note.'

"I went to my father on this occasion and said, 'I think I would like to establish my credit for $350.00 and I think we can do this through the Building and Loan, but of course I will have to have your signature. I'll have the money back within three months.'

"He said, 'That is the smart way to do business,' and he cosigned the note and I received the $350.00. I sent it to the Russel Lowe people and received the seat-type packed parachute. Now this came in a reasonably small bundle and the instructions for folding it that came with it looked something like the city directory for New York City. It was quite complicated, especially in the directions on how to fold the parachute.

"I gave it to Clyde and he said, 'We won't worry about the instructions. What we'll do is we'll take the parachute apart. We'll take it out of the pack and I'll note how its folded. We won't bother with the instructions and I'll fold it again just from looking at it.'

"We unpacked it. Then we made the mistake of putting the thing down and pulling the ripcord. Directly we had 500 pounds of silk in the air. That thing was all under pressure and it was a complete snarl of lines and what have you. The three of us, Dave Reed and Clyde Lee and myself, proceeded to try to get it back into the pack. We did. It took us about four hours and when we had it put together, it looked like a Christmas stocking full of nuts. It was a lumpy looking pack and I am sure there were four or five things that weren't quite right about it.

"I said, 'Clyde, you're going to jump this parachute. I'm a little nervous about this—it doesn't look right.'"

"He said, 'Don't worry about it. What we'll do is we'll get up about five thousand feet and I'll get out on the wing. I'll wear the parachute and I'll hang on to a strut and then I'll pull the rip cord and if it doesn't open, there's no harm done.'"

"I said, 'Now this doesn't make good sense to me because it will certainly come out of the pack and if it comes out of the pack and doesn't open, I don't think you are going to be able to hang on to the wing. I don't think you'll have time to get out of the harness of this thing.'"

"'Well....,' he said, 'I am reasonably sure this will work. Don't worry about it.'

"The morning came that we were to test it. We went out to the airport very early in the morning and Clyde got into the harness and buckled himself in and climbed in the cockpit of the OX5, Jenny. In those days, it took about an hour to get up to five thousand feet in a Jenny. You had to clean the jets before you took off and you had to circle and circle and circle and circle, and finally we were up about five thousand feet over the airport.

"He climbed out on the wing where we could see him and he pulled the ripcord and just like I said he didn't stay on the wing. It came out of the seat pack like a necktie and that was as big as it was from where we sat. He came off the wing like he had been shot out of a cannon and he started down and the parachute didn't open and it didn't open, and it didn't open.

"There was just a ribbon of silk, and then it partially opened and it was probably two-thirds open when he hit the ground. He hit the ground so hard you could hear it from a quarter of a mile away and not only did he hit the ground but he popped up and passed the parachute when it was still coming down. In other words he hit with a tremendous thump. Why he wasn't killed, I don't know. After he landed, we landed and we ran over and he was maybe four to five inches shorter than he normally was, accordian-wise. He had very flat, large feet and was humped back for many months after that. We had to take him, unconscious, to the hospital. The doctor checked him over. He had a cracked vertebrae in his back, and five broken ribs. He walked out of the hospital a few hours later.

"After that, we had a problem. Everyone said, 'Your parachute–this Russel Lowe outfit isn't such a hot outfit. The parachute doesn't work.'

"This worried me. I had invested $350.00 and that would take a lot of parachute jumps at $50.00 a jump that I was going to have to make to get this parachute paid for, so I immediately wrote the Russell Lowe people and told them what had happened.

"They said, 'Apparently you didn't read the instructions carefully.'

"They sent me another set of instructions and they said, 'Now you read these very carefully and do exactly what the instructions tell you to do and rather than you jumping it yourself until you feel a little more confidence in it, put a 150 pound sandbag in the harness–strap it in–and get about 100 feet of clothesline and tie it to the rip cord and tie the bag of sand with the parachute on it on the catwalk of the plane; hang on to the end of the clothes line that's tied to the ripcord; get out on the end of the wing and kick it off. Hang on to it long enough to jerk the ripcord to open the parachute and you can practice with it this way. You can test it yourself without having to risk your life to do it.

"'The other alternative, of course, is to send it back to the factory and we'll pack it for you every time you jump, but there'll be a fee of about $20.00 for this.'

"Well I'm already on the hook for $350.00, so I decided that testing the parachute was good advice. I took the parachute up to my father's plant and laid it out on a long table in the cutting room,–a good 40-50 feet long. I proceeded to try to fold the parachute. I was the better part of three days trying to follow the instructions on how to fold this silly thing. And when I got through with it, it still looked a little lumpy to me. It looked as lumpy as when we had packed it the first time, when Clyde jumped in it.

"I finished packing it and went back to the airport. I talked to Dave Reed and said, 'Dave, I'm going to test this parachute. It didn't work too well the first time, so we're going to follow the instructions of the Russel Loew company and push a sandbag off the catwalk. Use a rope to open the chute. We'll test it that way.'

"'Well,' he said, 'I'd suggest you do it right away and have someone go with you.' There was a mechanic at the airport–an old timer–I can't think of his name.

"I approached him, 'I'll tell you what, Cap, I'll strap it on the catwalk. I'll be the guy who gets out of the cockpit.' This plane was one of those old tandem airplanes ...two passengers in front and the pilot sat in the back...a biplane type. Dave, by that time had graduated from the OX5 Jenny to a Wright Whirlwind Waco which was a step in the right direction for a red hot airplane in those days. I think this was one of the first ones that had a radial engine in it. I talked to this mechanic, encouraging him to go with me.

"I said, 'Now your job will be to hang on to the ripcord and when we get up a couple thousand feet, I'll get out on the catwalk and untie the ropes that hold the sandbag to the strut and kick it off and step back and hang on. You just give this a good hard jerk when it reaches down 100 feet and then I'll get back in the plane and we'll come down and check it out to see if it worked.'

"We flew up about two or three thousand feet and when we were over the airport, Dave said, 'All right, start working.'"

"Just about the time we got up there where we needed to be, I discovered I was sitting in the wrong seat. I would have to climb over the mechanic (sitting on my right) to reach the sandbag, on the catwalk, and shove it off.

134

"Unbeknownst to me–even though I saw him leaning over the side of the plane, fooling around with something–he had discovered I didn't need to get out of the cockpit. You can't very well carry on a conversation in an open cockpit plane. The noise is earsplitting. He couldn't tell me that he had discovered I didn't have to get out of the cockpit, but I didn't know this.

"He had just voluntarily gone ahead and untied the sand bag and was busy pushing it off the catwalk. In order to have both hands free, he tied a slipknot on the ripcord (clothes line) and slipped it around his wrist in order to have his hands free to push the sand bag off the wing.

Just at the time I stepped one foot over his shoulder–trying to get out on the catwalk–the 150-pound sandbag slipped off the wing caught up with his arm and not only did it practically pull his arm out, but he started out of that ship with my legs wrapped around his neck looking down about two thousand feet. We just hung long enough when the rope broke. Both of us were hanging practically by the heels of our feet in that plane by the time that rope broke.

"Well even though he had pulled the rip cord, the parachute didn't open! It opened partially. The chute came out of the pack. It came down, hit the ground and the sandbag burst open. This would have been the same results if a man had jumped with it. He'd have been cooked. It would have been fatal.

"Well, now word had gotten around that not only Clyde had nearly been killed in this thing, but two more men had nearly been pulled out of an airplane testing the chute with a sandbag. This was a very unhappy state of affairs for everyone concerned.

"Clyde and Dave decided they would not use this for their flying circus. At the rate we were going it was too unpredictable. They did not want to pay $20.00 to send it back to the company to have it repacked and returned every time they jumped with it.

"I was caught in the middle of something I was very unhappy about. I had $350.00 of frozen assets that nobody wanted to use and I owed the Building and Loan the money and my first payment was due and I didn't have that kind of money. I was considerably unhappy.

"Dave Reed came to me and said, 'You know I am going to enter a ship in the Thompson Trophy race.' He and Clyde were building a midget racer. Clyde was the only person who flew that plane–I remember seeing that. The midget plane was developed for Dave to fly in that race. It was about two feet shorter than Clyde. Dave never had the nerve to fly it. Clyde did. I remember that was the only time that plane was flown. There must have been four or five thousand dollars of time and material in it even in those days.

"Clyde stepped into it. He stuck out of it. He looked like a kid riding a tricycle. There was two thirds of him sticking straight up out of the cockpit, and he flew it. He did a tour with it and it went like a bullet. It had the gliding angle of a brick. It was a tremendous sight. That I recall.

"Dave went on to tell me, 'I am going to need a parachute for the midget plane race...the Thompson race in Chicago. But you've got to prove to me once and for all that that damn thing you've got will work.'

"Writing the Russell Lowe Company had been going on for some time. I had written my third letter, that the parachute wasn't working, and received the same answer from them. Sending it back each time we jumped was too time-consuming and too expensive.

"I had long ago decided I wouldn't try any more of the sandbag testing, which seemed more dangerous than jumping with it.

"Things were at an impasse. Nobody at this point was going to do anything about the parachute. I knew that if it was tested again, I would have to do it myself. I wasn't sure what to do about it.

"I took it to the plant and refolded it again. This time it didn't look quite as lumpy. After reading the instructions again, I thought I had discovered what we had been doing wrong. The shroud lines had to go up and it had to be laid out in a straight line—the shroud lines perfectly straight and then the tucks or the gaps in the chute, pleated in, because the shroud lines skip along the skirt of the chute about every six or seven feet. I think there were twenty-eight or thirty shroud lines. We had been very careful about getting the parachute out of the way by pleating it in, rather than pleating it out, so the shroud lines were on the inside of the chute rather than on the outside and folding it back.

"It finally got through my thick skull that probably this might be it. I folded it and it wasn't quite as lumpy looking. It took me the better part of the next two days to do, but I got it all back in the chute and in the pack.

"Now I had the problem of proving that it was going to work. The only way I could prove it to Dave was to jump it. In the meantime he wouldn't pay me any money, but, he said, "I'll give you flying time. You want to learn to fly, I'll solo you for that parachute."

In those days it cost about $25.00 an hour for flying time. "This is a bargain because I don't think you could get ten lessons for $350.00." Dave said, "This is the only way you are going to get your money back, but you've got to prove to me that that parachute is going to work."

"I had been taking private flying lessons from Dave for several weeks. If I couldn't prove to Dave this parachute would work I would not only owe $350.00 for the chute, but also $25.00 an hour for the lessons.

"I had run up my original investment into a sizable figure and at this point I was getting a little desperate. How would I come out of this situation?

"It's getting pretty close to the Thompson Trophy Race. His plane is pretty near finished and Clyde had test piloted it. That was something to see. It was a damn sight smaller than any midget plane that Wittman or anyone ever flew–why you could almost reach across the wingspan of that thing.

"Well at any rate, we were all gathered at this tavern having some of this needle beer and there was quite a crowd collected and I think I was on my third bottle, feeling as if I was made of stainless steel, standing about sixteen feet tall, weight two hundred pounds. Dave said, 'When in the Hell are we going to decide whether or not this parachute is going to work?'

"Belching a blue flame, I said, 'Do you think for a damn minute that I would let you take that parachute without I, myself, jumping it personally?'

"'And he said, 'Yes, I think you would.'

"I said, 'Well, you get your plane out there tomorrow afternoon. I've got the parachute ready and I'll jump that damn parachute.'

"Well, of course, this was said under the influence of this strong drink– in front of witnesses. I had never jumped before and after the experiences I'd seen other chutists have with this chute, and what had happened when Clyde jumped. I was a nervous wreck. I was drunk at the time I made the statement.

"By the next morning I had forgotten all about it. As a matter of fact the next morning I had the granddaddy of all hangovers. Dave called me while I was still sleeping it off, and said, 'El, I'll get the plane ready and you be out there with your parachute this afternoon and we'll try her.'

"And it got all over town. The Boy Scouts, the Girl Scouts were there– the entire Middle West showed up or so it seemed to me. Hamburger stands and marching bands and what have you!.

"Well I showed up with the parachute and this was about as reluctant a hero as you have ever seen in your life. Fear! I have never known fear like that! But I had high hopes that somehow I would get out of this. And believe me I was going to try anyway I could. When I first showed up, Dave came over and said, 'El, I've got a funny feeling about this. You're a friend of mine and I just don't want to be a party to this, so I'm going to ask Elwyn West to fly the plane for you.'

"I was hoping he was going to say, 'I'm not going to let you go through with this.' But he didn't and he was pretty emphatic about it. After all, he has an investment of flying time in me and wanted me to prove once and for all whether or not this chute was going to work. I said, 'Well, all right if that's the way you feel about it,' and I proceeded to get into the parachute. Not knowing anything about parachutes I got into it quite tight. I figured the tighter you were laced into one of these things the better off you were. The straps go around your shoulders and in back and around your thighs and your crotch and one thing and another. In itself it was not a comfortable sort of an arrangement.

"Well at any rate, Elwyn West sauntered over and said, 'Inasmuch as I've done quite a bit of this work, flying circuses etc. and flown for quite a lot of parachute jumpers, I want to tell you exactly how you are going to have to do this.' He pulled out a hunk of rubber hose which was about–oh, give or take about two feet long and filled with lead shot. He had a cork in the end of it.

"He said, 'Do you see this?' and he waggled it under my nose and said, 'We're going to get up as high as we can go.' "He was flying Dave's Wright Whirlwind Waco and he said," 'I'm going to get up about–oh, five, six, seven thousand feet and you are going to get out on the catwalk and you are going to face me. As soon as I give you the signal, I am going to tilt the plane and you are going to dive head first–you're not going to jump–you're going to dive head first. If you reach for that ripcord at any time that you are in the vicinity of where I can belt you, I am going to give you this rubber hose as hard as I can right across your skull–I'll kill you!'

"Well, I said, Hell–well what in the Hell is–Why?

"And he said, 'Item one. If you pull that ripcord too soon, you'll shoot back into the tail surfaces and I'll go with you and I won't even have a parachute. And,' he said, 'On the other hand if you jump up in the air with the parachute when you jump off–it just could be these tail surfaces will catch up with you and cut you right in two–the blast of the wind blowing you off. I've made it a standard rule that when I pilot for a parachutist that he dives head first. There can be no hanky panky business about this.'

"Well I couldn't visualize myself doing this, and I saw that at the worst, I had visioned that I might shut my eyes and back off or fall off or have some temporary amnesia of some sort so that I wouldn't have to think about it. But now he tells me that if I look cockeyed, he is going to belt me with a rubber hose, and if I don't dive I'm going to be decapitated, and I'm not sure the parachute will open, and then to crown it off–he says, 'I'll tell you furthermore at about five, six, seven thousand feet we're going to jump you over the middle of Lake Winnebago. It's an east wind and I figure that at about the middle of Lake Winnebago at seven thousand feet you'll drift over and land at the airport.'

"'No,' I said, 'Let me call something to your attention, assuming that I go ahead with this silly arrangement, this is what they call a Russell Loew parachute. It's not built like an umbrella, it's built like a doughnut. In other words, the shroud lines skip from a skirt half-way up the parachute and then to the vent which gives it a flattened doughnut effect and they say that these damn things don't drift. In other words there would be negligible wind resistance in any sort of a wind.

"I said, 'Now what happens to me if I come down in the middle of Lake Winnebago? We have no boats out there and this is what–seven or eight miles out to the middle. What in the Hell happens to old El? Now assuming that you don't brain me with this damn rubber hose you have, and assuming that I'm not decapitated because I falter and fall into the tail surfaces, assuming that the parachute works–and even if it does work there's a damn good chance I'll drown before anybody will get to me with a boat, just what are the odds for me on a deal like this?'"

"'Well.'" he says, 'Nevertheless, that's the story right there. Now when I tell you to jump, you jump! There's no fooling around about it. You do it just that way and if you look cockeyed you're a dead man anyway you look at it.'

"Now, I am not used to the parachute, it hasn't worked twice before, I'm not sure of my own ability–I'm half out of my mind with worry. Well as the roar goes up from the crowd, they have to lift me up and put me in the plane. I'm too weak to get in it on my own strength. I don't mind telling you...with my hangover and all...I'm in a hell of a shape. I got in the plane and we flew and we flew and we flew and finally we got over Lake Winnebago, way up to 7,000 feet and then he tapped me on the shoulder.

"It was a good twenty minutes before I had strength enough to even try to stand up. But I tried and I got one foot on the catwalk. I got two feet on the catwalk and I was hanging on to the cowling of the cockpit and I held on with my left hand–facing toward the pilot. He waggled the rubber hose at me and he said, 'Now.' And I couldn't let go–and I couldn't let go! I'd reach over to try to force my other hand to let go and I'd hang on with both hands. It was just dreadful! Well, we flew around and around and he kept giving me the signal and waggling the rubber hose and finally he shook his head, 'no', motioned me back in the plane, and we started back for the airport.

"I thought to myself. My God, there are maybe five hundred people at the airport, and I have always prided myself on my bravery–I'd been a semi-professional prize fighter, a ski jumper, I'd always prided myself on a reasonable degree of courage. I thought, my God, I can just visualize landing in that plane and getting out of it in front of all those people and I just didn't have the guts to do that. And it became a thing with me on the basis that it was either–I'd actually come to the conclusion–it was either facing that kind of an ignoble ending of a career or committing suicide by jumping. It almost came to that point. I had gotten one foot back into the cockpit and I was still facing him and he put the rubber hose away and he was gliding down and heading for the airport. I should say we were just about over South Main Street and I don't know what possessed me but I let out a yell and I jumped. And I did everything backwards. He didn't have time enough to get the rubber hose out again.

"I exploded the theory of the tail surface and it was a peculiar thing–from standing on the wing of a plane and the roar of the motor and this tremendous rush of air and then all of a sudden it gets deadly quiet and there is no sensation of falling. There is just nothing! The only thing was I'd see a flash of white and a flash of black; a flash of white and a flash of black so obviously I was going end over end and I was seeing the earth and sky alternately. This was something that was happening around me and I felt perfectly stationary. I had no feeling of moving. There was a strong breeze blowing from the ground up or from some direction, but this seemed nothing unusual and then it came to me. My God, I've jumped! Somewhere around here there is a ripcord which has to be pulled and now! I got ahold of it all right and I pulled it so hard that I must have spun like a whirling dervish and I hung on to it like death. I was hanging on to anything I could get a hold of. And I must have been upside down when it opened because I saw a flash of white which must have been the parachute and then I got the damndest jolt I ever had in my life. It snapped me...apparently...from upside down to right side up and I thought every bone in my body was broken. It nearly snapped my head right off.

"I'd probably fallen, I don't know, about a thousand feet when it opened. I was still hanging on to the ripcord which was supposed to be a test of great foresight and courage. To me I'd have hung on to a porcupine if I could have gotten my hands on one. At any rate I'd made it! The parachute had opened. God, it was a glorious thing to see! God...I'd still had no sensation of falling. The only noise was a hissing from the air going through the parachute and up through the vent, Other than that I felt I was stationary. I was far enough away from the ground so there was no relationship to anything that feels like speed. I was real happy to be alive.

"Elwyn was flying by–he was still, I think, contemplating whether or not he could whack me one on the skull with that rubber hose. He was so Damn mad! I had scared him so bad–almost into a conniption fit–the way I went out of that plane and what happened and one thing and another.

"I was so happy to be alive that I didn't care at this particular point where I came down. This was the big test!

"Then I began to look around a little bit and saw that I was coming down right into the jungle of South Main Street. They still had the car tracks–interurban–and there were buses and highlines. I never realized how many peaked roofs there were with spires, lightning rods, and brick chimneys, and junk yards and automobiles. Very slowly it dawned on me that I was coming down on probably what was going to be a very uncomfortable spot. I, then remembered reading some instructions about steering a parachute.

"You are supposed to grab one set of shroud lines and pull yourself up on it and it collapses the other side of the chute and you slide in that direction. When I thought I was coming down around Main Street, I began to realize that I was picking up a little velocity or at least I knew there was a definite rate of speed at which I was falling—I practically climbed up one side of that parachute, over the top and down the other side; I was so anxious not to land on Main Street. Then I was afraid if I kept on pulling the shroud lines the whole thing would sag and fold up and that I'd drop like an elevator, so I quit that and decided that what is to be will be.

"My eye centered on an old fashioned two-story house off South Main Street. It wasn't too far from the airport, about half way between Main Street and the airport. It was an old fashioned gable roof and it had an iron ball that caught my eye—on the edge of the roof. This peaked roof—and I could just feel it. I just knew that was exactly where I was going to land. I was going to sit on that ball. I knew it!

"Well, landing in a parachute is about the equivalent of jumping off a fifteen foot wall and if you have ever jumped off a fifteen foot wall and pulled your knees up under your chin and put your fanny right on about a four-inch iron ball, you will find it can be quite a shock to your nervous system. That is exactly what happened. I landed on that roof right on my tail end. And I hung there just long enough for the parachute to fold up and then I came down on top of the parachute, from two-and-a-half stories up.

"It knocked me out. Fortunately, I landed on plowed ground, the vegetable garden, or it probably would have killed me. The plowed garden was adjacent to this house.

"When I came to, I was completely enveloped by the parachute. I had fallen into it in such a way that I was surrounded by it. It was a sunshiny day and I was looking through this silk into the sun and it was like a beautiful iridescent fog and I was practically shook out of my senses. I remembered that I had jumped and I wasn't too sure. I knew I could never have made it to heaven and so realized that it must be the parachute. And then I was afraid to move. I thought every bone in my body must be broken. In other words I was afraid to move and actually find out.

"Finally, I had courage enough to wiggle a little bit and I fought my way out of the parachute. By this time quite a crowd had collected. I had apparently knocked a good piece of hide off my left elbow and was bleeding like a stuck pig. I had worn some white duck pants—which was a mistake—and a white shirt. You know under great fear a man's kidneys can sometimes be unset and white pants aren't the best thing to wear, especially when you add to that having blood all over them. I wasn't too sure how bad I was, but apparently I was a sight, because as I came out of the parachute there were two old women who lived in this house and I discovered afterward that they were old ladies who took off for Fond du Lac.

"I must have hit their house with a helluva thump and then rolled off and landed in their garden. They came out to see what was going on and seeing the crowd and this apparition with blood and what have you all over it reeling around in their garden, they took off for Fond du Lac. I'd like to have had this guy, Nurmi [Olympic distance running champion] there to run along side of them. They took fences on a high hurdle–I'm not too sure that they made Fond du Lac–yelling at the top of their lungs.

"Well, finally...no one would come near me... I just lunged around there for fifteen minutes, half out of my mind. Finally, I got the parachute off and Dave showed up and put me in his car and took me back to the airport.

"Dave never did get his ship into the Thompson Trophy Race. Nobody trusted that parachute even though I had proved it would work. Nobody wanted anything to do with me for years afterward. To this day I can't stand the sight of beer. I sold the parachute for $160.00 to a fellow by the name of Jones who hung around the airport and I finally paid off the Building and Loan by going to work which was against my very nature. But that was the last venture in capitalism I ever made. I couldn't stand the sight of an airplane for years afterwards. I'd tremble and shake."

Enid

Enid Miller was employed as a clerk in the safety deposit department of the First National Bank. She lived with her parents on Wisconsin Avenue, one block from Cherry Avenue where Clyde lived with his Aunt and Uncle Bert Hough (Huff). Clyde and Enid met as strangers a couple of times on Wisconsin Avenue near her home. One glance and Clyde lost his heart!

He had to meet her. He had to find out who she was, this beautiful blue-eyed girl with the entrancing smile, who had captured his heart. Later that week he told me that he had just met a beautiful girl. "I don't know who she is," he said. "I think she lives near the corner of Scott and Wisconsin Avenue. I met her near there. When I glanced back to see her again, she had disappeared." From the glowing description he gave, I wondered if he was raving about Jeanette Miller's sister, Enid.

I remembered that Jeanette and her close friend, Marion Torreyson, both teenagers, were lost in a romantic haze over Rudolph Valentino, who had recently appeared at the local theater in the movie, *The Sheik*. I was sure it wasn't Jeanette my brother was raving about and I knew Jeanette and her older sister, Enid, lived in the second house from Scott Street on Wisconsin Avenue. "Do you mean Enid Miller?" I asked.

"Is that her name? Do you know Enid? Can you introduce us?" He asked eagerly.

"I know who she is. She works in the Safety Deposit department of the First National Bank, but I don't know her well enough to ask her to come over here to meet you. Leighton works at the same bank. Why not ask him to introduce you?"

Leighton Hough lived a block from Uncle Bert Hough's house. Two sisters of Clyde's mother married two brothers named Hough. They lived a block apart on Cherry Avenue. Clyde lost no time in walking the block to Leighton's house.

He asked him to arrange an introduction for him and Enid. Leighton mentioned a mutual friend who knew both Clyde and Enid. Clyde immediately sought him out. The very next business day, just before the bank's closing, Clyde and the mutual friend, surprised Enid in the safety deposit department in the bank. There they were introduced and Clyde asked Enid if he could walk her home that evening after work.

That was the beginning of their courtship. Enid had a very close friend, Alice Speigelberg, who had a boyfriend named Bob Morgan. Soon the two couples were double-dating and Clyde and Bob became very close friends. They were four good friends, who went to movies and dances together. After dates they would go to Alice's house and make popcorn or fudge candy, or just spend the evening dancing to the music from the radio.

These were the early years of the Great Depression so few young people owned automobiles. They walked on dates. When Clyde and Enid went to the movies, they walked about a mile to the theater. It was usual to stop in at the Peacock or Coe's after the movie for a sandwich and a milk shake or a sundae.

Afterwards they walked to Enid's home. Occasionally, Clyde and Enid spent an evening flying. They flew to the Larson Brothers airport to visit his cousin, Viola Larson, and his flying pals, the Larson brothers. Clyde was very proud of his girl friend, Enid. They flew to Winchester and drove to Larson so Enid could meet his grandmother Lea. On one visit, Grandma Lea told Clyde he shouldn't expect young people to want to meet her because she was so old.

Clyde retorted, "We'll all be old some day."

Enid and Clyde became engaged in 1929. While he was in Miami in 1930, he called Enid and asked her if she would go to Waukegan, Illinois with him the following weekend so they could be married. Enid agreed. She and her mother went shopping for bridal clothes, the kind women wore in those days for an elopement.

Clyde flew to Oshkosh, incidentally setting a record for speed from Miami, and they drove to Waukegan–at least almost to Waukegan. Between Milwaukee and Waukegan they began discussing where they were going to live. Enid said she wanted them to live at her home with her parents. Her parents, she told him needed the money she was contributing to the household expenses.

144

Clyde refused absolutely. He wanted them to have a home of their own, just he and Enid. They were unable to resolve their differences so they never reached Waukegan.

Living with the parents of one or the other of a young couple was not an unusual arrangement during the hard times. Many young couples could not afford to be married unless they did live with parents.

I learned about the intended elopement the day after Clyde called Enid. The telephone operator who handled the long distance call listened to the conversation. She told her sister about it. Her sister was my classmate in school and passed the news on to me. The telephone operator listened because a call from such a distance was a rare event. I was really excited. I liked Enid and looked forward to having her as a sister-in-law.

The next week Clyde was still at home and I asked him when the big event was to occur. Clyde, slightly discomfited, said embarrassedly, that they had postponed it. "We're still engaged," he added. "We just have a few matters to iron out before we tie the knot. Enid is still wearing my ring."

Enid's father was strongly opposed to her marrying Clyde. "He lives a risky, reckless life," he said. "I don't want my daughter left a young widow. If Clyde wants to marry you, Enid, let him get a regular job and settle down, buy a house and be a family man."

Clyde applied and was hired by the Axle Company. He had worked there about six weeks when a long, heavy bar of iron fell on his foot and he had to wear a heavy, cumbersome cast for several months. How ironic for him to have a serious accident in a factory as opposed to climbing around on the top wing of an aeroplane 5,000 feet above the earth.

Although the leg injury put a stop to his exhibition flying for several months, a broken arm had not deterred him. He broke it while crank starting his Ford car–an accident not uncommon among Ford owners. Still, he put on an wingwalking exhibition at Menominee Park for the Fourth of July. A doctor attached a prosthesis from his shoulder to the finger tips of his broken arm. It had a hook on the end for a hand. He climbed on the wings and hung from the ladder the same as at any other exhibition. He pulled himself back up on the ladder using only one arm and the hook.

Clyde also made the parachute drop into Lake Winnebago. Arrangements had been made for a boat to pick him up immediately after he hit the water, but the wind blew him off the center point where he was to land and the boat was slow getting to him. The wet parachute settled over him in the lake and pushed him under. With only one workable arm he had difficulty holding the canvas above his head and swimming at the same time.

Clyde had actually hired another parachutist to make the jump, but when Clyde told him he would land in the middle of the lake, he decided he didn't want any part of it. Since Clyde was under contract to make the jump, he did it himself. When he set his mind to do something, he did it even if his life depended on it.

He had a very square chin with a dimple in his cheek, from a boyhood injury, and the laughingest light brown, hazel eyes. Because of his narrow hips and broad shoulders, Jane Labudde, one of our neighbors, described him as "that Greek God, Clyde Lee."

At age ten, he was living with his grandfather Cross and attending Ball Prairie country school near Winneconne. One day Clyde walked home from school with a friend and distant cousin, Gearhart Anderson. They were bragging, as boys do, as to who could throw the highest and began throwing their lunch buckets into the air. That wasn't difficult enough, so they began throwing gravel stones at the lunch buckets before they hit the ground. One of the stones Gearhart threw struck Clyde's face hard enough to penetrate his cheek and enter his mouth. When it healed, it formed a small hollow in his cheek. Thus my one-dimpled brother, whom I always teased about it.

In the 1920s and '30s, it was still considered demeaning and fast for a girl's picture to appear in the newspaper. It was not considered "good ton." When the reporters began following Clyde around and the publicity became almost constant, Enid's father became upset and put his foot down. "My daughter's picture will never appear in the papers." he said. He didn't want Enid followed by reporters and written up in the newspaper.

Clyde protected her from publicity but he continued to see her secretly until he left Oshkosh for Vermont. At that time, he was driving an old Packard car he borrowed from Earl Iverson. He would call for Enid after dark and they would drive to another city to the movie or a dance. The reporters never discovered the relationship between Clyde and Enid and her picture never appeared in the paper.

In 1926, the year he began courting Enid, Clyde kept a diary. One entry reads, "Enid is a lovely person, I love her so much. I wish we could be married. Her personality is like my mother's. She reminds me of my mother."

Clyde's memories of his mother were very private and very intense. He was five years old when she died of peritonitis following an appendectomy. He carried her living image with him always in his mind. The greatest compliment anyone could receive from him was to be compared with his dearly beloved mother.

Early on, he took Enid out to the airport and talked her into flying with him. Daredevil though he was, Clyde was a careful pilot and he always checked his plane carefully before take off. He checked the water, the gasoline and the air in the tires.

He helped Enid step up on the wing, then make the very long step over the side of the cockpit and into the passenger seat. Leaping in beside her, he began setting the spark and gas levers. He kicked the ailerons and rudders to make sure all was in order. He stepped out again and, facing the propeller, began turning it first to his left and then to his right. When it began turning automatically he removed the chocks from the wheels and vaulted into the cockpit. They taxied out to the runway, with Enid's stomach continuously sending up complaints and distress signals. When the plane lifted off, it seemed to fall out from under her. She looked down and it seemed as if the ground was moving back and the plane was standing still. There was no feeling of motion. A bit timid by nature, Enid's hands were clenched into fists, except when she tightly clutched the side of the cockpit. Updrafts and downdrafts made her head spin. She saw the beautiful scenery of the countryside in miniature and the mirror of water as they passed over Lake Winneconne. As Clyde maneuvered for position to descend, the right wing of the plane dropped almost out of sight. As he banked and began diving it seemed as if they were headed straight down towards the cluster of farm buildings that made up the Larson Airport.

The ground was coming up at them at a tremendous speed, Enid thought, as she grabbed the edge of the cockpit. Soon, the plane was on the ground rolling along without trouble on a grass landing strip. It taxied along until it stopped of its own momentum. Clyde had cut the motor just before the wheels touched down. Despite her preflight fears, Enid admitted to Clyde as he lifted her down that she had enjoyed her first ride very, very much. But when she tried to stand, her legs betrayed her.

Romance of another sort also was part of Clyde's life. When Art Bradley joined Earl Iverson as co-manager of the flight to Norway he thought there should be some rumor of romance in Clyde's life. The publicity it would attract would create interest on a personal level and help raise badly needed funds for the flight.

Art had two children, William and Helen, who often accompanied their father on his flights with Clyde. Helen was willing to help promote the romantic interest. She liked Clyde, enjoyed his company, and his flying. Helen was a pretty blonde, college student, and a member of the Alethean Society at the Oshkosh Teachers College. I was also an Alethean at the college and knew Helen well.

The news hounds gave the supposed romance lots of space in the papers, especially just before the final arrangements were made and they took off for Vermont. Helen was naturally thrilled with all the attention she received from the reporters and with flying. One day she accompanied Clyde, his father, her father and Earl Iverson on a business trip to Milwaukee to pick up some parts for the airplane. They received lots of publicity that day, with one reporter asking them if they had eloped and were married in Milwaukee. Both denied the rumor and stated firmly they were just good friends.

I was Clyde's sister, and his closest friend and confidant. At that time we both lived at Hough's and Clyde often spoke of his thrilling, hair-raising escapades. The usually close-mouthed airman did not confide in his friends and even Enid didn't hear about many of his adventures. His friends knew only what they saw at the air shows. He was not one to brag but he did not consider talking to his sister as bragging and I made a suitably impressed audience.

Clyde was my wonderful big brother, my hero, and I was the only fan he needed. We had flown together many times and I shared the thrills of the stunting and the dangers of flying in an open cockpit Jenny. Not only flying, but flying upside down without a seat belt. It was a real thrill to look up where the sky should be and see green grass with barns, houses and cattle in the fields. The only thing that kept us in our seats was air pressure.

Immediately after the Oslo flight, while we all were agonizing over losing Clyde at sea, a reporter did find me outdoors at Clark's Point, and took my picture when I wasn't expecting it. That picture later appeared in the *Chicago Tribune*, along with those of other members of Clyde's bereaved family. It never appeared in the Oshkosh paper. My family wouldn't allow it.

Before Clyde left for Vermont, he asked if he could take our mother's ruby engagement ring along as a good luck charm. He knew I had the ring and cherished it, but I gave it to him. One of the last things he did while still in Vermont, was to return the ring. "I know how much this ring means to you, Bernice, and I don't want to risk it going down with us in the plane if we don't make it. I am giving it to Helen and asking her to return it to you."

Clyde did not return, but I still have the ring he sent back to me.

Miami and Al Capone

The winter weather grounded aircraft in the northern states so many flyers moved south to enjoy the warm air. Clyde was one of them, and one of the more fortunate ones too, since he was able to find work.

"I spent two winters in Florida," he later recalled. "One in Daytona Beach flying news reports of Don Campbell's racing exploits to Washington, D.C. and New York City. The other in Miami.

"Bob Morgan, a close buddy of mine, had an uncle in Miami with whom we stayed part of one winter. I flew exhibition flights there and sold rides. It was early days for flying in Florida and the people in the surrounding areas were attracted to the air shows and unable to resist an occasional plane ride.

"In 1929, Miami was a great sprawling giant city with whole blocks vacant within the populated area. It was a city attempting a comeback from a severe depression plus a great real estate bust. There were sewers only in the densely populated area downtown. The other people had cess pools. Telephones were a rare commodity. There had to be a valid reason for having one—medical or VIP. Employment was difficult for snowbirds. Snowbirds were people from the North who needed a place to live while awaiting a divorce or to wait out the cold northern winter. A divorce could be accomplished in three weeks time. These people often sought temporary employment to maintain themselves during that time. It was felt they were unemployable as they would leave for the North as soon as the divorce was granted or spring arrived.

"Flagler Street was a main artery running east and west to Bayfront Park. Biscayne Boulevard crossed Flagler running north and south along the bay. It was a beautiful drive with its stately royal palms gracing the middle of the boulevard. The causeway ran from Miami to Miami Beach. It was a beautiful and interesting drive. Even more beautiful to view from the air.

"Miami Beach was mostly a composite of hotels. At the end of the causeway Lincoln Boulevard lead to Collins Avenue, running parallel to the Bay. Many beautiful and unusual hotels had been built along the beach from one end of Collins Avenue to the other.

"In the early evening with the coral sun setting over Biscayne Bay and the lights of the hotels shining, it was a veritable fairyland. The soft air and the beauteous sight of the lighted hotels at night were impossible to describe. Emotionally, it clutched your heart. The song, "Moon over Miami" is a beautiful song, but it cannot compare with the sight of the full moon shining on the rippling water of Biscayne Bay."

Clyde and Bob became tourists and visited the zoos and unusual parks etc. They visited Indian Village and Orchid Grove, which were lovely and enlightening places.

They were greatly impressed with the Everglades and flew over them many times. Clyde wrote me that he had been very interested in that area and he had read about it. He described it to me. "The Seminole Indians," he wrote, "lived in the Everglades and so did the alligators and thousands of exotically beautiful birds.

"The Seminoles," he said, "lived in homes or chickees, as they called them, with thatched roofs, thatched with palm leaves. The sides of their homes were open and built on stilts, high off the ground. They averaged about 9 x 16 feet and were usually built of palmetto wood. Torrential rains kept the Everglades wet and soggy. Unlike the other Indian tribes in the U.S. they, at that time, had never signed a peace treaty with the U.S.A.

"Divorce among the Seminoles was even simpler than the 3-week waiting period in Miami. The husband simply walked away from the chickee and never returned.

"The ever-hungry alligators ran up to 15 feet long and had a broad snout. Adults were grey/black and the young were black with yellow crossbands. Alligators like to live in fresh water and brackish marshes.

"Alligators are very noisy. During mating season you could hear their full-throated bellowing rend the swamp for several miles. The female is a good parent. She builds a nesting mound near the water and lays 15 to 80 eggs. She covers them and guards them for about ten weeks. After they are hatched the mother stays with the young ones for about a year, sometimes longer.

"When there are no people around, alligators live on crustaceans, frogs, insects on water, small fish, birds and small mammals. Occasionally one has been known to have eaten a small child."

150

On a lazy day, with nothing better to do, Clyde and Bob would fly over the Everglades, out of curiosity, to watch what was happening. "The birds were so exceptionally beautiful and of such an unusual variety it was much better than attending the zoo." he wrote.

"We checked the plane very carefully, especially our gas, before we left to fly over the Everglades. The Seminoles who lived deep in the Everglades did not take kindly to uninvited guests we were told. Alligators, on the other hand were most welcoming and gave very large open mouthed voracious smiles showing lots of large white teeth."

Flying over the Everglades, they buzzed the Seminoles frequently and flew low to get a close up of the alligators sunning themselves along the banks of the many creeks running throughout the area. The large flying birds created a hazard. They could fly into the plane or its propeller. The boys flew much too low for safety, but it was a great excitement for a couple of twenty-year-old thrill seekers.

They flew to Key West and buzzed the ferry boats carrying passengers from island to island. Planes were rare in 1929 and 1930 and passengers swarmed to one side of the boat to view the aerobatic antics of the flyers doing loops and barrel rolls as they flew circles around the boat. Some boats nearly capsized when too many people stood on one side watching them.

They buzzed the gambling ship just outside the coastal limits. The gamblers didn't appreciate it. They probably thought the flyers were revenue officers coming to arrest them. The shots they fired at the plane deterred Clyde and Bob from doing their usual aerobatic antics around and over the ship.

They flew over Homestead, the last town before the Keys. People ran out of doors to see the airplane. It was a novelty. So the boys gave them a treat and buzzed them a few times. The people waved and laughed and screamed. The view of the land was palm trees everywhere and the landscape sandy and flat.

Someday, the boys decided, a road would have to be built to the Keys from Miami. They noted that boats were the only means of transportation besides Flagler's Folly, the railroad Henry Flagler built at the cost of the lives of many men. The construction of this gargantuan project took years of planning and nearly bankrupted its founder and his partners. All the materials had to be brought to the islands by boats. Huge concrete pilings had to be constructed between all of the islands to erect the railroad bridges from Key to Key and eventually to reach Key West.

"The railroad was finished and the first train whistled into Key West in 1912," Bob told Clyde as they followed the tracks on their flight to Key West.

151

The islands–Key Largo, Islamorada, Marathon and more–were left behind as they continued flying south.

Homes were scarce on any one of the keys as transportation was difficult and hurricanes were devastating. The boys thought seven mile bridge was unbelievable as they flew over it, following the tracks on their flight South.

Flying over the city of Key West, itself, was an interesting adventure. "The people," Don told him, "are called 'Conch People,' a name that began with the early settlers. The city is dubbed "Conch." I expect it is because of the use of Conch shells and the sea snails who dwell in them." The sea snails are basic food and are listed in menus in all the restaurants. The shells are beautiful and are utilized for decor in the homes as well as used for horns.

The island was small. It was a little over three miles long and slightly over a mile wide. It separated the Gulf from the Atlantic Ocean. The boys' reaction was, "What happens when a hurricane strikes? It is almost at sea level." They saw many large rambling houses topped with Captains' Walks. Since this was a seaport town, and in the beginning wrecking was the main industry, it was not unexpected to see 'Captains' Walks on the houses. "It has been hinted," Bob continued "that some of the sunken vessels were lured into the shore and onto the shoals for wreckers to benefit from the treasures recovered from the sunken hulks."

Everywhere, the foliage was lush and green. Bushes colored with gorgeous blooms blended in a near carpet of flowers. It was a most enjoyable day, the golden sunshine bathing the landscape furnished the boys with a perfect day of flying.

One night, friends took them shark-viewing on the ocean in a barge. When they were far out, they saw movement in the water and from the fins just above the waves, knew it was a school of sharks. One of the men threw his white shirt in the water near the sharks. In their great rush to eat the shirt some of the sharks bit others as they swarmed to reach it. As soon as one of them shed blood, they all began eating the bleeding one, and the same thing happened again. In their eagerness to reach the bloody one, others were bitten, drawing more blood. Real carnage was going on. The sharks, hungry for blood, went after the wounded ones and tore them to shreds. The water was red with blood.

The violence of their swirling caused a tremendous surge of water. The barge began to rock dangerously and the owner quickly drove back to the harbor. Clyde and Bob had seen enough. They were not hungry for food that night.

On one lazy day in Miami, Bob was working with his uncle. Clyde, bored and alone, sauntered slowly along Flagler Street. As he neared Bayfront Park,

152

he was far away in thought, but was aware of people meeting and passing him as they hurried along. At one point, he became aware of two tall, very heavyset men pacing along beside him, one on either side. A prickle of alarm went down his spine and he thought, "hm-m, I have a feeling a situation is developing which I am not going to enjoy. What have I done to incur someone's wrath, because we buzzed the gamblers' ship? These two don't appear to be here by happenstance."

As he attempted to turn left towards the Mayflower Hotel, he felt something press into his ribs, something hard and blunt. At the same time, a menacing voice spoke in a low tone, "That is a gun in your ribs. You are to come with us. The boss wants to talk to you. Continue walking, straight ahead."

Surprised and startled, realizing he actually was in a dangerous predicament, Clyde wondered who "the boss" could be. He carried on with his usual calm aplomb. He said nothing and continued walking on Flagler Street with his two unusual and burly companions.

It would have appeared to anyone nearby that three friends were out for a stroll on a lovely sunny day. They directed him to the Marina. A Cris Craft with motor running was waiting and the three stepped into it. With the captive in the middle, they headed out towards Palm Island.

Being a curious tourist, Clyde was looking around, especially at his would-be kidnappers. They were heavily muscled swarthy smooth-faced men with unfriendly expressions on their faces.

"If you know what's good for you, you won't do much looking around," one said to him.

As they approached the island, Clyde, despite the creepy feelings crawling up and down his spine, noticed the exceptional beauty of the whole area. The house was unpretentious, very much like any other three bedroom, one-story, stucco house in Miami. A wall enclosed a beautifully manicured garden which encircled most of the house. The bougainvillea, poinciana and various other exotic tropical plants were in full bloom and presented a picturesque and pleasing background for the house and wall.

The inside of the house was simply but luxuriously furnished. There were no women to be seen. The two men–goons as they were called then–led Clyde down a hall to a large room furnished as a study. A long table, much like a conference table, was in the center of the room. Ten to twelve men were seated around it, and the room was thick with smoke. Although they looked up expectantly as Clyde and his escorts entered, they showed little interest and gave the appearance of boredom.

153

At the head of the table sat a man with the unmistakable face of Al Capone A feeling of foreboding shivered down Clyde's spine as the gangster looked him up and down. Clyde felt justified for his feelings of apprehension as he stared into the hard cold eyes of the most notorious gangster of the times, sitting exactly across the table.

Al Capone, the recognized leader of organized crime in Chicago, had retired to Florida to get away from what he called "abuse" by law and order and the news reporters. "I have become such a figure of brutality and murder," he stated in an interview, "and it has reached such proportions that a woman in England wrote me the other day, she would pay my passage to England if I'd kill some neighbor she'd been having a quarrel with."

He was also considered to be a millionaire and Uncle Sam was interested in why he wasn't paying income taxes.

At a gesture from Capone all the men except four body guards left the room. Two standing, one on each side of the door by which they had entered, and one standing on each side of the door directly behind Capone. They were very large, heavily muscled, loutish looking men. Not appearing to be outstandingly intelligent, but men with whom one would not care to tangle.

Feeling slightly out of his depth and a bit nervous, Clyde reached into his left hand pocket. Instantly a loud menacing voice boomed, "Hold it right there." He withdrew his hand holding a cigarette between thumb and middle finger. That was when he saw both guards holding revolvers pointed at his midsection. Nonplused, he continued very nonchalantly to light his cigarette, closed his lighter and returned it to his pocket.

That deliberate and casual action seemed to amuse the gangster and he invited Clyde to sit down. "Do you know how close to death you were just then?" he asked.

Clyde shrugged his shoulders and said, "Why am I here?"

"I need a good pilot," Al replied. "I want to know a whole lot about you. How old are you? How many years have you been flying? In what areas of the country have you been flying? What kind of planes have you flown? Are you your own mechanic?

"I am going to buy the best and fastest plane I can find and I need an excellent pilot to fly it. The newspapers refer to you as 'Daredevil Lee', Why?"

His mind distraught with astonishment at his predicament and feeling a great deal of apprehension, Clyde explained he was called 'Daredevil Lee' because of the many close encounters with death he had had through stunting, parachute dropping and with his flying circus exploits. "As for my flying experience, I have flown from Mexico to Canada, throughout the Midwest and east to Massachusetts. I soloed at the age of 16 and have been flying ever since. I will be twenty-one next month."

154

Maintaining his usual imperturbable expression and preventing his astonishment from showing while wild thoughts whirled through his brain was not easy. As Capone began talking again, he thought, "This is madness!. This is mind-boggling insanity! I, Clyde Lee, am sitting in front of Al Capone, the most notorious gangster in the world, listening to him offering me a job flying him and his murdering, thieving, liquor-smuggling, gang of goons about the country. And if I don't agree to this lunacy I may be shot right here in my chair, and no one knows where I am. Surely he won't let me go and I can't possibly accept his idiotic offer. Not on any terms will I become one of them. This is worse than jumping out of an airplane 2000 feet up, wearing Elmer Clark's parachute.

"If I do get out of this, I shall end up stark raving mad! I think I am now! Oh, he is through talking and wants my answer."

Capone continued, "The pilot I need would have to be available to fly at any moment anywhere in the U.S, Canada, Mexico and even to South America. In other words, where ever the whim suits me to go. You would become a part of my group and live here with us. Once involved with us you could never leave. The pay would be $250.00 a month and keep. Think it over, if it appeals to you, the job is yours–a lifetime job and a dangerous one. Rival gangs might resent my having a private plane and eliminate it and the pilot. It's been known to happen to people associated with me."

He realized Capone wanted an immediate answer. He took a last puff on his cigarette and put it out in Capone's ash tray. Standing up, all six-foot four inches of him, he said, "Mr. Capone, I like a free life. I need to be able to go where I want to go when I want to go. Your offer of $250.00 a month plus living accommodation is hard to refuse, but I must refuse. I have to be free. I'm sure it would have been exciting and dangerous being in your employ. It was interesting meeting you as I have read so much about you in the papers.

"I have a luncheon engagement with a friend at the Mayflower Hotel at 12:00 noon. I'm afraid I must leave now or I shall be late."

He held out his hand and without standing up Capone shook it and said, "I'm disappointed at your decision, but you may go now, and my men will escort you back to Bayfront Park. If you should change your mind, get in touch." He gestured to the guards.

They stepped aside, opened the door, ushered Clyde out and followed him through the front door. There the original two guards took over and conducted him to the speed boat, and on to Bayfront Park.

All the way back in the Cris Craft his mind seethed with thoughts of cement shoes, a dip in the Bay, and every other horrible end he could possibly conjure up. He well knew Capone's reputation for not accepting, "No" for an answer. When Bob met him at the Mayflower Hotel, Clyde said, "I've gone stark raving mad. I'm having nightmares in the daytime, like this morning! I can't believe it," he told Bob.

"You know, Clyde," Bob said. 'You not only live a dangerous, risky life, flying around in that crate of an airplane. You also somehow court dangerous experiences, all unknowingly and unwantingly, but there you are. That's you!

"But what in the world does Capone want with you for a pilot? And as the reality of Clyde's experience burst upon him, he exclaimed, "Al Capone! Clyde! My God, Clyde! Al Capone! You don't realize how lucky you are to be out of his clutches. No one, but no one ever says 'No' to Capone and gets away with it. You are beyond praying for! What can I say?...WOW!"

*(Top) Sixteen-year-old Clyde Lee, right, with his cousin Walton Johnson.
(Bottom) Clyde's first Jenny waiting for spring to arrive, so the wings can be
mounted, and the flying begin, 1927.*

Clyde in his "Gin Bar" days in Oshkosh in the late 1920s.

Flyers at the Larson Airport, 1926: Roy Larson is in front of the plane; Dave Reed wears a leather coat and flight helmet; Clyde Lee sports a fedora, with Walton Johnson in the soft cap. Man not facing camera is unidentified.

(Top) Don Campbell's land speed record team at Daytona Beach, Florida in 1930. Clyde, who is standing on the truck in a dark suit, flew news reports and photos of the event to northern newspapers. (Below) Clyde in a publicity photo for the transatlantic flight and (Right) setting off for Vermont from Oshkosh.

LA MAR 14 30

Clyde painted his Stinson to promote Oshkosh's most famous industry in an unsuccessful attempt to raise funds for his Norway flight. (Coincidentally, Clyde's plane is parked in front of a Ryan aircraft, the same model that Charles Lindbergh flew across the Atlantic in 1927.) Clyde had better luck raising funds in Vermont, where the Stinson became "The Green Mountain Boy" to promote the "granite center of the world." First co-pilot Julius Robertson stands next to Clyde.

(Top) The crew for the Norway flight (left-right) Earl Iverson, Fred Sensiba, Knute Hansen, Julius Robertson and Clyde. (Bottom) One of the postcards Clyde took along to mail to collectors from Oslo. The route shown was not the course Clyde flew. He used a more southerly route that passed over Ireland, England and the North Sea coast of Germany before swinging northeast to Oslo.

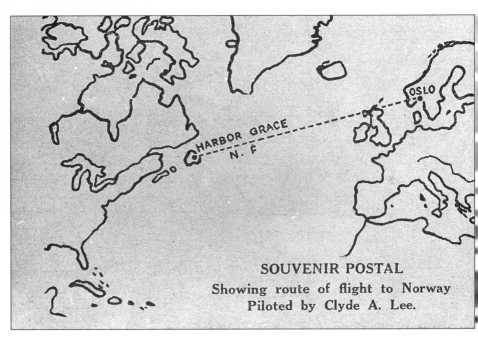

SOUVENIR POSTAL
Showing route of flight to Norway
Piloted by Clyde A. Lee.

The engine of the Stinson was warming up in the background as Clyde and co-pilot John Bochkon stood for the camera just before takeoff. A Norwegian naval pilot who paid for his passage, Bochkon was a late replacement for Julius Robertson.

MOTOR CEASES SUDDENLY, THE REPORT TODAY

Patrol of the Automobile Association Asserts That Plane, Believed to be That of Local Flyer Was Well Over the Ocean

London. –(UP)– An airplane, possibly that of Clyde Allen Lee and John Bochkon on their attempted transatlantic flight, was heard off the Welsh coast Friday by a patrol of the Automobile association, officials of the association announced today.

The plane was well over the sea, the patrol reported, when the noise of the motor suddenly ceased.

Lee and Buchkon were not reported after leaving Harbor Grace for Oslo thursday in the monoplane "Green Mountain Boy."

The patrol was on duty on the shore near Talybont when the motor was heard. Visibility was bad. The patrol believed that the motor stalled.

RELATIVES STILL HOPE

(Relatives and friends continued to hope today for the rescue of Clyde A. Lee, missing since he and John Bochkon of Brooklyn, N.Y., took off from Newfoundland last Thursday to fly the broad Atlantic.

They reposed their hope in the promises of Lee's navigator at Barre, Vt., and were greatly encouraged by the message received from England, where it was said members of a Welsh coast guard unit Friday heard the motor of a plane they thought might have been the "Green Mountain Boy."

"We are sure Clyde has landed, and that he was near his goal when his flight ended," a member of the family stated.

RECEIVE MESSAGE

Huntington, Lee's navigator, told the flyer's sister Sunday that the youthful pilot and his companion could have gone down on a remote island somewhere near the coast of Ireland, and not be heard from for a week, until he was able to communicate with some point in direct contact with the outside world.

Lee flew a 1928 Stinson monoplane which he brought to Oshkosh last year from Negaunee, Mich., and rebuilt at the Oshkosh airport with local aid and largely with materials bought in Oshkosh.

There appeared no authenticity to the report that Lee was promised a cash offer and a new plane if he would postpone the ocean hop until next year. Lee attempted for months to obtain financial backing in Oshkosh, but meeting with no success he turned to Barre-Montpelier, Vt., where a civic organization presented him with a check for $1,000 to make the flight from that place.)

Probably the last notice of Clyde Lee and John Bochkon was the sound of an aircraft engine heard off the coast of Wales as reported by the United Press Service and reprinted by the Oshkosh Northwestern on August 30, 1932.

Norway Bound

By 1932, Clyde had definitely made up his mind to attempt the flight to Norway. He brought his five passenger Stinson cabin commercial plane from Negaunee, Michigan to Oshkosh and made plans to redesign and reconstruct it for the flight. It had been in a minor accident in 1931 and he wanted to make sure every part of it would be in perfect condition for ocean flying.

The amount of fuel the Stinson could carry was crucial so Clyde began by stripping the plane down to its minimum weight. He then redesigned the fuselage to carry a 100 gallon fuel tank. New wings were designed and built to house a 50 gallon fuel tank. Space also had to be provided for fifty 5-gallon cans to carry another 250 gallons of fuel. As gas in the fuselage tank was depleted, it would be replaced with gas from the 5-gallon cans. The total amount of gas, 450 gallons, should have been able to carry the plane over the ocean for 37 to 40 hours. It was enough to complete the flight–unless, and this was a very big unless–the plane encountered severe headwinds or a storm.

The Stinson's maximum speed was estimated at about 135 miles per hour. At the start of the flight, while carrying the full weight of 450 gallons of gas, flyers and gear, would probably be about 95 miles per hour. As the tanks emptied, speed could increase.

Fred Sensiba of Crystal Falls, Michigan, an experienced assembly expert in airplane manufacturing, became a member of the team. He was the chief mechanic. Later, Knute Hansen joined the team as an assistant to Sensiba.

The markings on the plane were the license number which permitted Clyde to attempt the flight. The government had stepped in to stop many young men flying less than well constructed airplanes across the Atlantic, and being lost at sea. Clyde's plane was licensed with the lettering NR7576. The "N" denoted the plane was from the United States. The "R" limited his license to transocean flying. The lettering appeared on the upper side of the right wing, the lower side of the left wing and on both sides of the rudder area.

In 1928, a Norwegian newspaper offered a prize of $10,000 for a successful flight from America to Oslo, Norway. In 1932, the prize was still listed with the National Aeronautical Association and it gave Clyde added incentive for his flight.

Many times he was asked, Why are you so intent on making this flight to Norway? Are you seeking glory? Looking for adulation such as Lindbergh achieved? Is it the prize money offered or is there a deeper, singular purpose driving you on? He replied:

"I do have a singleness of purpose and have had ever since my first airplane ride with Roy Larson in June, 1923. I believe in and predict a great future in flying. I envision very large airplanes flying all over the world carrying unbelievably large cargoes (as much as trains) and flying much faster than trains travel. I want to be a part of that incredible progress.

"With the rapidly advancing technology of the first three decades of this century, we will be performing events previously undreamed of such as building space craft amd even landing on the moon during our lifetime.

"Of course, the prize money will help me attend college and achieve a degree in aviation engineering. One has to have a Bachelor of Science degree in engineering in order to be employed by Stinson or any of the other aviation manufacturing firms today. I want to get on in aviation into some phase where I can make a substantial contribution to its progress, to be able to contribute to its future.

"A successful flight now, will encourage others to invest in its development; both in commercial and transport flying.

"If I can't realize that career, then the money will hold me over until I am twenty-eight and can become an airmail pilot. I passed the test to become one, but am too young, they said. It is useless to continue attempting to earn a living barnstorming or flying 'small-time' commercial during this Depression. I need to get on with a career.

"However," Clyde said, "I am determined to make the flight regardless of whether the award is still in effect or not." He made it clear that prize money was not his major motive for flying to Norway.

Young Julius Robertson, the copilot, would navigate, assist Clyde at the controls and empty the five-gallon cans into the main fuel tank in the course of the flight.

Once the Stinson had been rebuilt, flight tests were conducted. The length of the runway and the time required to lift that heavy weight of fuel also had to be ascertained. In the course of the tests, Clyde learned that his plane needed a new engine, which would be a source of a major delay.

To commemorate the event, a special catchet for mail carried on the flight was designed by the Oshkosh Philatelic Society and sold to the public. Letters to be carried onboard were received from stamp collectors in every state in the Union, Canada and Mexico. F. M. Getchel and D. W. Bronson, members of the Oshkosh stamp club, volunteered to prepare the letters for these collectors. The Oshkosh post office staff volunteered to stamp with the special catchet any mail leaving the Oshkosh Post office on the day Clyde left the city on his flight. He also carried approximately 3500 souvenir cards which he would mail from Oslo to the collectors.

Funding the flight was a major problem. Clyde was a young man who had worked at odd jobs when he was not flying. He got by in the 1920s, but jobs were few and far between in the early 1930s, which were the worst years of the Depression. Of all the difficulties involved in preparing for the flight, none was more frustrating than finding sponsors to underwrite it.

Since he had flown for local businessmen there and since it was the hometown of Julius Robertson, Clyde had hoped that Negaunee, Michigan, might put up the funds. If so, he would base his flight there. Those plans fell through, so Clyde focused his attention on his own hometown of Oshkosh.

"There were six business men in Negaunee, Michigan who helped make it possible. They banded together and hired me to live there and fly them to other cities on business trips, mostly to Chicago, Milwaukee and Detroit. I met a young man there, an enthusiastic would-be flyer, Julius Robertson. I taught him to fly and he became a follower of mine, even to the extent of asking to be my co-pilot on the trip to Norway. After a couple of years the six business men decided it was too costly maintaining a plane and paying a pilot for the few flying trips they made to their business appointments. They were several months delinquent in paying my salary. They gave me this plane in lieu of wages. Having my own plane made everything point to a trip to Norway for me. A chance for my dream to come true.

Saving The Bank

In the early 1930s, banks throughout the United States were in crisis. Many failed and millions of stockholders, businesses and depositors lost all their money. The atmosphere was so volatile that, immediately after his inauguration in 1933, President Franklin Roosevelt declared a bank holiday. All banks in the country were temporarily closed while federal officials examined their assets. Many banks were sound, but many others had to be reorganized and their assets combined with other institutions. Others were ordered to remain closed with all accounts frozen. It is in this atmosphere that the following story must be read. The characters are fictitious, except for Clyde Lee and Don Agrell, but the facts are true. The daredevil flyboy really did save the banks of Oshkosh in the spring of 1932.

Ted Reuter was standing at the cashier's window watching Tom Scott stuff a large wad of bills into his billfold when Oscar Perkins, a business acquaintance, overheard him say, "I'm glad I found out the bank isn't opening next Monday, so I can withdraw my money."

"What! The bank won't be open next Monday?" exclaimed Oscar.

"That's right," Ben Pritchard, the cashier nodded. Ted confirmed this by a nod of his head. Oscar hesitated, then turned to the next teller's window, withdrew all of his money in large bills and stuffed them in his wallet. But after he left the bank he began to worry about what to do with his cash.

Fred Heinz, from the Diamond Match Company, tapped him on the shoulder as he walked through the doors. "Passing me by Oscar, old friend, without a hello, what's wrong?"

"What's wrong!" growled Oscar. "The damn bank has gone bust and isn't going to open its doors Monday."

Fred frowned doubtfully at Oscar. "Are you sure?" he asked. "Who gave you this information? Personally, I don't believe it."

"It came right out of the horse's mouth." Oscar replied. "The cashier and Ted Reuter were discussing it when I came in. I asked them if it was true. Ted's a member of the Board of Directors. As a matter of fact I'm so damn sure I'll bet you $25.00 the bank won't open next Monday."

"Thanks Pal." Bill said and hurried to a teller to withdraw all his money. "Whew," he said to himself. "Was I ever lucky to meet Oscar just then, or I wouldn't have been able to pay employees' wages this month." But, as he went out the door he thought disconcertedly, "What in thunder am I going to do with thousands of dollars until payday? What if someone finds out I have all this money on me? What should I do with it?" Put it in another bank? No! If there is a run on this bank, they'll all be closed!"

He thought it over as he walked slowly down the street. Suddenly he turned around, and returned to the bank. He put three-fourths of the money in his safety deposit box, keeping out only enough for next Wednesday's payroll.

Later, both men returned to their offices. They began to puzzle over what they had heard and called other business associates to find out if they had heard anything about the bank going 'bust' and not opening the following Monday.

Bill called Sam Belding at the Trunk Company and advised him to withdraw his next week's payroll money from the bank today as the bank was not going to open Monday. He further predicted the American and National banks would have to follow suit. "When the word gets out, panic like you have never seen will set in and there will be a 'run' on all the banks in the area."

Wasting no time, Sam requested an immediate meeting of the board of directors of his company. He needed a decision as to whether or not to withdraw the company's money and what to do with it. "We could put it in a bank in another city." he suggested.

"Personally, I don't believe this," stated one director resolutely. "Ben wouldn't allow his bank to get in a financial crisis."

"My God!" Sam replied, "How can you not believe it when Oscar verified it with both Ben and Ted Reuter? What better word do you need? Can you visualize the repercussions to us and our payroll not to say anything about our future business if that bank does not open next Monday? The newspapers will report it tonight and there could be mass hysteria tomorrow. We need our payroll money for Wednesday. We have to get it today."

"People become frantic when their money is involved. In order to meet the demands, which is impossible in a run, it often becomes necessary to close the bank. It will go into receivership and it will take months to get our money out, if ever. I can see no way of keeping that news quiet. The rumor is already spreading like wildfire throughout the town. Pete Manning from Wolf's Department store, called me a few minutes ago, saying there are two lines, two blocks long waiting outside the bank. He asked me if I knew why? Said his wife heard at the bridge club the bank was closed, busted! He asked me if I knew anything about that. I didn't then, but I sure do now."

Sam became so wrought up over his conclusions in regard to the matter, that he called John Lister at the Overall Company. Sam explained to John his concerns about Monday and that word was spreading all over town. "They will have to close the bank Monday for good if this keeps up." he said.

"It might not even stop there, he continued agitatedly. "People in neighboring cities might become uneasy about their money and start a run on their banks. One rumor could start another. Once it develops into mass hysteria all the banks will be closed. Can you tell me what in Hell we can do to stop that bank from being closed Monday?"

"Calm down, Sam," John advised, "Don't get so excited. You are just assuming this vicious rumor is true and that it is all over town. I have known Ben a long time and I also know a lot about the condition of the bank. I am sure it is not going 'busted.' Furthermore, I am sure it is solvent," said John. "There is something fishy about all this. I shall call Jess Doty at the Stock Exchange and ferret out his information and suggestions on this matter. We must not let unfounded rumor stampede us into withdrawing our money, ruin a bank and along with it the economy of a whole city. What is your proof, Sam?"

"All right, don't believe it, John. Check for yourself. Call Oscar. He knows for sure because he bet Fred $25.00 the bank would not open." Sam argued.

"No, I won't call Oscar," said John, "but I will call Jess Doty at the Stock Exchange. I think you have your story all wrong. Of course, right or wrong, if a run starts on any bank it can close in a day. We all know no bank carries enough cash to return all the customers' money on demand in one day."

John called Jess. "If the rumor is correct and the bank is 'busted,'" he told Jess, "we can look for a shut-down of all business."

"It's true we would have a major disaster on our hands." stated Jess. "The lumber company, the axle company, the shoe company, the match company, department stores, grocery stores and meat markets. It's all too true. Without money, mass hysteria could certainly take over and we would close all the banks for good. We, John, we: Sam, Fred, Oscar and the rest of us. We are the ones who will have closed the bank by withdrawing our money and passing on false rumors. Frankly, I don't believe this rumor either. Why hasn't anyone called Ben? I am going to call him right now and find out how this all began and how true it is. In the meantime try to quash the rumor and don't pass it on to anyone else."

Shortly after Oscar and Fred left the bank that morning, Ben noticed business had picked up to an alarming degree. Most of this sudden business was withdrawals, not only of checking accounts, but also of savings accounts. Some were withdrawing all the money they had in the bank. The tellers were busy making trips to the vault, handing out more and more money to customers. The money in the vault was rapidly dwindling. Ben became puzzled and suspicious. A three-day-weekend wouldn't call for a person using his life's savings. Everyone was certainly going all out for this holiday.

It was about 3:00 p.m. when Jess called and asked Ben what was going on at the bank. "I have had at least three calls today with rumors about your bank. They said it will not be opening next Monday and there is a run on the bank right now and that it isbankrupt. Is this true?"

"Of course the bank will not be opening next Monday, Jess," Ben said. "Monday is Memorial Day and a national holiday. Every bank in the United States will be closed. Call your stupid rumor mongers and enlighten them. But thanks for the call. That rumor explains why the sudden surge in business and the urge on the part of our customers to withdraw all their money from the bank. I thought they were all going on a world cruise this weekend. Your call may have saved my bank and my hide, Jess. Hell! if this keeps up we could very well have a serious run not only on this bank, but all the banks in town. They could all be closed not only Monday, but forever! I'll be hard put to ward off a serious run as it is. Thank God you called me!."

Ben called an immediate meeting of the cashiers and tellers in the vault to assess the situation. He explained the cause of the business suddenly escalating that afternoon.

"You all know there is no basis for the rumor. We shall have to convince our people as soon as possible that there is no basis for such gossip. Try to allay the fears of the customers. Surely they must remember we have always been closed on Memorial Day. Why should we be the only bank in the United States to stay open on that day? Can we hold out until 6:00 o'clock with the amount of cash we have on hand?"

The Assistant Cashier thought the bank could hold out as it was only three hours until closing. "If we send home two of our tellers now, and the two remaining can stall for time by talking to each customer at length explaining there is no basis for the rumor and reassure each customer that the bank is solvent and will remain in business, we can make it through today O.K., but" he went on, "the situation does not look favorable for next Tuesday. Without additional funds, something like a half-million dollars, we may not be able to meet the payroll demands.

"Tuesday, the industries in town pick up their funds to meet payroll day on Wednesday. We can't finance those withdrawals with what is left in the vault."

Ben sent two tellers home and advised the others to talk to the customers as long as they could, delaying giving them their money on any pretext, making sure that each one understood Monday was a national holiday, and that every bank in the U.S. would be closed.

Immediately after this meeting, Ben called the Marshall and Ilsley Bank in Milwaukee and requested funds. The bank president agreed to release a half-million dollars, but couldn't provide transportation to Oshkosh.

"With the weekend holiday beginning tomorrow," he said, "and it is now after three o'clock and Friday. I know Brinks would never do it before Tuesday."

Again, Ben called a conference in the vault. He explained the circumstances to his employees and said, "I hope someone can come up with a good solution to our problems."

"Anyone know where Clyde Lee is?" Evelyn, one of the employees, asked, "I'm sure he would fly to Milwaukee and pick up the money. He could fly there and back in a couple of hours. His plane cruises at about 90 miles an hour."

"Great idea," said Ben. "We all know Clyde. He's just the guy that can do it. What's more we can trust him. If he will do it, we can have the money here tonight and available for Tuesday morning. It won't matter if the customers withdraw all they have here. We will be ready for any eventuality the day after the holiday.

"Marshall & Ilsley closes in two hours. Get on the phone and locate Clyde. Get him here as fast as you can."

Quickly, Ben called the Milwaukee bank again and set it up, tentatively, for the Brinks van to carry the currency in tens and twenties to the Milwaukee County Airport and transfer the bags of money to Clyde's plane.

Minutes later, Marty Peterson looked up and saw the lean and lanky pilot saunter in through the front door of the bank.

"Speaking of Angels," thought Marty as he hurried to Ben's office. "Your problem is solved, Ben." Marty told him. "Clyde Lee just walked in."

Ben hurried Clyde into his office and not wasting any time said, "Clyde, would you fly to Milwaukee right now and pick up a half-million bucks for us? There's a run beginning on the bank. Some blockhead started the rumor the bank is going broke because it will be closed Monday. Busted! Ridiculous! But nonetheless the run will make funds short for Tuesday opening. I'll need money to meet the business payrolls next week. The only way I can get it in time is if you will fly to Milwaukee and pick it up at the airport within the next hour and a half.

"Marshall & Ilsley closes in two hours or less. That is why all the rush. I need the money tonight!"

"I wouldn't mind picking up a half-million bucks any time, anywhere," drawled Clyde, grinning. "But, who started the rumor?"

"Some unthinking idiot spread the word that the bank is insolvent because we are not going to be open next Monday."

"Next Monday! Of course not! That's Memorial Day! Put a sign on the door, "Closed Monday for Memorial Day, open Tuesday for business as usual."

"We have," Ben replied, "but if people are reading it, they are not believing it. We can hold out until closing time today, hopefully, but it's Tuesday morning opening, we can't handle without additional funds.

"Marshall & Ilsley will have the money on the airfield in a Brinks truck in one and a half hours. I hope you can make it because they close in two hours. Later than that there will be no help from them until Tuesday morning. That could be catastrophic for us. Will you help us?"

"Sure thing," said Clyde, "but I'll need money for fuel to fly the plane. I'm flat broke..."

"If that's all" replied Ben, "here's twenty dollars. Get moving!"

"Well...that isn't quite all," Clyde drawled, "I need a lift to the airport. My car died and it's a long walk. If you'll let me use your phone, I'll call Don Agrell and see if he can drive me to my plane, and wait to bring me back to the bank with your money."

"Help yourself," Ben said. "Call anyone you need to get you there. I'll call Marshall & Ilsley again and confirm that Brinks will meet you at the Milwaukee County Airport in ninety minutes, and will load the money bags into your plane. You'll have to give them a receipt for the money and you'll have to accept their count. For your sake we don't want you counting bags of cash in the middle of the airfield in Milwaukee. To eliminate any waste of time, I will give them your pilot's license number and your plane I.D. number. When you show them to the Brinks driver at the airport that's all you'll need for identification.

176

"I am sure you realize how important it is that not a whisper of this reaches anyone now or in the future. Confidence in the bank would suffer drastically no matter how untrue the rumor is."

Don Agrell was a slight, blonde young man about the same age as Clyde. Although he was six inches shorter, he was well built. His smiling blue eyes and almost white thatch of blonde hair were quite attractive to the girls. Clyde and Don met one night when both were on the town. They had become friends, casual, but good friends.

Clyde stepped out of the bank just as Don drove in front of it. "Quick response," Clyde said as he opened the car door and settled his long legs inside, knees to chest as he accommodated himself to the space from the seat to the dashboard.

"Like I've told you before, Don, your car is too small for me," he complained.

Don smiled a greeting which was returned by Clyde. "What's up Sherlock? What is all this mystery about? he asked, "And why so urgent you get to the airport? I hate to tell you, but I am running out of gas. I don't think we'll make it."

"That cuts the mustard," Clyde laughed. "Don't worry about the gas, just stop at the first filling station and get 5 gallons. I'll pay for it. Then drive like Hell to the airport. This is a desperate situation!"

"What! Drive like Hell with this jalopy?" Don laughed, "You have to be kidding."

"All right, Clyde, spill it. What's going on and what's the mystery? I know you're not leaving for Oslo today. Why the rush to the airport, and why all the secrecy?"

"You are not going to believe this! We actually are on a secret mission." Clyde told Don with a Dick tracy leer. "Speed is of the essence. I am about to make off with half-a-million dollars. Boy Scout honor, and drunk or sober you don't breathe a word to anyone, not now nor at any time in the future."

"You do sound drunk, or addle brained. Have you been on Ninth street again? Drinking that "needle" beer? Made another drop in Elmer's parachute and landed on your head?. A half-million dollars, you say? How soon will the cops be after us? Where have you stashed the loot? Don't tell me you robbed the bank for gas money? Are we making a get-away?" Don demanded, looking at Clyde with roguish eyes.

"It's almost that bad," answered Clyde. "At least our gas money came from the bank, but there is a string to it."

"Come on, Clyde give, cut the stalling. Let's have it, this mystery of yours. If the cops are after us–like it sounds they are–I'd like to know. Also, where do we stash the loot or is it already at the airport and you are about to abscond with it?"

Clyde laughed. "You'll never believe this. It's the darndest story, and has such a kick to it. Hilarious! Ironic! It'll be interesting to see the end of it. I have to assure myself I'm not dreaming this farce. How men high up in the business world could bring about such a fiasco. It's beyond belief!

"Someone, I don't think they know who, spoke unthinkingly to another customer in the bank this morning mentioning the bank would not be open next Monday. That nincompoop, not mentioning any names, forgot about Memorial Day falling on Monday. Being a suspicious character, he jumped to all the wrong conclusions and started the rumor the bank was in trouble. He has half of Oshkosh believing it, unless they are smart enough to remember it is Memorial Day.

"Well, Ben was beside himself when he realized people weren't withdrawing money for a long holiday, and a 'run' on the bank was in progress. He called banks in Milwaukee for funds to see this thing through. Any bank could go broke when a run starts and goes on long enough.

"Ben put out a call for me, and asked me to fly to Milwaukee and bring back half-a-million dollars to save the bank. And here's the kick, I didn't have enough money to buy gas to fly to Milwaukee. I was leaving to pick up a half-a-million in unmarked currency in the plane, but no gas to fly there to pick it up. I was embarrassed. Ben gave me a twenty dollar bill.

"It must have added to your 'kick' when I told you I didn't have gas to drive out to your plane." They chuckled.

Clyde said, "They made a good choice of persons to trust with a half-million dollars, a couple of bums. I had neither car nor money and you had no money. At least you are getting me out to the airport. I wonder if Brinks would hire us?

"As a matter of fact, it was pure luck they found me, or rather that I came in today. I was at my sister's house on Mt. Vernon Street when a friend called her and told her about the bank. I wondered if they might need money pronto. Need it faster than Brinks could get it here.

"I couldn't bear to see my sister lose all her money, so I sauntered down to the bank. I certainly met with a cordial welcoming committee. Hustled me into Ben's presence before you could say, "Skat." I found out in the course of events, they had been calling all my hangouts with an emergency message that I come to the bank at once. Such popularity must be deserved. Do you suppose I am psychic and knew they needed me?

"Which sister?"

"Evelyn Baxandall. Ray's wife."

178

"The pretty red head who used to work in the vault at City National?"

"Yeah, that's her. Do you know her?"

"Just to speak to. Ray keeps her hidden. She's too pretty to let out of his sight. Speaking of Ray...he has lots of money, why don't you hit him for the $1,000.00 you need for a new motor for your plane?"

Clyde: "I already have and when I find the right motor, he will give me the money.

"I'll need you to hang around the airport for a couple of hours to drive me to the bank when I return. If anyone asks any questions stall 'em. You are waiting for me and we are going somewhere. Which is true. When I get back, we will be burning rubber to get that money to the bank before someone gets any ideas.

"I have a hot tip on an engine for my plane, available at a price. It's a reconditioned engine. The engine block is cracked. The German welder on the South side said he could weld it. He assured me it would be stronger than a new one.

"All kidding aside, this trip is super secret. Ben was adamant about it. The bank's reputation and prestige are on the line, in jeopardy, with this ridiculous 'run'. If he can't give them their money, there will be no more prestige, no more bank.

"Brinks would have brought the money to Oshkosh today but it is presently after 3:00 o'clock on Friday afternoon. Their day ends at 5:00. They couldn't make it to Oshkosh and back to Milwaukee by that time. So, I'm getting a free flight to Milwaukee to pick up the money. And you are getting a free ride to the airport and back.

"We'll stash the loot, as you expressed it, in the trunk of your car. Without transportation to the bank, I would be stranded in the middle of the flying field. I don't know how many bags nor how large they will be. It's all in tens and twenties.

"We don't want an audience while we transfer it to your car. I will land far out, on the south end of the field. Park over there, about half way along the road. Please be early. It's about an hour each way for me and if Brinks is on time, I will be back in just under two hours. Be sure to be there. If you are late, I will be in a ticklish situation.

"I need to give the newspapers the slip. They follow me around to find out everything I do and think. In short, I need you to help with the money and to drive us back to the bank very inconspicuously."

"You need me, Clyde, I should go along with you," Don said with a serious face. "Just think what we could do with all that moola. We could fly to Canada and they'd never find us in the backwoods."

"Who wants to hide in the backwoods of Canada?" asked Clyde, "If that's what you want to do, head south. Go where it is warm the year around. Lay on the beaches in Miami, buy a yacht and sail into the wide blue yonder."

"Sounds great to me," agreed Don. "Palm trees swaying in the breeze, beautiful seductive maidens sun bathing on the beach. What are we waiting for?"

"Bedazzled you are my friend, with moonbeams in your head, but keep on dreaming," Clyde humored him "Fat chance," he laughed, as they arrived at the airport. He climbed out of the car, grimacing as he straightened his long legs to take out the cramp from sitting in Don's car. "That is a Christmas that will never come. Here we are, here I go and here you stay until I get back with those bulging money bags."

"Aw Shucks, for a few minutes there, life looked beautiful and rosy," Don replied. "Maybe when you get back from Norway, we could give it a try."

Clyde checked his plane. He measured the water and gas with a wooden stick he carried in the plane. He checked the motor and the air in the tires. He was cautious when it came to his airplane. Sliding over the side of the plane and into the seat he began warming the engine and slowly taxied out to the gas pumps which were located beside the hangar.

The plane gassed and watered, he climbed into the cockpit and settled into the seat. Leaning over the side, he held out his hand, index finger and thumb forming a circle and shouted, "Wish me luck."

Don mimicked the gesture and heard Clyde say laughingly, "Meet me in Miami someday."

Clyde guided the plane into position for takeoff, revved the motor, and began taxiing down the field. The plane gained momentum, motor thundering louder and louder as it prepared for lift off. Gracefully, it took to the air, climbing and headed south disappearing quickly.

Don's thoughts as he watched the disappearing airplane, were mixed. He wished Clyde wouldn't continue planning his flight to Norway, but on the other hand, wished him the best of luck in his endeavor. "Damn," he thought, "you've just got to make it to Oslo and back. We need you here, Clyde." Another thought came to Don's mind.

"Just as your ancestors had the frontier of sailing on the Mayflower to the New World, so you have made your frontier flying the Atlantic to Norway. I can understand that, but wish you wouldn't."

Clyde's thoughts were mixed, too. He was worried. The deadline date when he should leave for Norway was fast approaching, and he desperately needed a new engine or at least a sound reconditioned one.

Why couldn't the city of Oshkosh back him to the amount of a thousand dollars? They were getting all this free advertising. The newspapers in the large cities were carrying the story about him and his Oshkosh plane. Pictures of the plane were in newspapers all over the U.S. he thought.

It was frustrating. He was frustrated. "I can't solve it now," he thought, better enjoy the ride.

"This is today, how nice this is today. I am getting a flight to Milwaukee on this beautiful day, the 29th of May at someone else's expense." The lure of the sky had always emotionally affected him. It was his real and only life, flying. Stunting and barnstorming added spice to his life. In an open cockpit plane he gloried in the freedom. Free as a bird, with nothing but air above, beneath and all around him. "All my problems are down there," he thought as he gazed at the checkerboard farms, their miniature red barns and white houses, basking in the sun. Farmers working the soil with horse-drawn plows.

"Soon, farmers won't need horses. Machinery will do it all.

"This trip of mine today should certainly prove airplanes are not just toys for fun. Where would the city be next week without the money I am bringing back to the bank for businesses to continue to function? Without the money there at opening time, Tuesday, customers would be storming the bank. Brinks couldn't help the bank. So who is helping? That 'Damn Fool', Clyde Lee is helping. Who will get nothing but a thank you for it? And the people will never know that Clyde Lee is saving Oshkosh from economic chaos. Oh, yes, I did get $20 for gas. I wonder what Brinks would charge? Only an airplane could get the money to the bank in time to avert utter chaos for a city."

He had almost an hour in which to muse and fly on. There was no turbulence, and he fell into retrospection. He thought about all the problems he was facing trying to get his planned flight to Norway off the ground, literally speaking. He needed money, at least a thousand dollars.

Last January, when he first announced his ambition to the public through the daily newspaper, people looked at him askance. "Crazy," they thought, and "crazy," they said to his face. Three other flights to Norway had failed and the flyers involved were all dead, lost at sea.

Why did Clyde want to take such a foolish chance, risk his life and for what? Lindbergh had already flown the ocean to Paris. What difference would it make flying to Oslo, Norway? It was just another flight across the Atlantic. Too many had already lost their lives in such foolhardy attempts.

And so the conversations were going on, all over town. Everyone in Oshkosh knew who he was. They ran outdoors every time they heard a plane to see if it was the big red bird that was going to fly to Norway.

On the other hand, people concerned for his life would tell him to his face, "Clyde, you are a damn fool to attempt this."

Now flying along on this balmy, sunny day and pondering his dilemma he thought, "I am just a damn fool I guess. Roy thought we could make it. Since he isn't here to go with me and make the try, maybe I can make it for both of us. It will be a memorial to Roy. I think I have a good chance if I can get a new motor. I have more flying hours than Lindbergh had when he made his flight. I have been studying ocean currents and air currents that cause drift and can chart them. I know of no aviator who has ever been able to measure drift accurately. I practiced it while flying over the ocean at Daytona Beach and Miami. The success or failure of the flight will depend upon the new engine and enough money for gas.

"It can't be worse than flying over the Blue Ridge mountains at night in a thunderstorm That was the worst I ever encountered. Pure Hell! I never thought I would survive it. Flying to Washington and New York City from Daytona Beach with pictures and news stories of Campbell and his racing car. Flying through those mountains in thunderstorms at night. It was flying blind."

All alone in the clear blue sky, relaxed and reminiscing; mentally, life looked good and he felt confidence in his plans for his flight.

"It's the money I need. A good new engine and it would be a cinch."

In the hazy distance he could see the smoke stacks of industrial Milwaukee and remembered the years he had spent at the Holterhauf Airport teaching flying. Pleasant thoughts of his students came to mind, particularly Don Toi who had become a fast friend of his.

How quickly Don had learned to fly. He thought of the wonderfully delicious meals Don had served him at the Toi Restaurant. He was sure Don's influence was behind the letter he had received from one of the top men in the Chinese War Department offering him a job. He had been invited to head up an aviation department teaching young men in China to fly. They needed aviators to fight the war with Japan. "I wonder if I should go to China instead of attempting a trans-Atlantic flight to Oslo. What would the public think if I bowed out on Oslo now. Probably that I had a sudden onslaught of cold feet.

"Perhaps I will accept that job in China pending my return from Norway. I will have to learn to speak Chinese before I can instruct the young would-be pilots."

Coming back to the present, his glance took in hazy smoke far ahead and he frowned. His reverie was interrupted. He was nearly at the Milwaukee airfield. "Here I come," he said to himself, "and ready or not, Brinks, I'll be on the field in ten minutes."

As he approached the field for a landing, he saw the Brinks armored truck driving onto the field and also two police cars posted at the entrances to the airfield and he laughed to himself. He wondered who would protect him for the next 85 miles on his return trip to Oshkosh. "What trust Ben has in me. All alone with half-a-million dollars and I so desperately need only a thousand to fly to Norway. Ironic!

"A turn south, east or west and I am a very rich man. Such thoughts belong to an ambition of flying to the moon. Not that I don't think that will happen in the not-too-distant future," he told himself. "I am sure it will.

"Motor cut, and gliding soundlessly, except for the wind singing in the wires, a nice smooth glide," he thought, "a slight bump and my wheels are on the ground. Another perfect landing, I hope that happens in Norway, too"

Taxiing across the field to meet the Brinks truck, he saw two armed guards walking toward the plane, guns very much in evidence, They requested Clyde's credentials: his flying license, his I.D. and the letter from Ben authorizing them to release the money. He also gave them a receipt for the money signed by Ben. "Now if I take off with it, Ben has signed that he has it. What fun! Get thee behind me Satan."

The armored truck men were surprised to see Clyde. "You all alone?" they asked in amazement. "No policeman with you? You must be a stockholder of the bank."

"No," Clyde answered, tongue in cheek, "in the Trust Department."

The guards and Clyde removed the money bags from the Brinks armored truck and placed them in the airplane, stacking them carefully, balancing the weight evenly. The men shook hands with Clyde, and wishing him "Good Luck" on the trip back to Oshkosh, they left.

Grinning sardonically to himself, Clyde stepped on the wing, swung his long legs over the side and slipped into the pilot's seat. He was definitely amused that it had been necessary for Brinks to have three armed guards in an armored truck and two police cars in the offing to deliver the money to him. He, unarmed and all alone, would take off and fly into the wide blue yonder with half-a-million dollars. His mind shifted to Don and him, picturing them, in Don's old yellow clunker, carrying the money from the Oshkosh Airport to the bank. "Our armored car," he laughed, "How ironic, ridiculous!

"Still, I flew a crew of mining engineers to Chiquita, Mexico for Bellstmore and Thomas when I was flying out of Negaunee, Michigan. And I flew a load of gold back to Kansas from the mines. I was alone then, too. Guess I am to be forever thwarted in the money business by carrying it for others. Wish some of it would rub off on me."

Taxiing north into the slight breeze to give the plane lift, he took off for Oshkosh. He felt like doing a few loops and spins just for the hell of it, but refrained. It always affected him that way. Flying on such a beautiful, balmy day. In fact flying on any kind of day. Flying! He had never gotten over that jolt of joy he experienced every time he lifted off in a plane. Today was no exception.

And then he felt the same sensations he had felt the first time he had flown at dawn. "The exhilaration of flying, itself, I suppose has something to do with my love for it, for it is magnificent. Dawn is breaking, you are sitting on a small board with a stick in your hand, flying. The noise of the engine is there, but you accept that and forget it. The earth below you is like some schoolroom sandbox project. There are the tiny white houses and red barns and checkerboard fields dotted with cows. Above you all is pale blue with patches of white clouds. Flying at dawn the air is damp with still falling dew, and the lushness of growing things is in the breeze as it slaps you in the face, pastes your eyelashes to your cheeks, and capriciously pulls and switches your hair into a tangle. In front of you the first pale rays of the sun are sending the signals of another day ahead as the red ball, old Sol, himself, slowly emerges over the horizon. I can't explain the feeling of exultation that seethed within me in those days when I flew in the early morn. It came from within and forced feelings of deepest emotion. I could have shouted except it was too awesome, or I could have leaped for joy, except it would have been dangerous. I was too overcome with rapture to move. With a moving spectacle like that in view, one can understand the savage Indian dances to the dawn, which caused them to thrust fire brands into their mouths and about their bodies in the frenzy of their ecstasy. I guess emotionally we aren't nearly as remote from the savage as we would like to think."

The plane was flying itself as he recalled his bygone emotionally rich experiences. Thoughts of his coming flight and the problems to be solved before he could leave for Harbor Grace returned. They were rarely out of his mind. He desperately needed a few hundred, possibly only five hundred dollars to buy all he needed to put his plane in excellent condition and put all to rights for that long ocean hop. He knew and appreciated the help his friends were giving him.

It was unfair! He was flying, unattended, in a plane carrying bags of money to save the city. "I do wish the city would save me. It is like the saying, 'Water, water everywhere and not a drop to drink.' This time it's 'bags and bags of money and none for Clyde,' or is it, 'Baa, Baa black sheep...and I am the little boy who cries in the lane?'"

184

His thoughts were on the things his friends were planning to do for his cause. Benefits planned in the near future: A pavement dance in Oshkosh, a dance at the Eagles Club House. The Junior Chamber of Commerce had donated $100.00 and members were planning other events to raise funds. The Chamber of Commerce had also donated a special leather jacket with the insignia, "Junior Chamber of Commerce" name and insignia on the back. Vernon Johnson donated money for 350 yards of special fabric for the 'skin' of the plane.

He thought about Roy and how he missed him and his advice. "He truly made history when he built his airport in 1924. His was the first airport in Wisconsin complete with hangar that succeeded. Doc Ross at Sturtevant in 1927 with his plans for an air city was a great dream but it folded during the Depression. And then Oshkosh, late in 1927, with Dick Lutz as president. He sold 100 acres of his own land to the city for their airport. Milwaukee County Airport and Currie Park weren't permanent airports until long after Roy's hangar and field–1927 at the earliest, I know. And Appleton was a year after Oshkosh.

"Hard times hit Roy too, but he persisted and succeeded. At one time he only charged 50 cents a ride per person...$1.00 for two. Roy, a legend in his own time...I like that."

His thoughts returned to other things needing to be done. He should leave within the next two weeks for the weather to be favorable. Chances of getting his new motor and fittings which he needed for ocean flying in that length of time were slim. His sister Evelyn and her husband Ray had donated $500.00 for the new engine, but he hadn't been able to find the right model engine at that price. The best he had been able to find was a reconditioned one with a cracked head. If he had to attempt the flight with that, he didn't think it would hold up.

Approaching the Oshkosh Airport, he saw Don's yellow car parked far out on the edge of the field. He began to laugh. "There sits my armored truck and Don the armed guard. Where are the two police cars? Just Don and I and all that moola."

He brought the plane down near Don's car. He taxied over as near as possible. Clyde handed the bags of money to Don who quickly packed them in the trunk of his car. Don drove to the parking lot at the airport. Clyde taxied his plane to the hangar, parked it in its slot, and left.

One of the hangers-on at the airport asked him where he'd been?

"No luck where I've been," he answered, walking over to Don's car.

Fitting himself into it again they took off for the bank. "Ya know," Don said, "I've been thinking the bank owes you plenty for this trip of yours today. Maybe they'll reward you with a healthy amount, a donation towards your flight, or just a generous donation to you for services rendered. You have certainly saved the bank from receivership. They should reward you in some financial way. They would've had to pay Brink's much more than twenty dollars and Brinks wouldn't come. Present the bank with a bill and see what happens."

"They don't consider flying a business, Don. No one does. People still think it's all fun and games. They wouldn't understand. I sure as hell hope they do pay me more than for my gas."

Further conversation was exclusively devoted to Clyde giving Don a vivid description of the handling of the money which was so vigilantly guarded in Milwaukee.

"Where's your gun, Don?" Clyde asked him, "and your armored car? What! No police escort? I expected better of you."

Don laughed. They chuckled most of the way to the bank.

The last hour of the banking day had been tense. The lobby was teeming with depositors determined to withdraw their money even though the rumor had been explained to them. It was so crowded in the bank lobby, it became impossible to maintain two lines to the tellers' windows. The people jostled each other for position and some, more rude than others, actually stepped in front of people who had been waiting in line much longer. Tempers flared! Fist fights threatened.

The relieved custodian closed and locked the doors promptly at 6:00 PM, telling those outside to come back Tuesday when the bank would be open for business as usual.

Two lines of people lined up outside, converging on the bank. The police were keeping them in orderly position. One line stretched a block North and the other line, South. They knew it was after closing hours, but still they remained. Some shook the doors, others pounded on the doors angrily shouting, "Open up!"

Ben walked over to the closed glass doors. He pointed to the sign stating the bank's hours, then pointed to his watch as he held it up for them to see the time. The custodian remarked he hoped they weren't going to stand outside in the street all weekend until Tuesday morning.

Customers still in the bank after the doors were locked were allowed to conclude their business. Ben circulated among them explaining the rumor and denying any cause for alarm. "The bank is solvent and will reopen on Tuesday, the day after the holiday," he reaffirmed time and time again. Some listened and understood the reason for the rumor. Sheepishly they stepped out of line and left.

As they went out the door, some called to those outside to go home, that it was all an April Fool joke. "The bank is fine and your money is safe. Enjoy your three-day-weekend holiday, especially Monday," one joked. Gradually the lines of people diminished and by the time it was dark the street was empty.

No one saw Ben, Clyde and Don Agrell carry the heavy money bags into the bank and place them in the vault. "A half-million dollars," said Ben, with great satisfaction. "That should do it."

"Don and I are thinking of going in competition with Brinks come Tuesday," quipped Clyde.

He never did bill the bank for his trip to Milwaukee, nor did the bank ever offer to help fund his flight to Norway. Like most of the people of Oshkosh, the bankers couldn't take one of their own seriously. He was just Clyde Lee, that crazy flyboy. They couldn't believe that he would ever do anything great.

A Farewell Party

On the last Sunday night in July, 1932, we had a picnic farewell party for Clyde at Clarks Point on Lake Winneconne. The pretty little lake was aglow with moonlight as we sang the old songs around the flickering light of the huge bonfire. It was a beautiful, pleasantly warm night following a day of festivities and party making. Later, after several of the guests had left for a dance at Waverly Beach, we gathered around the low burning campfire. Looking through the hanging leafy branches across the lake, we observed unusual phenomena taking place in the sky. It appeared to be the northern lights flashing brightly. So clearly I could see the reflection plainly on the rippling water of the lake.

Although the earth lay in greatest stillness, the skies themselves were sportive in gleeful play. Giant pincers of light flashed upward from the horizon on all sides. Tapering fingers of light reaching up and over the middle of the sky, quivering there, bursting with light and retreating back to their source only to start all over again, pulsing, straining to reach some goal we knew not of. These pincers of colors came from all sides like a gigantic bombardment. They dwarfed the large yellow moon flanked by millions of stars. We were silent, hushed, almost cowed by the unusual manifestations of nature and the heavens. Observing it, I became aware of a feeling of breathlessness, of suspension, and at the same time glory flooding through me, leaving me awed, humbled, and yet somehow gratified. Pleased that I was privileged to witness such a show.

Nothing stirred. It was too quiet there, too peaceful. It was as if the birds and beasts and in fact the whole world had found itself in some giant cathedral and prostrated its very soul in prayers of adulation and thanksgiving.

After a few minutes, I felt as if I had to speak and yet I was too full of emotion to speak. I glanced at Clyde standing near me. He, too, was watching the panorama before us. He sensed my glance. He suddenly bent and seated himself at the foot of an oak tree and leaning back said softly, "I wish I were up there in my ship. I wish I were on my way to Norway tonight, watching that glorious sight from up there over the ocean. The outcome of the flight wouldn't matter too much one way or the other and what better finale could one ask for?

"It is predicted that at about midnight tonight we will see the greatest spectacle of northern lights of this generation. It is an aurora borealis that will not appear again until after the year 2000.

"One man's importance in this world is even more infinitesimal than that bonfire as compared to God's handiwork up there. God or nature," Clyde said, "can you distinguish between them. Are they the same? Or if they be different can one tell where one begins and the other ends?"

The shimmering, radiant lights, myriad with rainbow colors streaked from the horizon to the very zenith over head. Then shiveringly retreated, only to streak outward and upward again in a constant pulsing movement from the entire horizon upward. This was the greatest display of fireworks imaginable. Awesome!

As I stood there my very soul seemed to expand. The magnificence of the spectacle gripped me and I swelled with emotion. I thought magnificent thoughts about the immensity of the universe, the puniness of man, compared with God's great powers. His wonders to conceive were striving for articulation from my lips, but I could not express them and so was silent.

Our friends were totally silent, in awe as were we. It was a long time before anyone moved or spoke. A bird chirped, breaking the stillness, someone sighed deeply and the spell was broken. Each tried to express his reverence, his amazement at the wondrous spectacle, but how puny were the words. Again, silence prevailed. The twittering of the birds grew, the light was so bright they thought it was morning. They were awakening for the day to come.

"Clyde said suddenly, "All things pass, but His wonders never cease."

It was with a strange mixture of emotion that these words struck us. Was he thinking of himself and his flight to Norway?

He added, "Tis like a life span. Man forges ahead, is defeated, timidly ventures again, succeeds, streaks boldly forward into the zenith of his career

190

and in old age shrinks back to the beginning as his powers wane, weaken and he dies. And the life he created, the next generation, forges anew again ad infinitum."

I added a mental "Amen."

It was a night in which one had to give thought, deep thought and search one's soul. A deep humility dwelt within me. I did not, now, attempt to speak. I thought of people in symbolism, artists statues of the pioneers forging ahead, some falling by the wayside. Thinking further of the myriad of colors in this spectacle before us, it seemed to me that those giving forth color were the kindly people, the understanding ones, who paused in their progress to give a lift to their fellow man, a pat on the back, a kind word, a kind deed or even just a friendly smile.

An atheist could quickly gain religion on a night such as this. The sun, moon and stars are an accepted fact, but a mystery. This is complete mystery. "Soon, during our generation's life span," Clyde predicted, "We will land a man on the moon. It is inevitable that we do. Our technology is moving ahead in leaps and bounds. I am thankful to have been born at this time, to be a part of that progress.

"I am an example of the swift progress we have made in the last 25 years. I was born in a log cabin built by my parents. They sawed the trees for the logs to build the house. They split some to make furniture.

"Now, I am about to fly the ocean in a single motor monoplane. That progress seems impossible. People were travelling by horse and buggy when I was born. Some were using teams of oxen. Trains were the newest form of transportation. Airplanes were in the vision of three or four people in the world, and the Wright brothers.

"Whether we are successful in reaching Norway, or not, we are blazing a trail, others will follow, technology will expand. The future is limitless or complete extinction."

Vermont

On July 23, 1932 Clyde visited Barre/Montpelier, Vermont to seek backing for his flight. J. Carleton Jones, manager of the Appleton, Wisconsin airport and a former resident of Barre, accompanied Clyde and introduced him to Emory Denis, Airport Manager, and Paul Marsigli, who would be handling local arrangements for Lee. They drove to Vermont by automobile. Clyde inspected the flying field and found it to be suitable lengthwise and groundwise for his needs.

Clyde remained in Barre a little over a week. While there he attended the Charity Air Show at the airport and talked with several men who were likely to sponsor the flight. They felt that the flight would promote Barre's granite industry and more than return their money.

Mayor La Point urged the city council to investigate the idea thoroughly, and the city fathers considered it favorably as an advertising stunt for Barre/Montpelier which, they believed, had the finest granite in the United States.

Within the week after his return home to Wisconsin Lee received a telegram from Barre officials offering him $1,000.00 if he would change the point of origin of the flight from Oshkosh to Barre/Montpelier. Barre promised $500.00 and the same sum would be forwarded from Montpelier. A few days later a check in that amount arrived and Clyde immediately paid for and received the newly reconstructed motor and some necessary instruments.

The transatlantic airmen left the Oshkosh airport at 12:30 PM Friday, August 5, 1932 bound for Barre/Montpelier. Along with Clyde in the airplane were Earl Iverson, manager; Fred Sensaba, mechanic; Knute Hansen, assistant mechanic; and William Bradley, son of publicist Arthur Bradley. They planned to remain over night in Buffalo, New York, but encountered a severe storm at Erie, Pennsylvania and remained there until the next day. Clyde wired Oshkosh friends that they had landed in Erie, after five hours and twenty minutes of flying, at an average speed of 114 miles an hour.

The airplane was operating well. After taking on 60 gallons of gasoline, Clyde left Erie on Saturday morning and arrived at Barre at 3:30 P.M. Saturday afternoon. They were warmly welcomed at the airport where a large group of people were waiting to greet them.

The civic organizations of Barre/Montpelier had named the plane the *Green Mountain Boy*, in honor of a Vermont State hero. The plane was red and the letters spelling "Green Mountain Boy, Barre/Montpelier Vermont, Granite Center of the World" were in white.

Julius Robertson, co-pilot, arrived by automobile at Erie airport just as Clyde was taking off for Vermont. With him was Fred Meyer, a friend of his. Bradley changed from the plane to the car at Erie, Pennsylvania. Speed Holman had expected to make the trip by auto in three days. They arrived in Barre on Sunday, the day after Clyde.

Arriving at their Vermont destination on Saturday, August 6, Earl and Art, business managers of the flight, began making arrangements to have benefit flying exhibitions to raise money to pay their daily expenses and gas for the trip across the Atlantic.

The pilots held exhibitions on two Sundays and carried passengers aloft. Attendance was much larger than anticipated since people were excited and eager to meet the two flyers. They wished them the best of luck on their trip. Reporters interviewed them and extolled their courage and enterprise in attempting the flight.

"If this trip across the Atlantic is successful," Clyde stated to a reporter, "I plan to attempt a return trip by plane to the U.S., west across the Atlantic. I would follow the route of Captain Wolfgang Von Gronau via Iceland and Greenland. I would then be the first pilot to fly round trip crossing the Atlantic to Europe and home.

A "Bon Voyage" meet was held at the airport for Lee and Robertson on Saturday and Sunday, August 15 and 16. Prominent eastern flyers took part in the meet. It was planned for the residents of the Vermont cities to meet the flyers and have a close look at the plane. On Saturday a noon radio program was broadcast from Waterbury, Vermont with pilots Lee and Robertson and members of the Barre, Montpelier flight committee as speakers.

The following Thursday, August 19th, Clyde flew the *Green Mountain Boy* to Portland, Maine where he obtained final clearance papers for the flight from the Department of Commerce.

The trip was delayed in Vermont nearly three weeks awaiting arrival of 40 extra five-gallon gasoline cans. Then once the cans arrived it was necessary to check any magnetic attraction the metal cans might have toward the compass. Any deviation in accuracy could lead the plane far off course and would be a life-and-death matter.

A few days before taking off for Harbor Grace, Clyde flew to Roosevelt Field, near New York City. There, he was told the red Stinson Senior Cabin plane he was piloting was the most beautifully designed plane to ever set down in that airport. *The Green Mountain Boy* attracted lots of attention while it was at the flying field. Crowds of people, mostly flyers, gathered around to admire and talk about its finer points.

The plane received a final check and Clyde also purchased navigational equipment which he needed for better directional flight over the ocean. The newsreel people were there and took footage of Clyde and his plane. Pictures appeared in the Gotham newspapers and on newsreels in the theaters.

At Roosevelt, he met John Bochkon, a former pilot from the Norwegian Navy. When he heard Clyde was flying to Norway, Bochkon told him he was interested in going with him. He had six years experience flying in the Norwegian Navy and money to pay his passage. He added that he would like to go home and visit his parents. A tentative agreement was reached and he flew to Vermont with Clyde to talk to Julius Robertson. He agreed to step down and John Bochkon became the copilot.

Twenty-eight years old, four years older than Clyde, Bochkon began his flying career at age 20 in the Norwegian Naval Air force. Unmarried, he had migrated to the United States seven years earlier and had worked as a pilot and an engineer.

On August 22, Clyde and his new co-pilot learned that two other pilots were planning an immediate flight to Norway. Now Clyde's flight might turn into a race. Thor Solberg and Carl Peterson, Viking descendants, planned to take off from New York at daybreak on August 23. They were to follow, in reverse, the route of the first Norsemen to cross the Atlantic ocean to the North American continent.

Thor Solberg was an old time motorcycle racer and Carl Peterson was with Admiral Byrd in the Arctic. Both were experienced adventurers who

195

planned to fly a Bellanca Sesqui airplane out of Harbor Grace, Newfoundland on the same day the *Green Mountain Boy* was leaving Barre for Harbor Grace.

With Thor Solberg piloting, they lifted off from Bennett Field in New York at 4:43 AM, headed for Harbor Grace, ten flying hours away. They planned to refuel at Harbor Grace and takeoff immediately for Norway. Their route would carry them first to Scotland and then to Oslo, about 24 hours away.

They were observed flying over Port Greville, Nova Scotia, in the Bay of Fundy, about 800 miles from Harbor Grace at 12:25 PM. They were spotted over Hermitage, on the southeastern coast of Newfoundland at 5:26 PM.

Back in Vermont, the departure of the *Green Mountain Boy*, was delayed by dense fog. Clyde was at the controls when the Stinson finally lifted off at 10:18 AM, with John Bochkon in the co-pilot's seat. Approximately 1,000 enthusiastic people witnessed their departure. They shook hands all around as the admiring crowd wished them the best of good luck and bon voyage.

Shortly before take off reporters of the United Press questioned Clyde, regarding the race. He told them, "I don't know whether it is a race or not. I had heard nothing about it or their flight plans until yesterday. We had planned on beginning our flight as soon as we were ready. Today we are ready.

"We will know more when we get to Harbor Grace. They may get a considerable head start over the Atlantic. Our departure today has been delayed because of the fog.

"Whether it is a race or not doesn't matter. We are looking forward to setting our plane down at Jkeller Field, Oslo, Norway, 32 hours after leaving Harbor Grace."

At takeoff, the *Green Mountain Boy* was carrying 200 gallons of gasoline and a load of empty cans, which would be filled with 400 more gallons at Harbor Grace. Their itinerary ran via Augusta, Maine; St. John, New Brunswick; East Point, Prince Edward Island; and Cape Ray, Newfoundland. They expected to make the 977 mile flight in approximately nine hours.

A plane believed to be a red Stinson, the *Green Mountain Boy*, passed over St. John, New Brunswick at 1:00 PM, flying toward Harbor Grace. The plane was too high to be definitely identified but no other planes were expected to be in the area that day.

As both planes headed towards Harbor Grace, they flew into an unexpected and severe storm with hail, blasting rain and even some snow. At Harbor Grace heavy rain was falling and a strong east-northeast wind was blowing. Towards evening a thick fog settled over the airport. The latest report of a plane flying towards Harbor Grace came from Belloram, 120 miles away. That was shortly before nightfall and the plane was not identified.

As dusk settled in, and no word was received from either of the planes heading for Norway, Harbor Grace became quite anxious. Officials there placed lighted flares around the edge of the airport to guide the flyers to the airfield. To further illuminate the airport, they parked automobiles with their headlights switched on in a circle at the center of the field. But no aircraft landed there that night.

When Clyde encountered the storm he recognized its dangers and reluctantly set the Stinson down on a barren beach at Burgeo Bay to wait it out. Since he had decided that a radio–whose battery might emit sparks that would ignite the fuel carried in the fuselage–was too dangerous, Clyde and Bochkon had no contact with the outside world. They were cold, wet and uncomfortable, with one wing of the Stinson slightly damaged. On the other hand, they were alive and well and could continue on to Harbor Grace and the ocean at daybreak–if they were not too late.

The dawn of August 24 saw the pilots of the *Green Mountain Boy* making minor repairs to the damaged wing. To gain traction in the sand for takeoff, they softened the tires by taking air out of them. All this effort took time and would delay their departure from Harbor Grace. They had no way of knowing how Solberg and Peterson had fared in the storm. While Lee and Bochkon were stuck on the beach at Burgeo Bay, their rivals might have made Harbor Grace, refueled overnight and could now be over the Atlantic on the way to Norway.

When they first encountered the storm, Solberg and Peterson also considered landing at Burgeo Bay, but decided it was unsafe. The storm worsened and Solberg attempted to force his plane to 5,000 feet to get above the turbulence. Instead, he flew into a snow storm. His engine stalled as he climbed and, before he could restart it, the Bellanca nose dived and crashed into the frigid waters of Placentia Bay.

Fortunately, both men were uninjured and the plane remained afloat. Fishermen soon discovered them and towed the Bellanca ashore at Darby's Harbor. It was a very small settlement of five families, isolated from the outside world, with no way for the flyers to tell anyone in Harbor Grace–or anywhere else–of their whereabouts. They were feared lost until the next day, when Douglas Fraser, a St. John's aviator, spotted the plane at Darby's Harbor, flew home and reported the crash.

Now all thought of a race to Norway between two contending teams of aviators was over. The Bellanca was too severely damaged to fly. The assault on the North Atlantic was reserved for John Bochkon and Clyde Lee.

Harbor Grace

After they got their plane off the sand of Burgeo Bay, Clyde and Bochkon headed for Harbor Grace. They set the *Green Mountain Boy* down on the airfield there on Wednesday August 24, 1932, more than 22 hours after they had left Barre/Montpelier.

Both men were weary and strained from the struggle with the plane during the storm and the forced landing. They had spent a freezing, tense night in the unheated, uninsulated cramped cabin of an airplane, with wind and rain howling outside, their heads only inches away from a tank containing 100 gallons of aviation fuel. They could take some comfort in the knowledge that they had weathered the storm with better luck than their rivals Solberg and Peterson–but neither was the kind of man to find joy in another's misfortune.

Weary, but undaunted, they set about making preparations for departure early the next morning. John topped up the gas tanks and filled the empty five-gallon cans. They needed a total of 450 gallons to sustain the plane for 37 hours. The price of gasoline was much higher than expected at Harbor Grace so Clyde was forced to contact his managers, Earl Iverson and Art Bradley, to forward money for it. They didn't have enough to cover the cost, so Clyde had to call his cousin, Leighton Hough, in Oshkosh, who forwarded more.

The damaged wing, slightly torn and bent in the storm at Burgeo Bay, was repaired. New spark plugs were installed, and other necessary adjustments made. Clyde checked every inch of the interior and exterior of the fuselage for any undetected damage. The wing caused the greatest concern, but he was confident the repairs would work.

"I believe that will do it," he said. "Now I am satisfied the plane can weather any conditions or crises we might encounter on our journey. Everything has checked out O.K."

Then they checked their supplies: five gallons of water, sandwiches, a quart of milk, a quart thermos of hot coffee, and enough concentrated food tablets to last about a month. Besides extra underwear, the only clothing they carried was on their backs. They also brought a bottle of ammonia to whiff when sleep threatened to overtake them.

Also included was a one-and-one-half-inch, foot-long, silver-colored, metallic cylinder, containing their identification and destination. It would lie loose in the fuselage in the hope that, if they ditched, it would float to shore and somewhere, someone would find it.

They put a large open-mouthed sack in the tail into which they would toss the 5-gallon gas cans as they emptied them. The air trapped in the sealed cans would–they hoped–keep the plane afloat if they had to ditch into the ocean. To carry more gas cans and make the plane more watertight, they had sealed the cabin doors and cut a hatchway in the roof so they could climb in and out. Also to aid flotation, they packed a hacksaw in the tool box. If necessary they would use it to lighten the plane by cutting through the engine mounts and dumping it.

They packed a 500-foot-beam flashlight and flares in case of a night emergency landing. An ex-Boy Scout, Clyde believed in the motto, "Be Prepared." Their tool box carried a pliers, screw driver, sand paper and a Boy Scout knife. A prankster donated a fish line complete with bobbin, hook and sinker.

"What, no bait?" quipped Clyde.

"That's us," laughed Bochkon. "Shark bait."

"Not funny." Clyde said, "Wittman at Oshkosh suggested we take along 100 pounds of hamburger to feed the sharks on the way down.

"I didn't appreciate his suggestion then, either."

At the last minute they scuttled plans to take a raft and paddles. That would reduce the weight of the loaded plane by 35 pounds and every pound dropped made for an easier takeoff. They kept the yellow silk kite for attracting ships at sea in case of an emergency landing. That is, if the plane floated.

"The plane, loaded, weighs 5,400 pounds," said Clyde. "That weight will determine our speed and speed is of extreme importance. The greater the weight, the less speed we will have in the beginning of the flight. With our planned load, the beginning speed will be between 80 to 90 miles an hour. As we use the fuel and the weight lessens, our speed will increase. Over three-fourths of the ocean it should average 95-100 miles per hour. From the British Isles to Oslo it should increase to 110 to 130 miles per hour. 130 miles an hour is the maximum speed this Stinson can attain."

When all the needed supplies were ready to board in the morning, the two exhausted pilots sought their beds in the hotel for a much needed night's sleep. As they walked along, they became aware of a light fog slowly drifting in. It brought uncomfortable memories of their problems the previous night.

"We should be over the British Isles in thirty hours, if the weather predictions hold," said Clyde.

Hubert Huntington was their weatherman. He remained in Vermont and telegraphed his predictions to Harbor Grace. He had been analyzing conditions over the Atlantic and had OK'ed the weather conditions for the next day. His telegram read, "The storm 600 miles at sea Wednesday has moved north and out of your path."

The weather report for the next two days also appeared to be excellent. "Sunny days and a slight tail wind to help them along." The two pilots decided that was the information they needed. They would take off early the next morning.

Lying in bed at the hotel, sleep eluded Clyde. Tired as he was, last minute thoughts troubled him. Thoughts of possible errors in planning ran through his mind. Had yesterday's storm and landing at Burgeo Bay damaged the plane more than he thought? Had the structure possibly been weakened?

Had the wing, slightly torn loose and bent by the emergency landing in that violent storm, been damaged to such an extent it might be unable to withstand the buffeting turbulence they might encounter on the flight?

Had their repairs been sufficient? Had some vital step in preparation been omitted, forgotten?

Could the weather report from Canada be erroneous? Was Hubert Huntington correct that the storm reported 600 miles at sea yesterday and directly on their course, had moved north as predicted?

Some storms didn't move for days. It was late August now, instead of early July. The ocean was much colder. Would ice forming on the wings be heavier now than in July? If so, would the extra weight force them to use more gasoline to stay aloft? If that happened would they have enough fuel to carry them to Norway?

Theirs would be the fourth attempt by Americans to reach Norway. All the others had failed, and been lost at sea. Lieutenant Umdahl and Francis Grayson left Old Orchard, Maine in 1928 in the monoplane "Dawn", and were never heard from again. Bert Hassel and Parker Cramer tried in 1929, but cracked up in Greenland. In September, 1931, Cramer made a second attempt, but the wreckage of his plane had been found floating in the Greenland sea, a grim sight.

"Well," reflected Clyde, as he drifted off to sleep, "three times and out. We will be the ones to make the successful trip."

They arrived at the air field Thursday morning at 4:00 AM cheerful and refreshed. Clyde was wearing a special leather jacket bearing the inscription of the Oshkosh Junior Chamber of Commerce. He was the first and probably the only transoceanic flyer to wear a jacket bearing that inscription during a flight.

The lettering on the plane's wings was "NR7576." According to international code, the "N" designated the plane was from the United States of America, the "R" restricted the plane to cross-ocean flying.

The pilots checked everything once more. John had supervised the loading of their perishable supplies. He checked again. They started the engine and let it warm up for nearly an hour. Clyde kept his eyes and ears open, watching for problems, listening for any engine noises he didn't want to hear. Everything appeared normal, ready for takeoff.

Before dawn a large group of people had already congregated to see them off. After hearty hand shakes and good wishes, the flyers climbed into the cockpit, waved a last good-bye, closed the overhead hatch, revved the engine, and began to move out slowly. It was 6:02 AM in Harbor Grace, 5:02 AM in Vermont, 4:02 AM in Oshkosh.

The heavily-laden plane appeared cumbersome and sluggish. It would be hard getting the "lift" needed to raise it off the ground. Clyde taxied twice around the field to get the feel of it with the new load, then he turned toward the center of the runway. He revved the motor to full speed and slowly the Stinson rose into the air.

Once up in the air, he circled the field twice, dipped the wings in farewell and headed toward Goose Bay. The Stinson flew into a cloudless early morning dawn. Sunrise was peaking over the rim, streaking along the horizon, rippling across the waves.

As they flew over the bay, the Stinson dropped and nearly touched the water. Clyde regained control and the plane rose, but was still low enough to leave a wake of waves behind it.

They flew over the little village of Goose Bay and the waiting crowd went wild—waving, clapping, screaming and jumping. As a farewell salute, Clyde dipped his wings again and again while he circled the town several times. Finally, he turned eastward in farewell to the North American continent, bound for Norway, to make a reality of his dream.

Interlude

Clyde sighted down the nose of the Stinson into the rising sun. Oslo was 3,150 miles from Harbor Grace, at least 30 hours of flying–providing the weather was fair. Clyde had selected a route that would minimize the time they would spend over the ocean, without having to fly over the frigid wastes of Greenland or fog-bound Iceland. The route of the *Green Mountain Boy* arched over the Atlantic to Dublin, Ireland and on to Boston, England and Cuxhaven on the North Sea coast of Germany. Then the plane would swing northeast to make its triumphant landing in Oslo.

At this point, the historical record all but stops. We do know that the severe storm that was supposed to have moved past Clyde's route across the sea, did not move. We do know that all aircraft in the British Isles were grounded due to fog. At this point, newspapers reported that a patrol unit of the "Automobile association" heard the sound of an airplane engine off the coast of Wales at just about the place and just about the time the *Green Mountain Boy* would have flown over--if the storm delay had lasted about five hours.

I flew with Clyde many times in sunshine and rain and electrical storms. I know that if anyone could have made it through that storm, it would have been Clyde. But no pilot–no matter how skillful–can keep a motorized aircraft aloft with empty fuel tanks. The ultimate fate of Clyde Lee and John Bochkon is unknown.

The stories Clyde tells John in the following pages are all true. I have exercised the author's license to invent a scene in which to tell a true story.

Neither pilot spoke for a time. It was such an exciting phenomenon, just being there. Clyde broke the silence, his voice emotional, "In thirty hours, John, our dream will come true or it will become a nightmare. For better or worse, this is finally it, and we are on our way."

"Yes," John replied, "and with a good tail-wind just as Huntington predicted.."

"Right now I am not complaining," replied Clyde.

"During the next thirty hours, we will have the problem of staying awake. The monotony of the scenery will put us to sleep, Clyde. I think we'll have to talk ourselves awake. We don't know each other very well. Why don't we begin with you telling me your life story. From what little I've heard, that should eliminate any monotony from the trip. It sounds as if it has been pretty thrilling and full of surprises. Is it fame or fortune that drives you?"

"A little of both, I guess," Clyde replied. "What makes one follow a dream? That's the only answer I have. I had a dream of flying to Norway. Roy Larson conceived the idea originally. He often talked to me about it, making plans. We barnstormed together around the state of Wisconsin eight years ago. It was just one of Roy's dreams then.

"What happened to Roy?"

"He was killed in a plane crash.

"Roy began dreaming his Norway dream two years before Lindbergh made his flight to Paris. Who knows? He might have tried it.

"My first interest in aviation was encouraged by letters received from my dad who was in the 32nd Division in the First World War. He enlisted in Canada to be a pilot and took flying lessons at Croydon Field, London, England. He washed out as a fighter pilot. They only wanted daring young men in their twenties. Dad was thirty-five at that time.

"Because he was an excellent mechanic, they made him an inspector of airplanes in France. Flying wasn't ruled out completely. It was his job to test-fly each plane after repairs had been made and before it was returned to the pilot. He flew the planes behind the lines before he OK'ed them for the fighter pilots. A combat pilot he never was. Just a frustrated one. He recounted his flying experiences over there to me and stimulated my imagination. At first I flew paper airplanes as most kids do, even nowadays.

"When I was a ten-year-old kid, living with the Frank Clarks, Uncle Frank bought oranges by the crate. The wood of the crates was soft and I whittled airplanes out of it. The propellers were powered by rubber bands. Those were the most exciting and amusing childhood toys I had. My enthusiasm for aviation was fostered way back then.

"Roy Larson was my hero, teacher and friend. It all began for me when he made his first flight from the Larson Brothers' Airport.

"My grandparents Lea lived near Larsen and their daughter and her husband lived across the road from the Larson brothers' airport. Working as hired boy for Uncle Ted the summer Roy began flying, it was inevitable, I had to get into the act. Roy recognized and encouraged my enthusiasm for flying. He taught me to fly when I was sixteen and we did a lot of exhibition flying for money. We shared many harrowing experiences before I branched out on my own.

"When airmail became popular, I not only encouraged Mayor Oaks to become interested in getting that service for Oshkosh, I flew him to Chicago to convene with the people who might be interested in establishing an airmail route to Milwaukee, Oshkosh, Green Bay and on to northern Wisconsin and Minnesota.

"Speed Holman, an aviator well known throughout the Midwest, flew the first airmail to Oshkosh on that route. That was a red letter day for Oshkosh. It also stimulated my ambitions to become an airmail pilot.

"A year ago, I passed all the tests for airmail pilot but they turned me down as too young. I was 23 then, and you had to be 28 years old to qualify.

"A second Lieutenant, Yeager, was the officer who tested me. It was winter time and I had to fly on and off the ice. I passed with a 96 grade, but my youth was against me. They wouldn't hire me. Frankly, I think it was my reputation of being a daredevil that was against me.

"All those years, the idea of flying to Norway was in the back of my mind. A memorial to Roy Larson. When I couldn't find a lucrative way of earning my living flying, I heard there was a $10,000 reward awaiting the first person to fly transatlantic to Oslo, Norway.

"One time, while I was flying in Michigan, a wheel fell off the landing gear on takeoff. I wasn't aware of it, until people on the ground gained my attention. With hand signals they alerted me to the fact that one wheel had fallen off the plane. It was a stunner when I looked down and saw a wheel from my plane being waved at me in the hands of someone on the ground.

"I thought, 'Roy, here's a problem you never taught me how to handle!' I flew around long enough to use the gas in the plane before attempting a landing. I didn't want the gas to explode. Meanwhile, I was straining my brain to tell me how to land with one wheel. If I didn't do it correctly, I would crash and the plane would land sidewise wrecking the wing and probably me, too. When the gas was nearly gone, I decided to give it a try. I didn't have much choice. What goes up must come down.

"It was a crazy landing, but a successful one and the plane and I were both in good shape when it was over. I learned later that, to the best of anyone's knowledge, at that time, there had only been one other pilot who had successfully landed a plane on one wheel without crashing.

"I have had lots of crazy adventures. One Sunday, Ollie Davies, William Bloechel and I were flying to Mercer, Wisconsin. Ollie had bought a Waco 8 plane, but hadn't taken any flying lessons. He always asked me to fly him wherever he wanted to go.

"We were over a thickly wooded area near Mellen when I felt a sudden jolt and heard a 'whack'. The propeller acted strangely, gave a lurch, caught and whirled on. Looking over the side of the cockpit, I saw a man standing below with a gun aimed at us and it looked as if he was shooting. Fortunately, by that time we were out of range. Had the propeller broken apart, we would have had no chance of landing safely anywhere near there. That area in Wisconsin is called the 'north woods' and it is very wild and rugged, almost solid trees.

"When we put down at our destination, I found bullet holes in the propeller. There were several pieces of lead embedded in the wood. The bullets had cracked the propeller and damaged it beyond repair. It was our lucky day. The propeller held together long enough to fly us to Mercer. Tongue in cheek, one man ventured to suggest the man was a hunter and mistook us for a large bird. 'We grow things big around here,' he added.

"Later, we talked to people who lived in the area. Some said they expected it was moonshiners. There were quite a few living around there. They probably thought Ollie and I were revenue agents sent to spy out and arrest them. I had heard moonshiners were pretty rough on revenue men, but shoot them?

"Another time, Carrold Manse and I were flying across Lake Winnebago. Half way across or about six miles out, the engine quit. I couldn't get it to start, blast or not, I had to glide it with the air waves. Touchy, a close call, a rough landing, but I am here today to tell you about it. I guess I am a pioneer in gliding an airplane. A first.

"I flew to Minneapolis one day and on my way home the motor overheated and I was forced to land in a farmer's field near Boyd, Wisconsin. The field was too short and I took out 75 feet of fencing. The farmer was very angry. I paid him what money I had. After taking on water, I took off again. The plane wasn't ready to fly. The motor was acting sluggish and when I was about 100 feet in the air it nosed down again. It was badly damaged. I hitchhiked home.

"The next day, a second cousin of mine, Vernon Johnson, and I took the train to Stanley, Wisconsin and walked from there to Boyd and to the farm. We dismantled the plane and stored it in the farmer's barn.

"We walked back to Stanley. We were hungry and had only 25 cents between the two of us. We saw Roy and Elwyn West and talked to them but were too proud to ask them for money to take the train home.

"There was a bakery truck nearby and we asked the driver for a ride. It was against company policy, he told us. We flipped a quarter to see whether we ate or bought tobacco and rolled our own cigarettes. The cigarettes won out. We walked on. The further we walked the hungrier we became.

"A few miles down the road, we saw the same bakery truck parked. When we reached it, the driver asked us to guard his truck while he found someone to sell him some gas. Mouth watering more and more at the sight of all those goodies, we agreed. It took quite a while for him to get the gas and we made up stories between ourselves as to how we could talk him into giving us at least one doughnut to share when he returned.

"He not only gave us one doughnut, but two, one for each of us. We didn't have to use any of the fantastic stories we had made up to win him over.

"We walked on to the nearest train depot and waited for a train. When one came, we hopped into an empty box car. A few miles down the track one of the trainmen discovered us and threw us off. We tried that again when the next train came along. It didn't work. We were thrown off again.

"We waited at the nearest depot and boarded the train as passengers. We walked into the coach, picked up a newspaper pretending to read until the conductor came along and asked for our tickets. When they weren't forthcoming, he was very angry and said if the train wasn't already behind schedule, he would pull the chain, stop the train and put us off right in the middle of the marsh we were passing through. He made us get off at the next station. We walked. At night it was so cold we found a straw stack and dug ourselves in. We stayed there until it warmed up the next morning. We finally arrived home, late night of the next day. I was still in my teens when that happened.

"Another time Ollie Davies hired me to fly him out of town on a business trip. We arrived back in Oshkosh very late in the afternoon. The sun was low in the sky and, in order to land into the wind, we had the blinding sun square in our faces. I knew the airport like the back of my hand. I should have had no trouble. A farmer had been cutting hay on the runway. At quitting time he left his rig in the middle of the runway. With the sun in our eyes we didn't see the hay mower. I set the plane down right smack on top of it. It badly damaged the plane and Ollie and I, too. That was a surprise ending for a day's jaunt. Ollie is going to sue the city and the airport for negligence in leaving heavy equipment on the runway.

"I worked at Holterhauf Airport in Milwaukee for a couple of years. I taught flying and mechanics to young would-be aviators. I managed the airport too for a while. As aviation progressed, and politics entered the picture, especially nepotism, I lost the job. I was later told I had lost out to a relative.

"Speaking of flying in Milwaukee, the first airplane flight at the State Fair there was September 16, 1910. Arch Hoxsey, landing in a Wright Biplane, flew straight into the grandstand injuring 8 persons. I wonder what his plane looked like. They were pretty open in those days, not much to them.

"I had a letter from the War Department in China six months ago. It nearly stopped this project. The head of the War Department offered me a job in China heading up the aviation branch, teaching young Chinese men to fly. China needs pilots to fly in the war against Japan. If the job is still open, when I get home, I am thinking of going over there. It sounds like a rare opportunity for a guy like me. I would have gone when the letter came, but I had this Oslo project too far along to quit. Then, too, there was the idea people would believe I had lost my courage to undertake this flight. Very often too much pride isn't good. Anyway, enough, today we are here...tomorrow Oslo!"

The Storm

The Stinson did a little bob and wheel as the wind began to pick up. The ripples on the waves below became ridges and the warm sun shining brightly as the plane now wove in and out of soft, fleecy clouds being blown in from the east. Clyde levelled the plane and his thoughts returned to the dream of Roy Larson that had become the odyssey of Clyde Lee.

"Not to change the subject," said John,"but the weather seems to be changing. There is a haze hanging in the air and the sun is fading. I seriously question the weather mans prediction of perfect weather across the Atlantic, Clyde. The haze is thickening and darkening. The sun is playing hide and seek through the clouds.

"That isn't all," John continued "Take a look at those waves and white caps, wild horses they call them, doubled! From here they look at least 40 feet high. I'll bet some storm ahead of us has whipped them up. I don't like the looks of this."

"I'm worried too," Clyde answered, "the wind is increasing steadily, and racing straight toward us, on a collision course. The gentle tail-wind following us has disappeared. Neither do I like the looks of those clouds forming on the horizon.

"Our sunny skies are rapidly changing. Huntington predicted a clear day with a mild tail-wind. It looks like someone goofed and at our expense, probably our lives.

"It looks like yesterday's storm didn't move. If that's true, let's face it, we are in for one hell of a storm!

"According to both compasses, and both read the same, we are exactly on course, flying at 95 miles an hour. It is 11:15 and we should be about 600 miles due east of Harbor Grace. Right where that storm was yesterday."

John nodded, "If it's that storm, it means using extra gas against the wind and we don't have any. We're short on fuel because we were short of cash to buy the extra we needed for emergencies on the trip. And believe me it looks like we have one big emergency!"

"I don't like the idea of flying in storms, fog or rain. I've had to do that a few times, a flyer becomes so disoriented and misdirected he doesn't know whether he is flying up or down, upside down or sideways. In fact I found it very confusing whenever I was in heavy fog off the coast of Norway."

"I've heard that," Clyde said. "However disagreeable it may be, it looks like we're in for it. It's growing worse, thickening. Take a look at the dark clouds ahead of us. We're heading nonstop into one hell of a storm, a monster. There is no going around it, nor below it. With this heavy load we don`t have a prayer of flying above it, so it'll have to be straight through the middle. Our weight was fine for cruising in good weather. Coping with any storm, we are much too heavy, making our maneuverability, zilch!

"Fool that I am, I depended on Huntington`s weather report. He said he'd telegraphed the Canadian Weather Bureau for weather conditions. They predicted, 'Fine weather for flying the Atlantic. There may be a slight tail-wind. Perfect!' they said. They need to update their technology 100%... or better yet, I'd like one of them to be here right now.

"It makes me wonder what their idea of fine flying conditions over the Atlantic are. Anyway, we're here and flying hell for leather straight into the jaws of Hell! The storm is closing in. We'll soon be in the soup, or the Atlantic Ocean.

"Unfortunately, we've no alternative, there is no farmer's field for a quick landing, no turning tail and flying ahead of it, no choice. What we need is an angel on each wing.

"Our compasses show O.K., we're still on course. All I can hope for is that the wind will not be strong enough to blow us off course.

"You flew a lot in Norway, near the North Pole. Did you ever have any experiences with the Aurora Borealis changing the magnetic compass?"

"When I was flying for the Navy, I heard that it happened to some of the fellows. You see, we didn't have compasses years back and we flew blind. Mostly, we used geographical locations."

"We are going to be flying blind very soon, and we have no geographical locations. I wish I had Leonard Larson here to help me fly through those stormy clouds we have ahead of us today."

"Who is Leonard Larson?" John asked.

"One super flyer," declared Clyde. "I'll tell you later about him flying in clouds in a dense fog in Wisconsin. I'm going to be too busy getting us through this storm if I can. Talk later, if we still can."

Apprehensively, they watched the steadily approaching storm. They heard the distant rumble of thunder and saw flashes of lightning flickering through the clouds. As they drew nearer, they felt the air growing cooler and damp and knew they were flying through the calm before the storm. It became darker and the clouds thickened. Tension grew. Transfixed, they watched the steadily building storm rapidly approaching. Speared through with flashing bolts of lightning, the clouds rolled erratically.

Soon they were flying in dark twilight and it was difficult to determine the sea except for the white caps. A sudden gust of wind struck with full and raging force. The plane staggered under the impact, diving and turning sideways as if to escape the fierce thrust of it. Grappling the stick with strong hands, feet moving swiftly on the rudders, Clyde struggled to keep control of the plane. They felt it drop and rise. They fought to keep the overloaded bird on course...East to Norway. The wind, a banshee cry, whistled and screamed through the wing wires. It was terrifying, but also exciting. Their adrenaline was extremely high.

"It will take both of us to control her now. That wind is too strong. When I was in Miami testing the plane for ocean flying, I was told that in a hurricane these storms gather added strength over water. This is making a believer of me. I have never seen clouds roll over and under and into each other like these."

As he spoke, crackling lightning sliced through the black clouds as ear-splitting peals of thunder reverberated on all sides.

"Uff Da!" exclaimed John. "What a blast! How can we ever live through this! Looks like the end," he shouted over the thunderous noise. "Short and sweet, our trip."

"Yeah," shouted Clyde, "People are always telling me what a durn fool I am to fly. Get myself killed," they told me. "It looks like they're right. We are both a couple of durn fools to be caught out here in this today! Mostly fools for trusting that weather report. Tomorrow will probably be that perfect day they predicted for us today.

"The three sisters of Fate must be giggling gleefully at our predicament. Chanting, "boil and bubble, boil and bubble," while stirring their brew pot. At the moment, I could almost believe we are looking at the gates of Hell and the Devil busily mixing up a bitter brew for us.

"There was a man staying at the Larson Brothers' airport who took tickets for passengers buying a ride. If someone said, 'They didn't want to fly, they wanted to keep their feet on the ground.' He told them, 'That's all right, I have put a box of dirt in the plane for your feet.' Right now, I could use that box of dirt in this plane. It would feel good to have my feet on terra firma. Forget about Norway."

Brilliant lightning blinded them momentarily, surrounding them, lighting their whole vision. An unearthly light...luminous yellow, opalescent green and weirdly bluish-purple fiery lightning danced along the edge of the wings. Thunder crackled almost simultaneously as the lightning flashed and a violent blast of wind again struck the plane. It lurched and dropped. After quick footwork on the ailerons and rudders, the plane rose and steadied. The motor roaring at full speed to counteract the wind pressure against the plane barely kept them aloft. They realized they were not gaining much, if any, mileage.

"Even if the plane doesn't come apart in this storm, we may ditch for lack of fuel. I have it on full speed. That's my main worry. Gas! With this strong wind pushing against us, we may even be moving backwards. And unfortunately with this powerful wind we're burning twice as much fuel as we would normally. This isn't a brief storm. It's worse than anything I have ever flown in before, even in the Blue Ridge Mountains."

"Speaking of coming apart," John said, "We've a damaged wing from the storm at Burgeo Bay, yesterday. How much more of a beating do you think it can take?"

"If it can't take it, we swim," yelled Clyde through his teeth, as he clung grimly to the stick and rudders. John wasn't the only one wondering just how much more battering the frail craft could take before it ditched. There hadn't been enough time and materials available to properly repair the wing at Harbor Grace before their hurried take off for Norway. "Fair weather" had been predicted. The repairs they had made were extensive enough for fair weather conditions.

Suddenly, as if the weather weren't already severe enough, a pattering of rain began, quickly turning into a lashing storm, a sudden deluge battering the plane, blurring the windshield with a mat of water.

"That's adding insult to injury," muttered Clyde. "As if we didn't have more than we could handle with the wind and thunder and lightning."

"I've heard tell," said John, "that when it rains as hard as this, it seldom lasts more than fifteen minutes."

"I hope we last fifteen minutes! And I certainly hope you are right. I don't have any desire to visit Davy Jones' locker today. I'd rather visit Oslo tomorrow."

People who spoke of Clyde Lee through the years often said, "He has no fear. He doesn't know what fear is.

"Well," thought Clyde, "They should see us now. I am learning very fast to know what fear is."

The storm continued, the wind howling, thunder roaring, lightning shattering the black clouds, and the rain dinning on the plane. They fought to hold the controls and keep the plane on an even keel, stay in the air and remain on course. Both knew their chances weren't worth much. Hoping for a ray of light, they peered intently ahead into the black hole of cloud that encompassed them. Fervently, both prayed for the storm to end.

"If only the wind would let up," said John anxiously, for the umpteenth time. "It's too strong. Even lashing the stick can't solve our problem. It's too tricky, blasting off and on, we have to meet every shudder and lurch differently. We're using too much gas."

Lightning streaked intermittently across the sky, zigzagging through the black clouds, followed almost simultaneously by deafening crackling thunder, then rumbling off in the distance.

In the crowded cabin, tension increased, nerves strained.

John said, "If the lightning strikes the plane near the gas, it will explode and there'll be a ball of fire and then only debris."

"Keep such ideas to yourself." Clyde answered, "It'd be better for both of us if you just prayed."

Visibility was practically nil. The steady throbbing of the motor was music to their ears and kept their hopes alive. They were unsure of their whereabouts. They were not able to see anything nor determine how far above the water they were. They couldn't be sure they were making headway toward Norway, at least they hoped that's where they were still flying.

"I have a sensation in my bones, that we are going backwards with the wind, clutched in its grip, a hostage to its power. We haven't enough power against it to blast our way forward and be free to fly on.

"Flying backwards," said Clyde. "That would be a first. It also feels as if we're being blown northwest. That would be unfortunate and we wouldn't have a prayer. It would mean freezing air tonight and ice on the wings. Ice on the wings means more weight on the plane. More weight on the plane means using more gas. We probably don't have enough gas to make up the loss. When we left Harbor Grace, we barely had enough fuel to get us to Norway. I have to keep it at full throttle to keep us in the air. As it is, we'll be flying on fumes before we get there."

Feeling that things couldn't get much worse, John quipped, "Do you think our black clouds have silver linings?"

"A silver lining would help, but I'd rather see golden sunshine pouring through a very large hole in that cloud in front of us."

After another half-hour of grimly battling the bucking plane, as well as contending with the storm and its sound effects, it seemed the thunder wasn't quite as loud, the lightning less frequent and the clouds thinning. Gradually, the velocity of the wind lessened and the rain began petering out.

"Can you believe this?" Clyde said, a gleam of hope in his voice.

It's letting up," John exclaimed." If we can just hold together until it lets up completely.

"Pray as you have never prayed before," said Clyde. "I am."

No Nails and No Coffin

A wisp of pale sunlight momentarily peaked through the clouds. "That pale gleam behind us may be watered down sunshine, but its the most beautiful sight I have seen today."

"That is the worst storm I have ever weathered in my life, Clyde! A storm such as people on land never see outside of a hurricane."

"With that behind us and the plane still intact, things are looking up. The only worry I have now is the gas. How much do we have? Is it enough to reach Norway?"

"I don't know our location, Clyde, nor how many miles we have lost flying against the stiff head-wind. I have been pouring gas pretty often. And it burns up twice as much gas bucking a stiff wind as cruising, and that was a stiff wind and still not calmed down enough."

"Well, John, If we can't make Norway, perhaps we can make the British Isles on the gas we have. And, as a matter of fact, there is no perhaps about it, we have to. Those waves still look too humongous for us to land on.

"When my dad went overseas in the war he was on the sister ship of the Lusitania and his ship was torpedoed off the coast of Ireland. Smashed a big hole in it just at the water line. He said the waves were so high, after a storm, the ship nearly sank. All the soldiers stood on one side of it for a night and the better part of a day. The weight of them on one side raised the torpedoed hole above the water line. The ships' carpenters repaired it while the captain surreptitiously maneuvered the ship away from the German submarine and reached the harbor. Repairs were difficult to make at sea.

"Waves on the ocean were normally twenty feet high, my dad told me. Even on a calm day the waves were twenty feet high. 'That's normal for the ocean,' he said. We wouldn't stand much of a chance riding out the ones I see down there now. We need a good strong tail wind, but we are getting a strong wind coming from the east, a nice strong head wind trying to blow us back home.

"Keep a close watch for any ships below us, so we can signal them."

"We may not see any, Clyde. If we were blown off course, they may have been, too. Anyway our planned route was slightly north of the ships' lanes."

"We started this flight from Goose Bay following a little north of the regular ships lane from the U. S. to England. I am fairly sure the wind blasting us in the storm blew us quite a few miles off our course. We have a night to go and time to make up. I can't stop worrying about ice on the wings and the lack of gas Hopefully, we weren't blown very far north. If we are still near our course, it shouldn't be cold enough to freeze enough ice on the fuselage to matter. We are carrying less gas to weigh us down. Perhaps we have a prayer of making it despite the bad luck so far. I figure we have two worries: too little gas and weakness to the structure due to the storm."

"There is only one solution to your two problems, Clyde, and I am working on them both. Praying," John replied.

"I heard the guys talking about your daredevil flying stunts. Someone said you have flown many a time on a 'wing and a prayer.' I hope you can still do that for the rest of this trip. With our gas so nearly gone, we are going to need a lot of prayers and more than gas fumes to reach Norway."

"Right, John. I'm sure prayer has helped me out many a time and Leonard Larson, too. He was flying passengers out of Thorpe one Sunday, and half-way home he was suddenly engulfed in a very dense fog. He had never done any flying in fog before. He tried remembering all the things he had heard other pilots say they had done when they flew in fog. He had an altimeter in the plane and that helped. He told me he flew as low as he dared and kept on course by diving down as near the ground as he dared whenever he saw a light spot in the cloud of fog. He could get his bearings and tell if he was headed towards home. He didn't know it at the time, but he flew over the Larson Brothers Airport. Roy was home anxiously pacing the floor. He knew Leonard was inexperienced in flying in foggy weather. Roy was very worried. It seemed to him it had been too long a time they had been listening for the sound of his plane. Viola told me later. 'When Roy heard a plane flying overhead, the happiest smile she had ever seen appeared on his face, and he said, 'Good for little brother, he is going to make it.'"

"Leonard kept on and the fog became thinner. His next sight of the ground was over Winneconne. Breathing a sigh of relief, he veered in, banked the plane and landed.

"Leonard told me later, 'That was the longest one hour flight of my life.' he said. But his troubles weren't over. While Leonard was otherwise occupied, a friend of his decided to ready the plane for the trip to Larson. He set up the controls in the plane and standing in front of it pulled the propeller. The engine engaged, the plane moved forward (the friend had forgotten to put chocks in front of the wheels) and it started across the field. The friend desperately attempting to climb into the plane to kill the engine, slipped and fell. The plane moved on and rammed a Ford car parked on the field. The propeller broke and the front side of the car was badly damaged.

"A very unhappy Leonard called home and told Roy his tale of woe. Not only could he not fly his plane home, but he had to ask Roy to drive to Winneconne, bring another propeller and enough money to pay for damages to the Ford car. Leonard hadn't made enough money flying passengers that day to cover his new expenses.

"It looks to me, Leonard, as if it's more dangerous for you to have an airplane on the ground than in the air,'" quipped a bystander.

"I've had lots of interesting experiences where I was the dupe. When the Mississippi River overflowed its banks last spring, I volunteered my services to the Red Cross. The newspapers were full of pictures of people stranded on islands along the Mississippi. Boats, they said, couldn't get to them because of the raging current of the water. I offered to drop supplies to stranded people. After I removed all five passenger seats from my plane, I could carry quite a sizeable load.

"They accepted and sent me to their La Crosse headquarters. They loaded the plane with supplies for the stranded and homeless in the flooded area. I was sent to the critical, most deluged locality at that time–Iowa's Mississippi river banks and islands.

"When I arrived at one particular island, I could see it was nearly inundated with water. Several people were collected at the highest point of land. They were jumping up and down, waving and screaming frantically. They were desperately attempting to get my attention. They were in a hopeless situation. I could see the water rising rapidly. They had to be evacuated right away or drown.

"I had a reputation for being able to land a plane on a raft and for flying by the seat of my pants. I said to myself, 'Clyde old boy, you have to use all your talents on this one. There really isn't any place large enough for a landing, to say nothing of being able to take off again. This is really going to be like landing on a raft. With the extra weight of all those people, it is pure suicide.' I had already dropped most of my supplies at the first islands I had flown over, so... I thought, 'Maybe those people down there won't weigh any more than the supplies I dropped at the other islands.'

"I circled around the island a couple of times to find the best spot to put down. I kept eyeing the rapidly rising river. I was going to have to be quick in and out. It was going to be a race between me and the river as to who took over first. With prayers in my heart and mind...I banked her in and set her down.

"No one needed to be urged to get into the plane. They were sitting on the floor in my plane in nothing flat. How I flew off that island was a miracle. It was truly a wing and a prayer. We made it, but for a few minutes I thought we were going to have to change my plane into a hydra plane. I had been right...there was too much weight. We flew out and just skimmed above the raging river for a few miles before I could lift her up. Those few miles were precarious ones. I can still see how muddy that roiling water looked.

"Those people were so happy to reach safety, when the plane landed at a shelter, they jumped down to the ground without heed for life or limb and ran for the shelter. They forgot about me. No one thanked me. Not even the Red Cross.

"My next load of supplies routed me back over the same location. As I flew over and looked down, I could see the river boiling over the island. It was several feet deep, where those people had been standing, when they were signaling me. It made my stomach queasy to think what might have happened to them.

"I was frustrated for a time and annoyed with the Oshkosh B'Gosh Over All people. I gave them four weeks of free advertising in July after I painted their name on my plane. It was the *Oshkosh B'Gosh Over All* until I arrived in Vermont and changed the name to *Green Mountain Boy*. The Oshkosh B'Gosh Company offered to pay me $2,000 when I returned to Oshkosh after a successful flight to Norway. That looked good to me until I realized how much free advertising they were getting from the newspapers all over the U.S. There were daily articles and some pictures of the plane and stories of the progress we were making getting ready for the flight.

"Today's flight to Norway would have taken place last July, but two of Wittman's students delayed my departure. One afternoon, I was putting gas in the plane. The gas tanks were stationed at the side of the field, next to the hangar, off the field and well out of the way of the runway. Those two would-be pilots, students of Wittman, taxied toward me and kept coming until their propeller chewed over half of my left wing before they turned off their engine.

It had to be deliberate. They had to see what their propeller was doing. They didn't need gas. They weren't trying to taxi into position for gas. My bright red plane parked there, was glaringly easy to see. Oh, they apologized profusely, but they were laughing when they walked away. Wittman was good about it, he paid for the repairs, but he couldn't replace the time lost over the ocean.

"We had to build an entire new wing. That didn't take as long as waiting forty-eight hours for each of the six coats of dope to dry. It did put me back at least two weeks and as the ocean was cooling each day I was delayed, I was worried then and am now of ice freezing on the wings tonight.

"Who is Wittman?"

"He is a flyer. He began flying about the same time I did, perhaps a short time before that. He built a midget plane and participated in midget plane races at Miami and Tampa in January of 1927. He won the EHR Green trophy and the Glenn H. Curtis cup at Miami.

"Mayor Brown welcomed him home with a large celebration. All the city officials were there. He was twenty-seven years old at that time. He began his flying at Byron, Wisconsin and moved on to Oshkosh a couple of years after that airport was developed in 1927. The name of his plane was 'Chief Oshkosh'. It was a real midget. It had a wing span of 16 feet, 4 inches and was 18 feet long, weighed 530 pounds. He also entered it in the Thompson Cup race but didn't win that one. At the time, his plane was thought to be the fastest of its type and size in the country.

"One of the would-be pilots at the Larson Airport," Clyde continued after a moment, " took off one day and temporarily lost control. The plane dipped nearly to the ground. That wasn't unusual, but it happened in the field where Loyall Larson was plowing with a team of horses. The team terrified, reared and kicked at the traces and nearly ran away with Loyall, plow and all. I'll wager that was the crookedest furrow he ever plowed.

"Sometimes it was fun to buzz cows and even people. We didn't do that very much. If the cows ran very long they gave bloody milk at night.

"One Sunday some special event was going on at Winneconne. That was when I hadn't been doing much flying. I was just a green beginner. I decided to fly there and get a bird's eye view of the goings-on. When I flew over, I noticed fishermen anchored in the river, four or five boats with a couple of fisherman in each one. As usual, being a teenager, I was looking for some excitement. Taking a long look at the bridge, (an iron center-pivot bridge, replaced in the 1930s) Just for kicks, I thought, 'I am going to fly under that bridge. I'll bet no one has ever done that.' I forgot about the fishermen and concentrated on just how to approach the bridge to fly under it and not get my undercarriage caught on the wooden piles in the water.

"Well, I flew over and around it a few times and decided to approach it flying just above the water from the west side. I flew low, the undercarriage barely above the water. It looked good to me so I kept on towards the bridge. Just before I flew under, I saw those fishermen in the water, hanging on to the sides of their boats. Their fish poles were floating on top of the water. I heard later they had gone over the sides of the boats so fast they lost their poles.

"I don't know why they did that unless they thought I was going to crash. The plane was never near them, but my tail wind made some pretty large waves and rocked their boats pretty vigorously.

"My Uncle George Cross was the rural mail carrier out of Winneconne and he heard plenty from those fishermen about his nephew and his low flying. Anyway, I was the only person who ever flew under that bridge. At least I was the first...I always had to be first!

"Another flying pal and early pioneer aviator, Speed Holman, crashed and was killed. He was from Minneapolis. He flew with Hinks Flying Circus. Later he became an airmail pilot, but only for a short while. He bought into a company and became an executive. He still flew as a hobby and for exhibitions. He was flying exhibitions at the Iowa State Fair the day he was killed. After I had been pall bearer for Holman and Roy, I told my sister, 'If I crashed I would see to it, if it was over land I would go down at least six feet underground so they wouldn't have to bury me. I'd bury myself. Or if it happened over water I would bank straight down...Davey Jones' locker for me. I will not put my friends and relatives through the gruesome ritual of a funeral. There will be no nails in my coffin...actually, no coffin!'

"Speaking of Holman, he crashed in Iowa at the State Fair. He was putting on a flying exhibition there. He was a great flyer. He loved it, too. He was one of the best and a real daredevil. To give the audience bone-chilling thrills, he would fly upside down just a few feet above the ground. It made my skin crawl to watch him. When they reached him after the crash, his seat belt was ripped out of the side of the plane. They think it broke loose and spilled him on the ground. He died instantly and I lost another close flying buddy, a terrific flyer, sport, and best company a man could want.

"He and I had some crazy experiences. He hired me for my first parachute jump in Manitowoc, Wisconsin. He warned me about pulling the strings to guide the chute where I wanted to go. I was green at the job. All I knew was to jump and pull the rip cord. Well I landed on top of a car in the parking lot. It was a jolt I'll never forget.

"Another time, Speed Holman was at my house on New Year's Eve. We went out on the town. On a sudden inspiration, Speed called his wife in Minneapolis and told her we were flying there to spend New Year's with her.

He told me he was homesick to see his wife and wanted to spend the holiday with her. He had the airmail plane parked at the Oshkosh hanger, but he couldn't use it for personal flying so he asked me to fly him to Minneapolis.

"I had had just enough to drink to think it would be a great lark. It didn't take much encouragement to interest me in flying anywhere, anytime even without a drink. We started out. It was a cold, clear, frosty night. We were in an open cockpit plane with the wind whipping our faces and it was colder than anything I had ever flown in. Despite the cold, he still wanted to go.

"We were about fifteen miles north of Oshkosh when the plane gave the most God awful jolt and I thought I would go into a spin.

"When I got the plane under control again, I looked back and Speed had pulled the rip cord on his parachute. We were flying with his parachute in full bloom, mushrooming out, trailing thirty feet behind the plane. That was the end of the trip to Minneapolis that night. It's a wonder the plane didn't spin us right down and six feet under.

"To this day, I don't know how I managed to fly it back and land it at the Oshkosh airport without spinning in. When my wheels hit the ground the parachute stopped me with a jerk. I didn't need any other brakes. Perhaps having celebrated New Year's Eve a little too much had something to do with it. I wouldn't try it again drunk or sober.

"How is the gas holding out, John? I don't see land ahead of us. I'll be even more grateful to see land than Columbus was when he sighted the islands. We forgot to bring birds to guide us in. Seems like we are the birds, or one big red bird. It is almost dusk, just one long dark night and shortly thereafter we will see the mountains of Norway, and then Oslo.

"Roy Larson and his brothers, Clarence, Newell and Leonard, especially Leonard, Speed Holman, Elwyn West, Wittman, Doc Ross, Mel Thompson, Howard Morey and myself to name a few were really the first to make a business of flying in Wisconsin. There were other flyers, but they weren't in it to make a living. They mostly flew for enjoyment. I am speaking, now, of the very first pilots, in the early twenties, the ones I knew. There were earlier ones, but they were like a one-night stand. Flew a while and then were gone."

"There was a Thompson airline wasn't there?" John asked.

"Yes, Mel Thompson began building an airplane in 1919 near Valders, Wisconsin. It took him two years to complete it. He modified the standard model. He used it for barnstorming for several years. In 1929, he was the personal pilot for Governor Kohler and later for Walter Kohler, Jr. At that time he was flying a Ryan plane. He received his license in 1930. He had one bad accident when his plane went into a spin. At that time, it was almost always fatal when the plane spun in. Mel hired me for a while to work on another plane he was building.

"Is that my tired eyes or is it getting foggy ahead? We've had enough of clouds today! It looks like it. I think I see wisps off in the distance. God, we can't take any more of that! Do you see them, thin wisps floating in the sky? If that turns into the dense london fog, we are truly in the soup, and out of luck. No one can fly in that. When they have one of those fogs over Great Britian, the government orders all planes grounded. I wish we could be grounded! I mean on land, of course. I detest flying in fog. I always feel so helpless, disoriented, so muddled! And night is coming on fast. We are really in trouble, now. Thank God we have an altimeter to tell us how far we are above the waves. John, I think you picked the wrong horse this time. It's got to be in God's hands. Just pray.

"The most difficult problem in the beginning of aviation was to convinve people flying and airplanes were going to be the thing of the future for transportation, and commercial as well as passenger.

"I believe in sdome small way, I did help to convince some, at least in Wisconsin. I saved the bank when Brinks couldn't do it by armored car. I saved people's lives and delivered supplies along the Mississippi River when boats were useless. Roy used his plane to fight forest fires from the air. A thing unheard of before. We both furnished entertainment flying passengers and giving exhibition stuns for entertainment. We now have airmail, one-day mail.

"Soon better and larger planes will be able to fly the ocean more easily and more rapidly than ships. To be honest with you, I firmly believe that during our lifetime we will be able to land a man on the moon. Scientific knowledge is burgeoning and we will saee miracles never dreamed of. People will accept those things as common place in just a few years. A blatant example of that is the fact that I was born in a log cabin built using logs from trees my parents cut down with a crosscut saw. Twenty-four years later I am flying an airplane across the Atlantic Ocean. In just twenty-four years technology has moved ahead that rapidly.

There was very little talking in the cockpit for awhile except regarding the flying conditions and the plane, as they concentrated on trying to make out their position, read their altimeter and compass and most of all, stay above the waves while flying through the fog.

"You take over for awhile, John, I am exhausted. My eyes won't stay open. I am afraid I am going to fall asleep."

John had been concentrating on the fog and trying to figure out their position and if they were on the right course. Staying above the ever fluctuating, tremendous waves was the main concern. John was sleepy, too. He had helped work the controls in the worst of the storm and was tired. Both were exhausted.

"I will for a while and then I will have to have a short nap or I will snooze off and fall asleep."

The small plane dipped lower in the darkness, but kept on tenaciously as the waiting sea below hurled its forty-foot waves.

Clyde, reawakening, rubbed his eyes wearily, as he struggled to keep the plane airborne. Tired beyond words, exhausted and not certain where they were, confused by the compass reading and what he thought it should show. He couldn't believe the wind had blown them so far backwards and off course during the blasting wind storm. He was praying the gas would hold out. John had said it was almost gone. Nearly all the cans were empty.

They weren't flying as rapidly as they should be. With the weight of the gasoline reduced they should be moving at about 135 miles per hour. He feared ice had built on the wings. There had to be extra weight building on the plane, holding them back.

It was cold and completely dark flying in the fog. He sensed they were near land. He thought they must be near the British Isles. He had hoped there wouldn't be fog. Exhausted, he rubbed his eyes. God, if he could only keep his eyes open. He glanced at John. John had been desperately tired. He would let him sleep a little longer.

Sleep blacked Clyde out temporarily. His head fell forward. In his exhaustion something strange happened to him. It seemed that he became one with the plane. They were the same entity.

He jerked his head up and forced his eyes open. His whole life seemed to be passing before him. They said that happened just before a person died. He didn't like to think about that. Still, if death did come now, he would have lived a good and full life. He'd done more in 24 years than most men did in 100. His eyelids grew heavy. He fought exhaustion. He would wake John in a few minutes and have him take over. His head fell forward. He was a child again, back at Clark's Point with his sister, Bernice. They were flying the toy airplane he had whittled. The rubber band detached, the plane fell and the propeller broke. He returned to awareness.

The things he had done, he thought to himself. He smiled. Like the time when he was campin&g with Vernon and Walton Johnson on Mud Creek. They built a crude raft and put it in the water. They hadn't realized how weedy and mucky it was on the bottom. Vernon dove off and stuck in the mud. When he didn't come up, Walton and Clyde jumped in and pulled him out. Luckily for Vernon, he learned artificial respiration in Boy Scouts or he wouldn't be alive today.

He couldn't believe his eyes. He had just seen Uncle Charlie Hough motioning to him. "Go the other way, Clyde," he called loudly as he motioned.

"But Uncle Charlie is terminally ill in bed with brain cancer," he muttered to himself. "I must be hallucinating." He thought that over briefly and then his mind went back to the Larson airport.

He thought of his pal, Wib Zehner. Typical teenagers! "How hard he tried to beat me racing our cars around the square near the airport. A couple of times he came within six or seven feet of tying with me, but I always managed to get there first. Yes, I always had to be first.

"And when we would race down the road, our cars, tops down, side by side, until we were each traveling 40 miles an hour. How the neighbors exclaimed when they saw us stand up and each step into the other one's car, and continue nonchalantly driving on.

"What fun we had Saturday nights at the Larsons' home, singing around the piano with Verna playing. How she could play! And we all sang! Sang? I'm not so sure we all could sing...but they were hilarious times and ones I and they shall never forget."

"Oh my God, John," he yelled, "Wake up! Wake Up! We are going to hit. The motor cut out, John, wake up! Get out!"

With the motor dead, he couldn't keep the plane from ditching. It slanted in nose first. It was a God awful bump. It struck the waves with a terrible scream of wrenching, tearing metal.

When the plane hit, the entity parted. With painful force, he was his own individual again.

Water rushed in and John awakened, scrambled out. Clyde struggled from the sinking plane into the icy water. Buoyed by his jacket, "Oshkosh Jr. Chamber of Commerce" clearly emblazoned on it, he floated. The plane, a dark shadow nearby, riding high on the crest of the waves, slipped away, lost in a trough of water as the sea took it entirely. He hoped John would survive. It had been the gas, all gone.

He was losing his body to numbness, but before he lost consciousness, he fancied he saw the first rays of dawn through the mist which clung to the waves. He thought he saw mountain peaks. "Incredible," he thought, "We must have made it... Norway!

"There'll be no happy cheering crowds at the airport, no triumphant parades, no 'Conquering Hero' headlines, none of the glory, but we have the realization that we almost made it. And we still could make it, just swim through the icy water."

He began to feel lighter and lighter. He seemed to separate from his body. He saw something he could hardly credit, through a brilliant light he thought he saw Roy Larson walking toward him out of the radiant mist, over the waves, a warm smile of welcome on his face, his hands reaching out towards him.

Reminiscing

A conversation, conducted in 1968, on flying in the 1920s with pioneer aviators Leonard Larson and Elwyn West.

Elwyn: I began flying in 1921. When did you start flying, Leonard?

Leonard: In 1923, after our house burned down, Roy came back from Northern Wisconsin to help rebuild the house. Meanwhile, two airplanes arrived from Texas. Roy had bought them from the Government. He taught all of us right after that. We were all flying that summer of 1923.

Elwyn: Right after High School, I think that was 1920, I graduated and the next year I went to Diggins Flying School in Chicago. Roy went there too, later, didn't he?

Leonard: Roy went in 1919. That same summer he came home from the War. He didn't buy a plane nor fly until after Ma died in April of 1922.

Elwyn: My first plane was a Cannuck JNR. Everyone called them Jenneys. At that time flying was mostly for fun. You could hardly make expenses. By the time you paid rent for the field and the gas it was all gone. Passengers were scarce. Too often the people were afraid. The newspapers played it up too much when someone crashed. War movies were popular then. They showed lots of combat pictures, where the airplanes were shot down ablaze, in screaming flames accompanied by appropriately terrifying sound effects.

Those pictures froze in the minds of the viewers and fear overcame any daredevil instincts they might have had.

Only the young would take a chance and they had no money. Times were tight. A young man could be a hired man on a farm and earn a little money, but not many had hired men in those days. $5.00 was hard to come by.

The cities were far away from our airfields. Twenty-five miles was a long trip for a horse and buggy. Not many people had automobiles and even if they did, the roads were so bad, graveled and dusty and not very smooth. The speed limit was 15 miles per hour.

A twenty-five mile trip took an hour and a-half. The gravel roads were single lane with very few places for a turnout. If you met a car and you were driving a horse, the horse would probably bolt. Lucky, if that was all. Sometimes they would rear and buck and kick the traces to pieces before bolting.

Horses were terrified of the loud noisy engine of the horseless carriages. Besides that, the roads were single lane. There actually wasn't room for the two vehicles to meet without each vehicle having their right hand wheels partially in the ditch. A rearing kicking horse was difficult to handle under any circumstances, but with the right wheel off the side of the road, it was doubly difficult. Wise drivers of horses hitched to a vehicle would, when they saw a car coming stop, get out, and hold the horse by the bridle, speaking soothing words to it until the car had slowly worked its way around the horse and buggy. Occasionally if the ditch was deep and the shoulder of the road had a sharp slant, the vehicle or the car could tip over, killing or crippling the driver.

The first macadam road I ever rode on was near Winneconne. [This was one of the first paved roads in Wisconsin. A mix of gravel and asphalt, macadam was similar to what we now call blacktop.] Winneconne had no airport. That was 1921. Later, there was a field near by we used. Posted speed limit was 15 miles per hour.

The only way I could make any money flying was to go to County Fairs or special events looking for passengers. It was necessary to keep abreast of all public events and rent a farmer's pasture as near the event as possible.

By 1923, business began to get better. I remember one Saturday meeting Clarence Larson. He came to see me about taking over a job at Clintonville. The Larson Brothers were booked solid and couldn't handle it, he said. I was booked, too, for that weekend. Soon after that, I visited the Larson airport. I had just returned from the School of Engineering in Milwaukee. They accredited me in Electrical Automotive Engineering. I still have my certificate.

About that time, I began carrying young men who called themselves 'stunters.' We would advertise we were putting on a show. That would usually bring a crowd and maybe some of the crowd would pay for a ride. I carried a lot of stunt men.

When I got up to about 1500 to 2000 feet, the stunt man would climb out of the cockpit, walk along the entering edge of the wing to the outer strut and from there climb up onto the top wing.

There was one advantage of the World War I JNR. Their cables were round and you could hold on quite well. The wires on the later model planes cut too sharp as a hand hold. When someone was stunting, the pilots flew about 65 miles an hour The stunt man wore a harness in later years. In 1923 he wore a tumbling belt around his waist with a large ring buckle.

There were loop holders fastened on the top wing. The stunt man could slip his feet into them to give him added security, especially while the pilot did a loop over. Without those loops a stunt man might fall. If he fell, he would lay on the wing until the pilot landed. It was tough flying and landing with anyone laying on the wings that way, if they weren't right in the middle. I found it was easy to loop with them standing on the top of the wing. The wind pressure helped bring the plane right over in a loop. You had to be careful not to stall at the top of the loop, if you stalled they would fall down and could roll off and hang there by their tumbling belt wires. That was dangerous for the pilot as well as the stunt man. I used the tumbling belt on my planes, the stunt man just braced back with those wires. I never had the foot holds on my plane.

Leonard, did you ever fly any stunt men?

Leonard: Roy flew quite a few exhibitions. He flew Clyde quite a bit and did some stunt flying himself.

Elwyn: I never did any stunting. I flew Clyde several times at Appleton and Oshkosh in his early stunts. He always finished his exhibitions with a parachute drop. On my plane, Clyde never pulled the rip cord on his chute. He fastened it on the end of the wing and let the plane pull the cord. That was smart because sometimes when the stunter pulled the cord it wouldn't open. And sometimes when the stunter could pull the cord he had dropped some distance...too far for the chute to open in time to slow the fall.

We couldn't get those planes more than 2,000 feet altitude and if the weather wasn't good 1500 feet. If they dropped too far the chute wouldn't open soon enough to slow their fall. They needed 1500 feet after the rip cord was pulled, or they could be seriously injured. They couldn't wear a parachute when they were stunting. It was too cumbersome. The parachute was fastened to the end of one wing.

I heard Clyde had some narrow escapes several times, but not flying with me.

Leonard: He and Roy had a bad time one day at Oshkosh. The wind came up just as they arrived there. They had to call it off. Something went wrong with the plane. They couldn't get up over a thousand feet. Boy, that crowd was mad! Even made the papers. They went back again the following weekend and did the exhibition over again with a parachute jump.

I saw some stunt men, after they made a chute jump and the chute didn't open. They were killed. Their fingernails were ripped off their fingers. They tried so hard to pull it open. They hadn't succeeded. They fell at 117 miles per hour. That isn't much time to pull it open.

Elwyn: I heard Clyde had an experience like that, with a parachute Elmer Clark owned. It almost killed him too, but he managed to get the chute half-way open.

Leonard: I remember that. The doctor said if he hadn't landed in a newly plowed field it would have killed him. Hurt his spine...cracked it as a matter of fact and broke five ribs.

Elwyn: I remember Roy flying to our house one night. That was in September of 1925. They were having forest fires around Weyauwega. He had been flying there and a bad storm came up. He didn't think he could make it home, so he stayed with me all night and flew back to Weyauwega the next day to continue fighting fires. I was flying a Standard then, and Roy had his first Waco.

It was 1926 when Clyde and Dave Read bought that Cannuck from Roy. Roy had traded it from Howard Morey. We didn't see much of Clyde after that. He flew mostly from Oshkosh where he lived. He flew in for a visit occasionally for family affairs. He was Viola's cousin.

Do you remember that time you came down in a field just East of our airfield?

Elwyn: No, I don't remember that one. I had quite a few of those. It often happened in those days to everyone, that you had to make an emergency landing in someone's pasture or hayfield. I took out more fence posts because the fields were too small to fly out of again.

Leonard: You were having carburetor trouble and I saw you land and drove over there to see if I could help.

Elwyn: Roy and I went to the Waco factory in 1926 and we each bought a Waco 10. I already had one and I put a tank engine in both of them.

I bought another Waco 10 at Manitowoc one time. Advertised second-hand. It still had the wrappings on it. Some poor guy ordered it and couldn't pay for it when it arrived. It had to have been new. That time I felt I bought one of the best planes I ever owned at a really good price.

I sold a Waco 10 to Eddie Diefenbach. He was deaf and dumb. He had Eddie Burrusso fly it for him. Burruso bought a Standard from me in 1925. I heard he died in a crash a few years later.

Leonard: What planes did you use for stunting?

Elwyn: Anyone I had at the time. I've used Jennys (although I never owned one) Standards and Wacos. Curtis manufactured both the Cannuck and the Jenny. He manufactured the Jenny in Canada and the Cannuck in the U.S. The U.S. Cannuck was the best. It had double ailerons and was lighter. Later on they put double ailerons on the Jenny. Some Jennys had a top wing on the bottom and made a longer winged Jenny. The bottom wing stuck out farther and had an aileron on it.

Leonard: The American Curtis we had we flew with our rocker arms on the horizon in order to fly level. The Cannuck was set that way. The longerines and fuselage were set straight with them. The Jenny was tipped down. The motor mount wasn't straight with the top longerine.

Elwyn: I never liked that, the pull never seemed straight.

Leonard: What ever happened to Dusty Rhodes?

Elwyn: I'm not sure. The first or second year that I was flying. It was the first year that I had my Cannuck. I was flying up at Medford Fair and I was pretty green, you know, and I wanted to play it safe. I was out from the fairgrounds quite a distance, maybe two miles. I would get a passenger now and then.

Dusty Rhodes from Minneapolis flew into the field where I was. He had a new Standard with all the army insignia on it, you know, the stars. It looked good, but it made my old Cannuck look bad.

He was in the same field with me and didn't think the passengers were coming fast enough. He wanted to be closer to town. He moved into another field. I didn't think I wanted to fly out of that one. It looked too small for me. I had already taken out a couple of fences on different fields at various times. I had lots of experience in my time with that. I didn't move to the other field.

It was that kind of day with a little sprinkle of rain now and then. It would clear up and the sun would come out. There was a ball game being played in the center of the race track. There was a mammoth crowd in the stands. As I passed over I would get a glimpse of the game. The grandstand was just across the race track from the game.

Because of the thick clouds I wouldn't go over 1000 feet. I didn't like to fly in clouds. You can't see anything. You can't tell whether you are flying upside down, sideways or what. Also, in the cloud, you might meet someone head on. I kept watching for this other plane, because Dusty was flying above the clouds and I was afraid he might come down on me. He couldn't see me either. The clouds were so low, at one time, I was only up to 800 feet. I kept looking around and up, watching for Dusty.

I happened to glance over my shoulder as his plane come spinning out of the clouds. I was headed away from it. I saw it slightly slow up and almost come out of the spin, but it went right into it again. I watched. I thought, 'you'd better be getting out of that spin soon, because you can't play around much longer.'

I turned my plane so I could see him and looking from a thousand feet, I saw that airplane practically come out of the spin three times and each time, it went right back into it again. From above, it looked low as if it might hit the ground any minute. Sure enough, it came down in the middle of the ball game, smash, right where they were playing. The ball players had to run for their lives. It killed the passenger, but the pilot, Dusty Rhodes, came out of it. I can never forget that. I can see it yet.

The crowd came out of that grandstand in such a rush they tore down the race track fence, trampling each other to get there and gather around the airplane. I don't know whether it was curiosity or wanting to help. But there were too many there to do any good. You never saw such excited people.

I flew back to the field I had been flying out of and caught a ride with someone back to the fairgrounds. The plane was completely smashed, squashed, The dead passenger was there on the ground. He must have been practically doubled up when they went into the spin and when they smashed, he was almost cut in two.

I went back to the field and took off for home. I didn't feel much like flying any more that day. I didn't see anyone hanging around waiting for a ride either.

The next day Dusty was up and around again. Cracked ribs or something like that. He was very lucky.

Later on afterwards, I was talking to Lyle Throw. He taught Dusty to fly. He said, 'I never could teach him to come out of a spin. He wouldn't wait long enough. He would come out and then go right into it again'.

Lyle said he could easily understand how the crash happened, because Dusty would never wait long enough for the plane to get all the way out of a spin. I wonder he had nerve to take up a passenger.

We were all foolish back then.

Yes, well before I hit that chimney I took out quite a few fences. Some of those fields were so small. You would look at all your passengers for weight, figure how much you had to hold it down and figure how you were going to jump the fence and sometimes your wheels would touch on the other side and sometimes I didn't make the jump. One time I went to jump a fence like that and just one wing caught again like it did on the chimney, and it whirled me around and put me through a lane fence that had two more fences...three fences in one lick...I often think of these people flying today and wonder what they would do if something like that happened.

Bernice: You didn't have brakes?

Elwyn: No, we didn't have any brakes.

Leonard: They wouldn't get in with brakes, where we operated.

Bernice: How did you stop?

Elwyn: You were headed into the wind, and waited to stop. We cut the motor before we landed.

Leonard: Remember the old Aeronca, remember?

Elwyn: Yes, I remember, that set right down between the wheels. In those days even the army brass said that in order to be a good flyer, you had to barnstorm for a while. The army pilots were taught on these big fields and they didn't know what it was to stall in, fly by the seat of their pants as we called it. They got that from barnstorming. The fields were so small we had to learn, or else.

Once I was with Herb Smith. He was a very good young flyer and the first time I took him out barnstorming–one of those trips–we were up there by the Chain-of-Lakes. He was doing very well but he came to me and said, "I'm scared, this isn't right...I don't have enough room."

I told him, You are doing fine, you have been doing just as good as I have, and I talked him into going on and keeping at it. He wasn't in a really small place, but it was a little too tight for him.

Elwyn: When we were at Chetek...

Leonard: I remember. Roy introduced you and he named you "Vest."

Elwyn: Where was that?

Leonard: It was at Cornell.

Elwyn: When Roy come there and tied right up to the fence?

Leonard: He had a Hisso.

Elwyn: You were there then? You and young Clarence?

Leonard: Yes, and Roy said, "Boy, if I crack up again, you birds better take off the other way".

Elwyn: You were there then. I had a Standard. When Roy made up his mind to fly anywhere, you couldn't change him. You and Clarence came over to me and said, "See if you can do anything with Roy. Have him change to another field".

Roy says, "You aren't having any trouble," and he stayed there and he pretty near went into the nearby woods. He went against the wind, see, he took off crosswind. I wouldn't dare do that. I kept in the wind. I went around that hill. When he wouldn't change, I finally went over and talked to Roy and told him to push the heavy people on to me. After that he did all right.

Leonard: Yes, I remember that well.

Elwyn: Well I guess he got a downdraft. He almost hung the tail on the fence.

Leonard: I have thought so often, back in those days, no one ever sued us or made a claim against us.

Elwyn: Well in those days they didn't try to stick people for insurance. No, they felt it was all in a good cause and they wouldn't turn you away, nor get an attorney. They were glad to see we hadn't been hurt. We never had any trouble.

Leonard: People are so different today.

Elwyn: Oh, today, they are just waiting for a chance to sue someone. You know we had no seat belts at first. A couple of times I pretty near lost a couple of people. One time making a loop with them I stalled at the top of the loop and they hung in those wires, that was a Standard, there were crosswires up in the top in the center section of the front seat and they fell into those wires and hung on. I tell you I belted them in after that when I flew passengers.

Leonard: I often thought of that, too, because all we had was an "A" strap in there and that was nothing in case of a loop stunt.

Elwyn: It might have held them from flying up into the wires at that. Well those two got their monies worth. They got a real thrill.

Bernice: Did the farmers ever sue you for their fences?

Elwyn: Oh, no. The farmers were always good. Glad to see we didn't get hurt.

Leonard: Was that up at Shawano that the sheriff came out after you, or was it at Antigo.

Elwyn: That was not a telephone pole, though. That was a light pole. The electric company came after me. Oh, yes, they made me pay. They weren't so bad though...it would cost a lot more now.

Bernice: That must have damaged your plane didn't it?

237

Elwyn: Oh, yes sometimes, but not always. I took down a...

Leonard: That was with Ollie Davis, wasn't it?

Elwyn: Ollie Davis, that is a name that I haven't heard of in fifty years. Now that I think of him, did he ever learn to fly?

Leonard: Yes.

Elwyn: I can hardly place him.

Leonard: Yes he is with the Cab company, I think.

Bernice: Runs the Greyhound Bus Depot in Oshkosh.

Leonard: Yes, now. He cracked up that Waco 9 at Devils Lake, I think. North Dakota. When he first bought his plane, Clyde Lee flew it for him because Ollie didn't know how to fly. Clyde taught him. Clyde came in for a landing at the Oshkosh Airport one night facing into the setting sun. It was so blinding he landed on a hay rake someone had left standing on the runway of the airport field. Do you remember that? How long were you at the Oshkosh Airport?

Elwyn: I wasn't there very long. Maybe that one summer.

Leonard: I didn't think you were there very long.

Elwyn: You see, Appleton built an airport right after that and I moved to Appleton.

Bernice: There was a law suit about that hay rake. I typed it for the Court. It went to the State Supreme Court on an appeal. I remember the name of Elwyn being in the case.

Leonard: He may have been called to testify. I know Ollie called me, but I couldn't say too much because I didn't see it happen.

Elwyn: As you talk about it, it is coming back to me. Something about that, but I can't recall it offhand. I can recall a fellow running into a load of hay, but that was at the Appleton Airport, not at Oshkosh. That was at the old county airport, not at the new County Airport. He ran right into a load of hay, taxiing,

238

see, looking out the side (that was a Waco 10) looking out of one side like this here and he didn't see a guy making hay. He taxied right into the load of hay. The guy hollered and jumped off the hay and ran.

Bernice: But this man at the Oshkosh airport had gone home and when he did he left the hay rake out in the middle of the runway. Clyde was coming in from Milwaukee and he was coming in for a landing from the east he had to fly west to face the wind. He came down and the hay rake was there where he set down. He couldn't see it as the setting sun shining from the west, was directly in his eyes.

Elwyn: Well I can remember something about that, but I didn't see it. I am sure of that.

Leonard: I didn't see it either, but the only thing they wanted to know was ...they had a jury trial, but that wasn't until in the thirties..

Bernice: After Clyde left.

Leonard: But this lawsuit was later, I remember, it was Ollie who sued for damages to his airplane.

Elwyn: What year did Oshkosh Airport start?

Bernice: 1927.

Elwyn: I thought it was before that. The Appleton airport was built that year, I thought. Lindberg flew the ocean in 1926 and Appleton built that year of 1928 and Oshkosh was a year ahead of them.

Leonard: When it began, Bob Menning was operating out of Oshkosh, remember?

Elwyn: There couldn't have been more than a year's difference between Appleton and Oshkosh. Did Oshkosh build before Lindberg flew to France?

Leonard: No. I don't think so.

Elwyn: Lutz was the backbone behind that airport..

Leonard: Yes, that's right.

Elwyn: I remember when Lindberg flew the ocean that Ryan B1 came into the top seller. They sold for $5,000.00 and Hawkes (Lawkes) came to see me and wanted to buy one; and have me go in cahoots with him and fly it because he didn't fly. We planned to but they were selling so fast, they were behind with orders, and our plan never materialized. We didn't get our plane.

Leonard: But wasn't the Stinson better for a load carrier?

Elwyn: The Stinson? Oh, no. It might be when you got up there in the air. It might be like the difference between the Waco 9 and the old Eagle Rock.

Leonard: Oh, was that right?

Elwyn: You know when you got up in the air, the Eagle Rock for speed would beat a Waco 9. But the Ryan was the best. It would beat them all. That B1 Ryan would get right out. Then Ryan came out with the B5...that had the big tail surface...that was a very good plane. I had a Ryan. I believe Frenzel was in on that one with me. That was a Ryan B-1 with a B-5 tail surface. Oh, you could really get up there with a load. That beat the Stinson. But I think flying with the Stinson, out across country, level flight, Stinson was probably the faster airplane (with its horse power).

Leonard: The Stinsons built a very good airplane didn't they?

Elwyn: Yes. They did. Then he was taken over by Cord wasn't he? I remember Stinson was at Diggins School when I started there and he was flying then and oh boy, did he used to put on a show! I saw him take a person up in the air and start looping from several thousand feet and I've counted twenty loops without stopping.
    Now, you have to be pretty high to do nineteen or twenty loops in an old airplane. When they got down lower you would hear the fellow hollering bloody murder. The people around there...the students...they wouldn't ride with him if he offered to take them,. He always wanted to scare somebody!

Bernice: That was Stinson?

Elwyn: That was Eddie Stinson.

Bernice: And he later manufactured the Stinson airplane?

Elwyn: Yes, and then it was taken over by Cord. I went to Detroit to visit Apitz and I looked Stinson up and he had a time, then, to take us through the Stinson factory. They had bought him out, but he was still in the office and they had stopped all visitors. He couldn't get a guide to show me through. He put up a good argument and got us through and he said isn't that something when they won't let us through my own plant with anybody? I don't know why. There was nothing there that was secret. There wasn't a war nor anything.

Bernice: Competition.

Elwyn: I don't know. It could have been.

Leonard: They claim he was the first man to recognize the cause of the spin and how to recover from it.

Elwyn: Oh, yes they used to think if you went into a spin you were done for.

Leonard: He went into a spin and instead of pulling back on the stick like would seem the thing to do, he pushed forward on it and came out of it. When he came out of it, he told the others about it and then went right back up and tried it again and they claim that he was the first man to discover that.

Elwyn: Naturally, the nose is down and for a while everyone thought you couldn't come out of a spin because as Leonard said you pull the stick back and you are already in the stall and you can't bring the nose up and you just held her in the stall, so you should push the stick forward instead of pulling it back. Some said you had to use the motor besides pushing the stick forward in order to come out of it. You know, those early days Waco 10's were bad.

Leonard: Oh yes, one time Roy almost had to jump

Elwyn: Oh-o, I nearly had it, a couple of times. One time...I don't know how true. It was...you know that Scandinavia Free Fair? I was flying there. I had a Waco 10. That's probably one of the first ones I bought from Roy and you would be flying a passenger and they would hand back a $5.00 bill and make a motion like a loop or a spin or something, see, and so I would go up to probably twelve, fifteen hundred feet and I made a loop, and I was going to spin him down and land. Well gracious, if I had spun down over the field, I would have hit, but you know that lake across there from the college?

Leonard: Yes.

Elwyn: Well I went down that far part of the lake and the people who were watching the airplane said they would swear my tail skid hit the water. I looked back when I recovered and saw ripples, but I thought that was my propeller blast. I still think it was. I don't believe I dragged in the water.

Leonard: I remember that, hearing about that.

Elwyn: It was close. Oh, I fought that spin. I finally came out with blasting the motor. Oh, I've been in spins several times flat that way, and you can use the motor and come out of it...but when you began using the motor you could figure maybe you had three turns yet before you could bring her out...if you could bring her out at all. I was always lucky.

And then that time Mel Thompson spun that girl in and killed her. I always figure, Thompson said he done everything. That was the trouble, he didn't hold his controls in one place long enough to respond. If you don't hold and wait for it, and you figure it ain't going to respond and you put it back in the position it was, then there you are again. Just the same as if it hadn't started coming out of the spin.

Leonard: You get impatient because it doesn't seem to be coming out fast enough. I know on these programs and such, they wanted us to just really bat that rudder as hard as you could and that's what they recommended for spins. Very positive movement and maybe that would help, too. And like you said I don't think those pilots had patience enough to wait. They thought it should recover faster.

Elwyn: Well I'll tell you. You put those controls where you should come out and you keep on whirling you do begin to wonder, see, if you should change them someway. When it was too slow coming out I used to use the motor then, but I wouldn't use the motor steady, but just, they will almost stop, then snap, see, and I would always work the motor so that when I snapped around against the wind then I would try to get my blast. Then, in a taper wing, one time, I pretty near got it.

242

Leonard: I believe you mentioned that to me one time.

Elwyn: Oh, that was in a dive and the darn thing wouldn't come out. I had absolutely no feel of a stick and she come right on down...diving...and I've heard that the taper wing...the army, even had some of their fighter planes that acted that way. Some pilots claim if you got in a certain position you'd get no vertical response at all.
And now that time of flying is just nothing and they are flying to the moon. It's like a dream.

Elwyn: Anything that is mechanical, look at those outfits they've got. Just thousands of little working parts. Just one little connection goes bad, one little wire loosens, anything, and they're done for. There's bound to be an accident sometime. I figured when they went on that last flight that they were going to leave those two men on the moon. I never figured they'd come back.

Leonard: They've got a lot of nerve going up there, those boys, to do those things.

Elwyn: That's right, but everything went pretty good and they made it.

Leonard: The moon is one-fourth or is it half the size of our planet?

Elwyn: I believe it is a little under a half the size of earth.

Bernice: A little over a third the size, I heard them say.

Leonard: Anyway, when you think of it...

Elwyn: The wires of an old Standard.

Bernice: It was something about the construction of the plane...

Leonard: Oh, that Ryan you mentioned. Tail group or something, smaller or larger, or something.

Elwyn: Well, was it a Stinson that Clyde had when he started out over the ocean?

Leonard: Yes.

Elwyn: Well then he flew that Stinson around there quite a while before he left with it, didn't he?

Leonard: Well, that is the one he used to fly with up there in Michigan. He flew for those people up at Negaunee.

Elwyn: Oh, that's right. I'd forgotten about that. There was an early airport up there. It was a club or something wasn't it?

Leonard: Yes, I believe so.

Bernice: Six wealthy men banded together and bought the plane so he could fly them to Detroit or Chicago on business trips. They rented a cow pasture from a farmer and that was where he kept the plane. That was his airfield. They went broke. For several months, they couldn't pay him his salary. They gave him the plane in lieu of back salary. It was a five passenger Stinson plane.

Elwyn: Oh, Yes.

Bernice: Then he brought it to Oshkosh and rebuilt it for his flight to Norway.

Elwyn: I remember him flying through with it several times.
    Where did I break up airplanes? I broke one up at Waupaca I broke one up at Antigo...

Bernice: How did it happen?

Elwyn: Yes, I broke one up at Antigo. That was that Standard I bought from Roy. I put a Hisso in it and...made a five place out of it.

Leonard: I didn't think you ever cracked that one up.

Elwyn: Yes, I cracked that one up.

Leonard: Oh, you did hunh?

Elwyn: Yes.

Leonard: Oh, it was that blue one that you never cracked up, that went up to Woodruff.

244

Elwyn: I'm just trying to think how I cracked that five place Standard up...see I rebuilt that one myself.

Leonard: Yes, I remember that. You made a four place out of that.

Elwyn: I flew one summer with it and the second summer when I started out with it, I cracked it up between Antigo and Merrill, I believe. Or right at Antigo.

Leonard: Did you have a forced landing or what?

Elwyn: Oh, no, not a forced landing...on take off.

Leonard: Your motor conk?

Elwyn: Yes, you know we had no rules and regulations and the gas tank had been stored all winter and scales formed. I was having a little trouble with it trying to clean those scales out. Finally the scales shut my motor off completely.

When I crashed, I took down the telephone lines and some poles. I had to pay for that. The farmers, though, they were always pretty good. They figured you had hard luck. I remember one time we were flying, Roy and I, at Weyauwega at the fair and we were doing pretty good. We were making too much and the farmer wanted to up the price on us. I tied my airplane right up and went to arguing with him...talking with him... He said, "Look at all the money you could have taken in while you were here arguing with me."

Well, I said, that ain't the whole thing...you offered us this field for a certain price and now you want to raise on us. I said, now while that airplane is tied over there to the fence, I know it's safe, and I said, if I was flying it (and we were having trouble in that field...you know you had to sneak off across there between those pines and over the road and dodge that hill) every time I take it up I could crack up.

The farmer said: "If Mr. West doesn't agree with me, he can go east."

Leonard: And I remember you flew the KKK cross over Oshkosh. I didn't think much about it at the time, but afterwards, years later I thought, boy, that was really taking a chance.

Elwyn: Not any worse than running bootleg whiskey out of Canada, was it?

Bernice: What year was that, do you know?

Leonard: You had that old Standard plane when you flew the cross didn't you?

Elwyn: I don't know just when that was. It was in the early times. Wittman was just barely starting flying at that time. Wittman...wasn't he flying in on that field at that time?

Leonard: No he wasn't. He wouldn't dare have had anything to do with that because you know he is a very strict Catholic. He had a brother who was a priest. Naturally he wouldn't go along with the Klan.

Elwyn: I remember one time at Oshkosh, Roy and I were flying from that field and Wittman flew in. He was just getting a start then. He wasn't carrying many passengers.

Leonard: I remember that. He flew a double X Standard.

Elwyn: I don't remember what he had.

Leonard: He was in a motor cycle accident, you know. He hit the back of a car. I remember people telling about that. He operated out of Byron, Wisconsin, in the beginning, you know.

Elwyn: Yes... yes.

Bernice: Did Wittman take lessons from Roy?

Leonard: Who did he take lessons from?

Elwyn: I don't know. I don't remember where Wittman learned to fly.

Leonard: I don't know either. I think from around Sheboygan.

Elwyn: Yes, but who would be at Sheboygan to teach him to fly in those days? At that time there weren't many airports. They were just getting started.

Bernice: Do you know the names of the early airports?

Elwyn: Well, what was started began just about the time that Appleton and Oshkosh did. You see they all got the fever about the same time. There was Manitowoc...Schablaski operated out of Manitowoc for years...and...

Leonard: Sturtevant was quite early, I think.

Elwyn: Sturtevant? That was Doc Ross. That was one of the first airports in the state, wasn't it?

Leonard: Well, I think Doc Ross was at least as late as 1927.

Bernice: Yes, 1927...I researched it. Doc Ross was in 1927.

Leonard: Howard Morey used to be at McFarland. He was at McFarland at the time Roy sold him that Waco 9.

Elwyn: Oh, yes.

Leonard: You see it was Morley and Quinn at that time, when he was at Four Lakes wasn't he?

Elwyn: I don't remember.

Leonard: Yes, that was southeast of Madison. Then he went to Truax Field, and then he was west of town.

Elwyn: Middleton. That's where Morey was. I suppose he is practically retired now. He probably doesn't do much flying now.

Elwyn: Oh there are a lot of the older flyers. I don't know where they are. There's Lyle Throw. I don't suppose he's still alive. Then there was Holman barnstorming with Hinks. Both Hinks are dead. Elmer was killed. When I was still in Minnesota, I used to meet Clarence Hinks. He never flew, but he was always interested. It was always Elmer Hinks who flew.

Leonard: When I was taking a refresher at Minneapolis, it was under Elmer Hink. Clarence never flew.

Leonard: Did you ever hear of Dutch Fuller?

Elwyn: Yes, when Roy was in Minneapolis and St. Paul. Wein hadn't gone to Alaska yet. If I remember right, Roy had a chance to go with them.

Leonard: Yes, with Noel Wein.

Elwyn: Roy told me about that a number of times.

Elwyn: Harrington, who flew for me for several years at Ely, Minnesota, when he left me he went to Alaska and got a job with Wein. He was a bush pilot with Wein for quite a few years. We've been out of Minnesota, now, sixteen years and he's been with them so long he's one of their oldest pilots. Now he's on an airline for them. They had him stationed at someplace above the Artic Circle. Not Nome.

Leonard: Point Barrow?

Elwyn: No, he flew into Point Barrow some, but it was Port Yukon where he was stationed.

Elwyn: Fellows who flew at the Larson airport in the early days of aviation in Wisconsin were Stecker, Burruso, Reincke, Bill Radtke was always around, Frienzel, Clyde Lee. At first when I was flying, as far as flyers...there just weren't any besides you guys.

Leonard: No, there were very few.

Elwyn: You bet your life.

Leonard: I remember one time when Ernest Berg stopped in....

Elwyn: There is a name I tried to think of. He used to barnstorm with Hinks."

Leonard: Yes, that's right.

Elwyn: I've tried to think of who that fellow was...a big man...

Leonard: Yes, very big. He was an athlete.

Elwyn: Then there was Cash Chamberlain...he used to stop in sometimes and I remember when he was flying the mail from Milwaukee on the first mail route to Green Bay, You know in the thirties it was pretty tough going into an airport trying to find a place to eat. I used to tell him what a nice job he had, when he'd fly in because there I'd be working on that cinder floor, not even cement. "Why," he'd say, "You've got it so nice," he'd say. "Here I have to fly to Green Bay in the morning with the mail, stay there all day, and fly back at night and," he said, "I sit there all day in Green Bay," and he says, "I get to worrying about the weather until my stomach is so upset I can't eat." He says, "You don't have to worry," he says. "I listen to the radio and hear that there's a storm brewing between Green Bay and Milwaukee and wonder how I am going to get back to Milwaukee."

I often think of Bob Menning when he was flying the night mail from Milwaukee to Minneapolis and St. Paul. You know in those days they had no radio in the plane. They would just fly into a storm and that was it. It's just a wonder he ever made it all that time.

Bernice: How many years did he fly the mail?

Elwyn: Oh I don't suppose it was too long. He used to fly a taper wing. That's the taper wing I bought. I don't think he flew the night mail at that time for more than a year or so.

Leonard: He was killed.

Elwyn: Menning? I never heard that Menning was killed!

Leonard: Yes, he was killed in Oregon. He was never found.

Elwyn: Oh! Chamberlain was killed, too.

Leonard: Yah, in the Dakotas.

Bernice: Did Holman fly the mail from Madison to Oshkosh and on to Green Bay when airmail began in Wisconsin?

Elwyn: The first pilot to fly the Madison to Green Bay run was Cash Chamberlain, I think, wasn't it?

Leonard: What about...he's retired now. Holman inaugurated the runs between Green bay and Chicago. He flew the first few runs in a Stinson Detroiter, remember that? Holman was the first but he didn't fly it very long.

Elwyn: No, a biplane.

Leonard: A biplane, yes. A Stinson Detroiter biplane.

Elwyn: He didn't fly that run long though.

Leonard: No. No, he became a manager didn't he?

Elwyn: Oh yes, Holman got to be the big wheel out west, you know. Menning, I"m sure, flew there some of the time, and Cash Chamberlain flew there for quite a while too.

Leonard: Howard used to fly it once in a while, you know?

Elwyn: Where?

Leonard: From Chicago to Madison and Green Bay.

Elwyn: Well I remember way back in the late twenties Apitz went to work for Thompson Airline. That's when you could get a limited commercial license. He left Appleton with a limited commercial and the pilot who was the captain of the plane was the one who got him the job. Merritt, his name was. He flew the Stinson in and delivered it for the Appleton Airways. What did they call that?" *Pride of Appleton.* And when he left Appleton, he went to work for Thompson. Thompson took a liking to Apitz and he got a job flying for Thompson from Detroit to Cleveland. He called Merritt one day. Merritt couldn't get a co-pilot who would stay with him. He called Apitz and Apitz called and asked me what he should do. He was working on his license at the time and he hated to give up his instructions before he had his commercial license. Well I said you've got to get in your time flying before you can get your commercial. You had better go while you've got the chance. He began flying out there as a copilot. Merritt couldn't get along with anyone, so he quit pretty quick. Apitz with a limited commercial was breaking in these transport pilots and had never flown an amphibian, but to make the trip legal with passengers there had to be a first pilot in the seat. Because he was a second pilot, he asked me to take the first pilot's job.

He trained several pilots to fly, When he called me, that was one of the biggest mistakes I made in my life. He called me when Merritt left. He said, "You can go right on as first pilot. I'm the teacher here." When Apitz got his transport license, he had a pull with Thompson. Thompson just got his license for him. He said the guy never watched nor rode with him. Just took Thompson's word and wrote out the license.

Thompson was taken over by Cord. Apitz was transferred right along with the company. American Air Lines took over Cord and way back in the thirties, Apitz was one of the ten oldest pilots on American Air Lines. They gave their ten oldest pilots a present. An anniversary present.

I visited him one time when I was in Chicago. He was going to try to get me on, but I couldn't get on then because of lack of education. You had to be a college graduate. I remember Apitz telling one of the personnel on the United Airlines when I was trying to get on there, "Well," he says, "look at me, I am just out of eighth grade."

"Well," he says, "You got on before the qualifications were what they are today." Herb Smith went down and tried to get a job and he couldn't get on. They had so many applications then and he didn't have the education. Although he had graduated from Lawrence College that wasn't enough. His father sent him to Stanford and when he finished there and put his qualifications on the table, they couldn't refuse him. He had everything he needed.

It was at Antigo, on Labor Day, and I generally flew back to Russell Wisconsin on Labor Day. This time he went to Russell and I went on to Antigo. Along about two o'clock in the afternoon I saw another Waco 9 (I was flying a Waco 9) coming in to a landing, and here was Herby Smith. He said, "I guess I could have kept on flying there but every time I took off the wind wasn't right and it was just nip and tuck to land. I'd just rather not take in any money than smash up an airplane and kill somebody."

The Fair Association was mad at me. They went right to the telephone and called that Conrad, that old grandpa flyer from Winona, and he sent in a plane. I guess he got there at 3:00 o'clock or thereabouts. About his third take off (Conrad sent in a pilot, he didn't come himself) the pilot hit a little dynamite building just off the edge of the field. He broke a woman's arm and put her in the hospital. Well, after that I had no more trouble with the Fair Association. When I went in there some time later, the fellow said to me, "Boy that was a good pilot you sent in here he knew his business all right." He said, "We couldn't believe it when he said he couldn't fly in and out of there, but we found it out the hard way." No, he was a careful flyer. There weren't many that careful in those days.

There was a Bill Knoll around, too. He flew for the Appleton Airport for a while. That airport was named "North American Airways." They bid on that mail run from Milwaukee to Appleton, and they had it all planned if they got the contract they would buy more airplanes immediately. That was the time Northwest got the contract away from them. I was flying their Stinson for North American Airways at that time. If they had gotten the contract, I would probably have gone right on flying. I was a chicken flyer. I don't believe in all this instrument flying, even today. There is too much chance for human error, too much stuff that can go wrong. Now, even to have a private license you have to be able to fly instruments. I argue they are so dependent on them if they fly into any kind of weather, one of these times they will fly into a bad storm and they won't come out.

The way I used to fly, my compass was a railroad track and when the weather came on bad, I landed by that railroad track. I had my map, I knew just where I was. I was never lost. When the weather cleared, I would take off and go. I flew in Canada that same way.

Leonard: I have known pilots who flew by instrument and when they got off the instrument they were lost. They were so dependent on the instruments they couldn't find out where they were.

Elwyn: I used to fly all around Chicago. I used railroad maps. You crossed so many railroads and then followed the one going to the town you wanted to go to. You were never lost. I had my railroad map with me and my camping gear in case of bad weather.

When you go right out and start cross country and you have no landmark well I guess probably these homing radios that they had do a pretty good job, but if the motor quits on you, single engine you are in the soup.

Remember that jewelry man from Sturgeon Bay? I can't think of his name, he had a Fairchild, one of those that first came out, and he did a lot of flying. He was flying from Manitowoc to Sturgeon Bay and it was all clear when he left Manitowoc. There wasn't a cloud. He ran into some clouds and he thought he would fly up over them and come down at Sturgeon Bay. He got up there and that cloud kept getting deeper and higher and first thing he knew he was in it deep and when he came down he was somewhere near La Crosse.

I don't think he ever flew after that. He said if that plane hadn't flown itself, he would have never made it. He said he just kept it headed somewhere and he just sat there and prayed and cried. He did everything a person could and finally he found a little opening. He had headed away from the lakes in order to get out of the clouds and he did finally get out of that cloud when he was nearly at La Crosse, three hundred miles west of where he started or wanted to go. He said he was a wreck for days. He took a train or bus home and somebody flew the airplane back for him. He sold the airplane and I don't think he ever flew again.

Leonard: That was Nelson wasn't it?

Elwyn: No, it wasn't.

Leonard: The same thing happened to Nelson. He landed over by the Mississippi somewhere. He headed it west to get out of the clouds around the lakes and landed near the Mississippi River.

Elwyn: There was a doctor who was the head of the airport at Sturgeon Bay and I had quite an argument with him one day. I was barnstorming there. That's when old Hippo was flying with me. Hippo was flying a tri-motor. He was doing a good job of it, too. There were three army pilots who came in. They were putting on maneuvers at the airport and we were carrying passengers and that Stinson when you had it loaded hung in the air. If you were flying level the fellow in the tail seat felt like he was going right uphill. You'd swear, sitting in the tail seat, that you were going up at a 45 degree angle.

The army fellow looked at that plane flying in the air in that position about 12,000 feet high and he came over to this Doc and he said if you don't stop that fellow from flying there is going to be an awful smashup. Of course Doc listened to this army pilot and he came over and jumped me. Well, I listened to him a minute and then I said, "Doc, now that is just enough of that. You can tell me anything and I'll listen to you, but I am not going to listen to that army guy. That army fellow means nothing to me and you are running the show here. I'll listen to you, but don't bring something to me that he's told you." I said. "He knows nothing about that commercial airplane or how it flies." I said. "That's the normal attitude of that airplane, flying heavily loaded. That pilot is doing a good job of it and I am not going to listen to an army pilot." That was the end of that.

Leonard: Was that at Embarrass when you and Roy were flying that one time and your Waco started to roll? It started down the hill? That was a Standard though. And you took off after it running like a deer?

Elwyn: Oh there had been a couple of different times. One did get away one time. But one of the helpers got it by the wing and he held it in a circle until a fellow could get in and stop it. Somebody started that. I believe a greenhorn started it. Turned the switch on and went around and cranked it with no chocks in front of the wheels and the stick not belted back. It probably would have taken off if we hadn't caught it. It was two-thirds back.

The fellow that caught the wing, I don't know how he ever caught the wing, hung on and held it in a circle. We ran there and we had to run in as the plane went around, and dodge the tail. It was going around fast. After we got in and got a hold of the throttle and stopped the engine, that fellow who had held it in a circle was just all in. In fact we had to carry him away from there. He was that tired. It is funny he didn't have a heart attack.

Then there was one time I was at the Oshkosh Airport. I flew in with a Curtis Robin. I had just made a trade down at Racine and I had a dandy nice Curtiss Robin and I landed to visit with Steve Wittman a few minutes.

My plane was parked out there by the hanger and one of Wittman's students came in and got in the airplane and just like the student that I had that ran into the load of hay, he was gaping out of one side of the plane and taxiing in a circle and he taxied right into an airplane and chewed the end of the wing clear off with his propeller, chewed it off clear to the struts. I can still see Wittman, he was talking with me, his mouth came open and he couldn't say a word. He couldn't even yell at the student. He just stood there with his mouth open. That's one of the things in my life that I will always remember. Of course, Wittman paid for it.

Clyde was with us quite a bit. Stunting, rescuing other people, jumping parachutes. Clyde Lee was always around with us in the beginning. He was very interested in flying and stunting. He liked any kind of stunting maneuvers. I don't know if he ever sold tickets with us or not.

Leonard: Yes he did.

Elwyn: Yes, he was around quite a bit, especially in the beginning before he took off on his own. He did a lot of chute jumping.

Leonard: His first parachute jump was with Holman over at Manitowoc. That time he landed on the hood of a car. We went over to see him jump. I think that was the first jump he ever made.

Elwyn: It seems to me I can remember carrying him on several jumps. I carried so many who were jumping that I never paid too much attention to who it was on a particular jump.

You have never made a chute jump, have you?

Leonard: No.

Elwyn: Nor I either.

Leonard: The only thing that would get me out of a plane is fire. Because I know that if I didn't jump I would be killed anyway. It would be the lesser of two evils. I would be sure to be killed if I didn't jump and might be killed anyway if I did. I am too heavy to jump now.

Elwyn: Well Clyde wasn't very heavy. He was tall and slim.

Leonard: The weight made quite a bit of difference.

Leonard: Now our time of flying is history. We were the beginning. We were pioneers. We are no longer heroes. All that is forgotten. We led the field. In these times they are flying to the moon. It's like a dream.

Elwyn: There was a saying that always went with me: "There's old flyers and there's bold flyers, but there's no old bold flyers."

Sena (Signe) granddaughter of
Sena Anderson *(André Doe—who came from Norway)*

Halvor Lee

1
ichester area)

terson
Neenah

is
ine
id Schanke

id
Theresa Strum
Scott
Sarah

ert
Nancy Young
James
Angela

Hamburg
m. Bessie Cross
✓ lived ?

C:Evelyn
m. Ray Baxandall
c.Lee
m.? 1 child?
m.Greta
(lives in
Oshkosh area

c.Mary Ann
m.? Krooth
c.1 ?
lives in CA
Berkley

C:Clyde
unmarried/ died
air accident

C: Bernice
m. ? Krippene
c. 2 boys/1 girl
(live in CA
area) *Ripon Ca.*
Children in
Ca. ? ?

also TV show

Nalvor Lea, wife Kari, & son Nalvor came from Telemask Norway about 1850

LEE FAMILY

Sena (2 Anderson) ma
Children: (

Alice ---------------------------------- Hilda
| m. Theodore Larson | m. Arthur
V (lived in Winchester area) V (lived

C. Loyal Larson
    m: Georgina Schaefer (died about 1960)
        c. Barbara   see below
    m: Evelyn Cross

C: Dorothy
m. Albe
live

C: Viola
    m. Clarence Larson (died 30's) *(no children)* C: Ethyl
    m. Leonard Larson   m. Ralp
                                            C: M
      Viola's children *c̄ Leonard*   m
      Theda
        m. Abe Eckstein   C
           several children
      Judy
        m. Dean Chance (baseball player)
          divorced/one son
        m. briefly--don't know name   C
          (lived in Ohio until 80's)
      Zola
        m. Bill Hewitt -divorced
        m. Larry ? (Texas)
        (Have ? children)
        Larry & Zola are teachers
        employed in overseas schools
        by gov. presently in Germany
      Bonnie
        m. ? *name* lives in PA
          (? children)
          Bonnie was Air Line Hostess

Barbara Larson -daughter of Loyal
  m. Ralph Luedke there are 4 children
      c. Nancy married, 2 children, has Nancy's Notions Beaver
      c. Dean -married 3 children on Winchester farm
      c. Roy -single recruiter for Oakland A's
      c. daughter   getting married '95 several years younge